REAL-ISH

REAL-ISH

*Audiences, Feeling, and the Production
of Realness in Contemporary Performance*

KELSEY JACOBSON

McGill-Queen's University Press
Montreal & Kingston • London • Chicago

© McGill-Queen's University Press 2023

ISBN 978-0-2280-1640-3 (cloth)
ISBN 978-0-2280-1641-0 (ePDF)
ISBN 978-0-2280-1642-7 (ePUB)

Legal deposit first quarter 2023
Bibliothèque nationale du Québec

Printed in Canada on acid-free paper that is 100% ancient forest free (100% post-consumer recycled), processed chlorine free

We acknowledge the support of the Canada Council for the Arts.

Nous remercions le Conseil des arts du Canada de son soutien.

Library and Archives Canada Cataloguing in Publication

Title: Real-ish : audiences, feeling, and the production of realness in contemporary performance / Kelsey Jacobson.
Names: Jacobson, Kelsey, author.
Description: Includes bibliographical references and index.
Identifiers: Canadiana (print) 20220414297 | Canadiana (ebook) 20220414300 | ISBN 9780228016403 (cloth) | ISBN 9780228016410 (ePDF) | ISBN 9780228016427 (ePUB)
Subjects: LCSH: Theater audiences—Psychology. | LCSH: Theater. | LCSH: Emotions. | LCSH: Reality.
Classification: LCC PN1590.A9 J33 2023 | DDC 792.01—dc23

This book was typeset by True to Type in 10.5/13 Sabon

Contents

Table and Figures vii

Preface: A Crisis of the Real? ix

Acknowledgments xvii

1 Feeling Real: Realness, Affect, Audiences 3
2 "Everything is True, Some Things are Scripted": Documentary Practice and the Presentation of Multiple Truths 29
3 Talking to, at, and with Audiences: The Politics of Participation 77
4 "You Will Long Remember": The Nostalgic Real in Site-Specific Historical Re-enactment 103
5 Constructing Immersive Experiences for "Real" Engagement 147
6 Immersion and Exertion: Audiences, Feeling-Labour, and the Production of Real-ish-ness 189

Coda: How Real is it Anyway? 211

Notes 215

Bibliography 239

Index 265

Table and Figures

TABLE

1.1 Overview of interviews conducted and data collected.   20

FIGURES

4.1 The audience in St Paul's church interior in Trinity, NL, 27 August 2016. Photo by Kelsey Jacobson.   105

4.2 The pageant scene at Harvey's Cove set in 1760 in foreground, community fishers in 2016 in background, Trinity, NL, 20 August 2016. Photo by Kelsey Jacobson.   121

5.1 Performers Cyrus Lane and Katherine Cullen dance in the chapel at *TomorrowLove™*, December 2016. Photo by Neil Silcox.   148

5.2 Performers Paul Dunn and Katherine Cullen amidst the "bare-bones" aesthetic of the set and space in *TomorrowLove™*, December 2016. Photo by Neil Silcox.   160

5.3 Performers Anand Rajaram and Oyin Oladejo perform in front of audience members in *TomorrowLove™*, December 2016. Photo by Neil Silcox.   161

6.1 Performer Amy Keating filling in "I desire you because_____" at *TomorrowLove™*, December 2016. Photo by Neil Silcox.   207

6.2 Performers Damien Atkins, Paul Dunn, Amy Keating, Oyin Oladejo, and Anand Rajaram dancing in *TomorrowLove™*, December 2016. Photo by Neil Silcox.   209

PREFACE

A Crisis of the Real?

Amidst the *Oxford Dictionary*'s declaration of "post-truth" as the word of the year in 2016 and the fast propagation of terms like fake news, misinformation, and post-fact, the central question of this book seems critically important: What feels real to contemporary audiences? Using interviews with audience members about the perceived realness of their experiences attending documentary, participatory, historical, and immersive theatre pieces, this book's objective is to investigate the use, production, and perception of realness in current performance practices. The pressing stakes of such a research question at this critical contemporary juncture seem clear: from truthiness to deepfakes, and QAnon to anti-vaxxers, the cultural touchstones of the past several years are emblematic of the time during which this book was written, a time in which the tenuousness of the perceptual border between what is real and what is fake has been laid bare.

One of the best summations of this destabilization between real and unreal, true and untrue, and fact and fiction in contemporary discourse is comedian Stephen Colbert's term "truthiness." As a kind of harbinger of what was to come, in 2005 Colbert coined the concept to refer to things that seem like the truth, feel like the truth, or are desired to be true by someone, regardless of their actual truthfulness.[1] A year later, Colbert pointed to the prevalence of truthiness in his address to then president George W. Bush during the White House Correspondents' Dinner comedy roast:

> It is my privilege to celebrate this president, 'cause we're not so different, he and I. We both get it. Guys like us, we're not some brainiacs on the nerd patrol. We're not members of the factinista.

We go straight from the gut. Right, sir? That's where the truth lies, right down here in the gut.[2]

In his speech, Colbert gestures towards a growing distrust of institutions – the media, higher education, government – and the facts, expertise, and truths they produce. Instead, says Colbert, truth can be located in individual embodied, affective experience: "in the gut." Fast-forward fifteen years and what was an entertaining, if incisive, joke in 2006 has since ballooned into an epistemological way of being in the world: what is real, truthful, or factual is increasingly a question of subjective perception rather than an ontological certainty. From climate change deniers to flat-Earthers, for many people truth is debateable, facts are precarious, and the real is perilously difficult to discern. This has created a climate in which what is perceived to be real is an increasingly contentious, dangerous, and difficult determination.

An argument for the rising blurring between the real and fictive in the first two decades of the twenty-first century is that, increasingly, science and technology are challenging the real/fantasy binary. As Damian Sutton, Susan Brind, and Ray McKenzie write in their discussion of realness in modern culture in *The State of the Real: Aesthetics in the Digital Age*:

> Things hard to believe have really happened, *have* happened. We have seen mice with human ears on their backs and we have witnessed 9/11. We have seen it all on the news, so in some sense it must have happened ... these are the facts that can be verified and we have the images to prove it. The trauma of these "live" video images of death is that they look almost too real to be real.[3]

In other words, the unbelievable may increasingly be hard to perceive as such since the "unbelievable" has already happened. Take, for example, a video of former president Barack Obama with the title "You Won't Believe What Obama Says In this Video!" that has garnered millions of views on YouTube since being published in 2018.[4] About twenty-five seconds into the video – in which the former president appears to directly address the viewer from inside the Oval Office – Obama states, "President Trump is a total and complete dipshit." He then continues, "Now, you see, I would never say these things, at least not in a public address, but someone else would," and the video reveals that it is not actually Obama saying these words but a digital reconstruction of Obama's face superimposed onto comedian Jordan Peele's. Such "deepfakes" are manufactured videos of people that very closely resemble real videos: communication and media scholars Cristian Vaccari and Andrew Chadwick write that they are frequently convincing enough that they contribute "to a climate of indeterminacy about truth and falsity."[5] It is, after all, maybe not so hard to imagine Obama denigrating Trump, especially when cloaked in a convincing technological simulation. As the Peele-cum-Obama video goes on to say, "This is a dangerous time. Moving forward we need to be more vigilant with what we trust on the internet."[6] This is a particularly prescient phrase given the explosion of internet-based conspiracy theories and spread of misinformation in recent years. Communications scholar Bente Kalsnes writes in her analysis of fake news, "Manipulation, disinformation, falseness, rumors, conspiracy theories ... have existed as long as humans have communicated." What is different now is that "new communication technologies have allowed for new ways to produce, distribute, and consume fake news, which makes it harder to differentiate what information to trust."[7] Increasingly sophisticated technologies like deepfakes make perception of realness difficult in a very practical sense.

If we can't believe our eyes, what can we believe? How can we determine what is or isn't real? Whom do we trust? The decade from 2010 to 2020 is accordingly described by author and academic Rachel Botsman as a time of "dispersed trust," in which previously reliable systems and institutions are viewed suspiciously. Botsman describes in her book *Who Can You Trust?* a lengthy list of events spanning corruption, elitism, and economic disparity that have resulted in deeply reduced trust throughout society. One of the most prominent consequences of this "dispersal" of trust away from traditional institutions is QAnon, an internet conspiracy theory turned political movement that centres on the mysterious figure of "Q" and is deeply distrustful of the US Government. Q is purported to systematically release information related to a theory that all American presidents between John F. Kennedy and Donald Trump have worked with a group of self-serving elites called "The Cabal" to undermine democracy, with potential connections to Satanism, pedophilia, and blood sacrifice.[8] Believers in QAnon attempt to decode messages on social media for hidden meanings. Media scholar Ethan Zuckerman writes in his article "QAnon and the Emergence of the Unreal" of one such instance when an innocuous tweet from former FBI director James Comey about his first five jobs (in response to a viral hashtag #FiveJobsIHad) was decoded by QAnon conspiracists as a "Jihad" bomb threat towards a California charter school's innocuous jubilee fundraiser. As Zuckerman warns, "A movement like QAnon is an inevitable outgrowth of the Unreal, an approach to politics that forsakes interpretation of a common set of facts in favour of creating closed universes of mutually reinforcing facts and interpretations."[9] Regardless of the actual facts, QAnon clearly feels real to its participants: real enough that the Grass Valley Charter School Foundation fielded calls from concerned QAnon believers, and police actually urged a cancellation of the jubilee due to fears that QAnon supporters might show up to "protect" the event.[10]

As we are gifted – or cursed – with incredible technological developments and near effortless access to information, the challenge of sorting the information from the misinformation and the real from the fictive can have even more pressing consequences. The late 2010s and early 2020s have so far been marked by events that belie the stability of the categories of fact and fiction such that even if the information is fake, the consequences can be real. In 2016, for example, a man armed with an AR 15, a Colt .38, and a shotgun attempted to rescue children who were being hidden in tunnels underneath a pizza restaurant by a cadre of powerful politicians including Hilary Clinton.[11] There were, of course, no children, no hidden tunnels, and no connection to then presidential candidate Hilary Clinton despite online rumours. And yet, even when disproven, fake news, falsities, and fictions can continue to affect the real world.[12] In the case of this so-named Pizzagate, even after the event had been debunked, belief in the theory persisted: in online forums the gunman was dismissed as an actor and the reporting decried as a biased failure of liberal media.[13] As another example, when Joe Biden was elected president of the US in November 2020, the "truth" for a group of Americans was that Donald Trump was the real winner of the election. They were convinced enough by this alternate reality to stage a real insurrection at the Capitol building in Washington, DC, on 6 January 2021 that resulted in the deaths of five people.[14] This is because, for many, "Trump embodies 'truthiness': ideas which 'feel right' to many people," regardless of whether his ideas are actually factual, true, or real.[15] For anti-vaxxers in the US, UK, and Canada during the COVID-19 pandemic, what is real is not that the vaccines are safe and efficacious but that the vaccines are a cover for the government to insert microchips into its citizens, render them infertile, or alter their DNA.[16] Such contagious conspiracism[17] threatens real herd immunity since "Even if people don't believe that vaccines cause harmful side-effects such as autism, the power of anti-vaccination stories is they evoke fearful emotions that undermine our trust, no matter what we might rationally think."[18] These examples suggest the very real, very persistent effects that unreal, false, or fictional information can have even in the face of scientific evidence, media debunking, or official statements. Taken together, these representative events of the past few years make it clear that the past decade has seen an intensification of the tendency to make decisions about truth and reality through affective engagements – and this is problematic for democracy, science, and society: a kind of crisis of the real.

Indeed, like Colbert's invocation of his "gut" at the Correspondents' Dinner, many are pointing to emotion and affect as the new barometers of realness. The *Oxford Dictionary* definition of post-truth, for example, is, "relating to or denoting circumstances in which objective facts are less influential in shaping public opinion than appeal to emotion and personal belief." A marker of the post-truth era is therefore a turn toward individual conviction and feeling. As Kathleen Higgins describes, this isn't a case of truth versus emotion: "'Post-truth' is often understood as involving people's emotions rather than their critical abilities to make distinctions … it's important to keep in mind that emotion and truth are not two different things … The two have to work together." In other words, emotion has come to the fore as a means by which truth is actually determined and defined. When, as Higgins suggests, feeling becomes a way of knowing – and constructing – truths about the world, the cultivation, control, production, and circulation of feelings of realness is paramount.

This is where an analysis of theatre may prove beneficial: theatre, as an art form that revels in feeling, emotion, and the manufacture of affect,[19] may offer a perspective through which we can better understand how people perceive, understand, and *feel* things to be real. Theatre is, after all, also a field that inherently plays in perceptions of real and fake. Conventionally, theatre is oriented towards the fictive and illusory. To attend theatre is, proverbially, to escape reality, and the entirety of the business of theatre is to take "real" materials – props, set pieces, actor bodies – and transform them into the fictional: A stick becomes a sword, a chair a throne, and an actor, Macbeth. More recently, however, there has been a trend toward what performance scholars have termed "theatre of the real." Carol Martin's seminal books on theatre and realness describe theatre of the real as theatre that incorporates, or to use her word, "recycle[s]," some aspect of perceived realness in content, frame, or effect. Theatre of the real embraces site-specific, verbatim, documentary, and immersive theatre, among other forms. It is theatre that may make use of, respectively, real locations, real words, real events, or real sensory experiences. As Jenn Stephenson writes in her study of theatre of the real, *Insecurity: Perils and Products of Theatres of the Real*, "All theatre makes use of real materials to depict the real world but by extending beyond a familiar naturalism to align these two aspects of realness in iconicity – the self-identical material with the thing it presents – these kinds of reality-engaged performances constitute a distinct genre."[20] In other words, theatre of the real is a practice that attempts not to re-present reality on stage, as in theatrical realism, but to actually stage reality itself.

The ways in which theatre of the real toys with perceptions of realness make it an enticing site for exploration of wider discourses of the real. Considering fundamental performance concepts like escapism and the fourth wall, which confidently delineate the real from the fictive, putting "the real" within the theatrical frame is provocative. Theatre of the real, we might consider, is the effect produced by exposing the representative apparatus. Audiences are made aware of the illusive frame so that we might see "beyond it." What might present-day audiences of theatre of the real consider to be real when what they see is presented within what is often a highly representational art form? Does placing the real within a typically fictive frame encourage a blending, an oscillation, or even a destruction of the real/representation binary that is so thoroughly entrenched in Western metaphysics? Marvin Carlson writes in his study of theatre's relationship to the real across history, "the real and the represented are not a set binary, but are the products of human consciousness and ways of seeing and encoding."[21] If it is within the audience's perception that realness is conveyed and constructed, and that "ontological transformations"[22] from the real to the fictive and potentially vice versa occur, a study of audience perception of realness may offer important insights to wider conversations about blurred distinctions between the real and the unreal.

Theatre of the real's interest in placing the ostensibly "real" onstage is likely unsurprising in a society in which the ideas of fake news, post-truth, and post-fact circulate daily in discourse. Martin suggests that theatre of the real has re-emerged as a response to a period of international crises of war, religion, government, truth, and information: a time in which governments "spin" the facts in order to tell stories.[23] Theatre of the real, she implies, is capable of filling a void in discourse. Drawing on work by theatre artist Mark Espiner, Jenny Hughes similarly argues that the "prominence of verbatim theatre can be explained as an attempt to establish authentic or reliable frames of reference for thought, feeling, and action in a highly mediated society."[24] Espiner himself agrees that amidst a world of increasing theatricality, theatre is rediscovering its true role, "turning to what it does best: exposing the truth."[25] Alan Filewod, writing specifically on Canadian theatre, declares that "at the core of the documentary [theatre] impulse is an implicit critical statement that the conventional dramatic forms of the culture in question no longer express the truth of the society, usually because those conventional forms cannot accommodate rapid social change."[26] Filewod's comments, taken alongside Espiner, Hughes, Martin, and Little cumulatively suggest that performances of the real might help spectators (and citizens) find truth within the contemporary paradigm, in which mediation, theatricality, and illusion are commonplace.

However, it may not be the actual veracity of the "real" in "theatre of the real" that is attractive to audiences – just as the lure of Colbert's truthiness is not about actual truthfulness. Importantly, theatre of the real often achieves a kind of truth-telling by highlighting its own construction. It self-consciously points to one or more aspects of itself as real, thereby confessing its otherwise theatrical (or unreal) structure: verbatim theatre affirms that the words are true, site-specific theatre that the place is real, and documentary theatre that the events really happened – allowing everything else to not be real. Instead of attempting an aesthetic of realism in which the real world is convincingly represented onstage, theatre of the real acknowledges, forefronts, and confesses its necessary theatricality. In revealing its essential construction as a curated, designed, and manufactured art form, such forms of theatre might work to rebuild trust and re-establish truth. Not, I argue, by "exposing the truth," so much as by exposing the structures through which truth may be perceived and presented: it is not about determining the real but demonstrating how realness may be produced. And this is what seems to be most pressing in the contemporary moment. When faith in institutions, sources, and entire epistemological structures are disrupted and perceptions of what is real seem to vary widely, questions of *how* realness comes to be felt, rather than what is unequivocally real, become deeply important – if deeply fraught – to investigate.

Acknowledgments

In the words of one of my interviewees, "Who comes to help the PhD student from Toronto, eh?" and I am accordingly first and foremost grateful to the audience members who allowed me to interview them and provided inspiring, thoughtful, and challenging conversations. I am also grateful to the theatre companies who graciously welcomed me to their productions and lent me their audiences: Donna Butt, Rising Tide Theatre, Kevin Toope, and the cast and crew of the Trinity Pageant; Richard Rose, Anne Wessels, Maria Milisavljevic, and the Tarragon Theatre staff for facilitating my study of *An Enemy of the People*; Simon Mallett, Ellen Close, Downstage theatre company, and the cast and crew of *Good Fences*; and Mitchell Cushman, Michelle Yagi, Neil Silcox, Outside the March theatre company, and the cast and crew of *TomorrowLove ™*.

Jenn Stephenson has been a role model to me throughout my academic career – from my undergraduate degree to assistant professorship – and I have deep gratitude for all her support, advice, and championing of my work. My doctoral supervisor, Kathleen Gallagher offered me inspiring opportunities during the course of my degree, and I am immensely thankful for her mentorship and guidance. My postdoctoral supervisor Stephen Johnson models the kind of generous, gracious, and collegial professor I aspire to be, and I am grateful for his continued support. Kirsty Sedgman gave extremely helpful guidance on my manuscript draft and has generously been an ongoing source of valuable insight and advice. I am also indebted to the great many people who offered thoughtful feedback on various iterations of the content in this book and were generous and supportive with their advice: Jacob Gallagher-Ross, Chris Megson, Barry Freeman, Kim Solga, Kelsey Blair, Signy Lynch, Scott Mealey, and the anonymous peer reviewers engaged by McGill-Queen's Press. I am also grateful to my colleagues at Queen's University and in the Dan School of Drama and Music, among them Grahame Renyk, Craig Walker, Julie Salverson, Rebecca Draisey-Collishaw, Kip Pegley, Stephanie Lind, Colleen Renihan, and Margaret Walker. The Centre for Spectatorship and Audience Research has been my intellectual home since 2016, and I am grateful to the many members of that centre for their feedback, collegiality, and support, as well as to the members of the Theory & Criticism Focus Group at the Association for Theatre in Higher Education and the Canadian Association for Theatre Research. I also wish to thank my students over the past several years for their energy and inspiration and in particular those students who provided research assistance during various stages of this book: Hamish Hutchison-Poyntz, Hannah Samuels, Bethany Schaufler-Biback, Chanel Sheridan, Jacob Pittini, and Meghan Lindsay.

An early version of chapter 4 appeared in *Theatre Research in Canada* as "Through the Fictive to the Real(ish): Affective Time and the Representation of 'Real Newfoundland' in Rising Tide Theatre's Trinity Pageant" (https://doi.org/10.7202/1055467ar) and an early portion of chapter 2 appeared in *Canadian Theatre Review* as "*Good Fences*' Scripted Truths: Cultivating Dialogue in Post-Real Times" (https://doi.org/10.3138/ctr.175.002). Parts of these articles are reprinted here with permission from University of Toronto Press. I would also like to acknowledge the work undertaken by the editors of these journals: Kim Solga, Barry Freeman, and Matt Jones, as well as the editors of Etudes, Jennifer Goof and Julia Moriarty, who published my first piece on immersive theatre. Thank you for your support of my early work.

Finally, I am grateful to my friends, family, and colleagues who have inspired and supported me throughout the development of this work, including: Lisa Aikman, Ashley Williamson, Jessica Watkin, David DeGrow, Sebastian Samur, Jenny Salisbury, Charlotte Young, Dirk Rodricks, Rachel Rhoades, Sherry Bie, Nancy Cardwell, Rebecca Starkman, Christine Balt, Andrew Kushnir, Anne Wessels, Derek Louis, Matt Harper, Jenny Hwang, Karley Salsbury, Derek Colquitt, and countless others.

REAL-ISH

1

Feeling Real
Realness, Affect, Audiences

KJ: So I'm going to ask you my second question, which is how real do you think this show is?
AUD 2e: 74 per cent real. [laughs][1]

The above excerpt comes from an interview with one of the seventy audience members I spoke to for this book and is possibly the most revealing response to my questions about the realness of theatrical performance. The answer "74 per cent real" is playfully indicative of the ways in which the often nebulous, always contested word "real" seems to defy absolute measurement. The question also reveals my naïveté at the outset of this study during which time I felt intuitively that realness was somehow definable. In the early stages of my research, I asked audience members to attempt to communicate to me a definition of realness, though I myself struggled to pin a description to it.

Rather than aim for definitive answers, this book explores questions of realness by centring audience members' voices and investigating not how real a piece of theatre may be but how experiences of the real are constructed, evaluated, and, most importantly, felt. These arguably fundamental aspects of performance – audiences, feeling, realness – are often treated separately. Audiences are a central part of Peter Brook's famous definition of theatre: "someone else is watching."[2] Feeling is the currency theatre trades in as an "affect-producing machine."[3] Realness is constantly negotiated in relation to theatre's illusory, imaginative, fantastical qualities. Here, I bring these aspects of the theatrical experience together to ask poignant questions of contemporary theatre: what feels real to the people who watch it? Why? And, why does that matter? Given the contemporary culture of post-truth, post-fact, and feeling-knowing, innocent-sounding questions like these betray the complexity and weight of words like realness, affect, and audience. I start this book, therefore, by considering these concepts each in turn, before delving into particular theatrical case studies that highlight the deeply nuanced relationships between them and suggest how theatre studies may offer insights into perceived realness more broadly.

REALNESS

I have to begin by addressing the thorny complication of what exactly I mean by "realness." Or, rather, what I do not mean by "realness" (a word that seems to necessitate scare quotes for precisely this reason). Writing on the topic of "the real" feels, at times, like an impossibly complex matter: uses of the term are so varied and debate over its essential construction so thorough that, as Alexander Miller writes with regards to the general philosophical concept of realism, "No brief account of it will satisfy all those with a stake in the debate."[4] This summary is no different: its aim is to provide just enough of an overview to address the issues raised by the recent usage of "realness" in theatre and performance studies.

The real is, after all, a long-standing component of foundational concepts like reality and representation. At the same time it is an essentially contested idea that provokes diverse philosophical positions. Empirical realists like A.J. Ayer assert that the real world can only ever be experienced indirectly, through the mediation of sense data.[5] Ayer roots his definition in three historic sources: Plato, who famously drew a distinction between the ideal and the real; Immanuel Kant, who expounded on phenomena and noumena (phenomena is that which is sensible or the knowledge of perception, and noumena is the thing-in-itself or abstract knowledge); and Edmund Husserl, who introduced and delineated the notion of noema (the object being apprehended as distinct from the actual act of apprehending). Each philosopher puts a distance between the perceived and the real. If, as these scholars suggest, a direct experience of the real can never be produced, the possible mediations, adjustments, and filtrations an individual's hermeneutic schemas might effect are only distillations and half-perceptions of reality; this makes the "really real" unattainable. The closest possible experience of reality is through the senses.

The poststructuralist view argues conversely that reality is not simply out of reach but is itself constructed and contingent. Philosopher J.L. Austin, whose work influenced poststructural thinkers, responds to Ayers in *Sense and Sensibilia* in 1962: "However much our everyday linguistic habits might suggest otherwise, there is in fact no one property that is being ascribed to things when we designate them as real." This "exposes the bizarre conclusions we are led to when we try to erect an epistemological system on the basis of something as insecure as optical illusion."[6] To illustrate his argument, Austin uses the analogy of a straw whose shape is distorted when it is in a glass of water. He asks whether the straw, which appears perfectly straight when out of water, is somehow more real out of water than when it appears as distorted in the glass. In presenting this analogy, Austin underscores the instability inherent in basing notions of what is real on sensory perception.

Austin's argument, replete with the fluidity or impossibility of defining the real, echoes Jacques Lacan's notions of the impossibility of touching the real. In their fittingly titled *State of the Real*, Sutton, Brind, and Mackenzie write that, "In the 'mirror stage', Lacan believed, the infant becomes aware of difference (between self and other) and subsequently functions in the world through the operations of the 'symbolic order' – that is through image and language. With the awareness of separation, the connection with the *real* object is, Lacan argues, always eluding us and can never be fully described."[7] To put it differently, "the Real is intrinsically elusive, resisting by nature capture in the comprehensibly meaningful formulations of concatenations of Imaginary-Symbolic signs. It is, as Lacan stresses again and again, an 'impossibility.'"[8] The real thus achieves (incomplete) existence only through the use of symbols and language. This perception of the real is manifest in Jacques Derrida's deconstruction of logocentrism in "Structure, sign and play in the discourse of the human sciences" in 1966. Derrida essentially argues for a reality constructed by discourse. In other words, the real is linguistically determined, and thus indeterminate; there is no independent reality object (or logos or signified concept) but only a never-ending chain of signifiers.

Turning to more recent invocations of the term in performance studies, the term realness has found specific use in queer theory and cultural studies. In ballroom culture,[9] according to Marlon M. Bailey, realness denotes "adherence to certain performances, self-presentations, and embodiments that are believed to capture the authenticity of particular gender and sexual identities."[10] It is the means by which members of the ballroom community design performances to compete in runway events, but also a means by which members might avoid violence and discrimination by achieving gender and sexual conformity in the outside world.[11] In their analysis of *RuPaul's Drag Race*, a reality television competition between drag queens, Sabrina Strings and Long T. Bui agree that realness can be considered the "ability to convince the judges that [the competitors] look and act the part of a typical woman (or man) who would inhabit said category," including adherence to not only gender and sexual identities but potentially also racial and class identities.[12] Paradoxically, this means that "realness signifies the possibility of deception – an enduring illusion – positioned at the crossroads between the ballroom world and the 'real world.'"[13] In this understanding, realness often denotes a credible illusion; a reading of "the real" that is not ontologically stable but constructed by and through a convincing performance.

Authenticity has also been connected to ideas of the real, especially as it relates to aesthetics and representation. Philosophers Somogy Varga and Charles Guignon articulate two understandings of authentic: in the "strong sense" of being "of undisputed origin or authorship," or in a "weaker sense" of being "faithful to an original" or a "reliable, accurate representation."[14] These definitions are interesting given that the first seems to indicate "the real thing" itself, while the second indicates a representation of the real thing; already the lines between real and representation are blurred as both are potentially "authentic." Varga and Guignon go on to offer another understanding of authenticity as "ideal"[15] and it is this idea that literary scholar Antonius Weixler picks up on to define authenticity as "the desire for the natural, the real, the original."[16] Weixler states that "Authenticity and popular culture seem to compensate for a reality that is perceived as being unreal and artificial."[17] This understanding of authenticity as desire, prompted by an inauthentic reality, is particularly relevant to this book as related to consumer culture and tourism, wherein the most authentic experiences are judged to be the most valuable[18] and travellers yearn for "real" local experiences in foreign places.[19] Consideration of authenticity in this text is primarily related to an analysis of historical re-enactment as a form of theatre of the real in chapter 4. In this case, authenticity need not be a tangible object but a constructed concept, or experience, that is contextual and shifting.[20] Indeed, what is deemed by the audience to be the most authentic representation of history may not necessarily also be the most accurate.

Wolfgang Funk, Florian Groß, and Irmtaud Huber in their introduction to *Aesthetics of Authenticity* suggest three further main findings regarding authenticity that are relevant to theatre and performance: it is fragmented, contested, and performative. They write, "Rather than a unified inherent quality an aesthetic analysis of authenticity reveals it to reside in fragmentation, in the piecing together of disparate elements, an idiosyncratic collage which can serve to construct the authentic beyond and in spite of essentialism – and yet may very well lay claim to essential truths."[21] Funk, Groß, and Huber argue that fluidity, instability, or multiplicity are fundamental to a feeling of authenticity: "As an aesthetic construct, authenticity is deeply implicated in the process of communication that is realized in the interplay between production, aesthetic object, context, and reception. Authenticity, in this regard, becomes a matter of form and style in which the authentic is realized as a performance effect."[22] Authenticity, then, is less an ontological surety and more the result of a nuanced discursive or performative process that allows for interplay between multiple perceptual processes and multiple understandings of what is real. This understanding of authenticity is particularly important to the theatre of the real case studies considered herein, which make use of different real-world materials and cultivate different perceived experiences of realness in individual audience members.

Liveness, too, has been connected to ideas of realness especially as regards performance but in similarly flexible and non-determinative ways. Philip Auslander describes that "The common assumption is that the live event is 'real' and that mediatized events are secondary and somehow artificial reproductions of the real."[23] This value-laden judgement, which Auslander refutes, implies a superior real, live event and an inferior mediatization. Lindsay Brandon Hunter in *Playing Real: Mimesis, Media, and Mischief* uses Auslander to interrogate these assumptions and closely examine how mediatization and liveness operate to create "playful" reals that are pleasurable in their confusion of boundaries and refusal of the real/not-real or live/recorded binary.[24] Her analysis of livestream and broadcast events that combine recorded performance with live audiences and live interaction suggests that such events can create a feeling of the real even in the face of an ostensibly unreal performance. Media studies scholar Karin van Es also usefully describes liveness not from an ontological, phenomenological, or rhetorical perspective but as *"constellations of liveness."*[25] Her understanding, similar to Funk, Groß, and Huber's findings regarding authenticity, sees liveness as constructed through multiple processes of perception and valuation including but not limited to unpredictability and unrepeatability. In this book, such understandings of liveness are particularly useful when considering affective experience as relates to being in a shared space wherein liveness is collectively created through the immediate experience of attending theatre as part of an audience. Such ideas are further explored both as related to documentary theatre practice in chapter 2, and in immersive theatre in chapter 5.

A discussion of performance's relationship to the real also needs to consider the real/representation binary, which is both a fundamental and disputed component of theatre. Plato's allegory of the cave, in which an ignorant man living in a world where all he sees are shadows of the real, argues that representation and imitation is suspicious at best and dangerous at worst.[26] Jonas A. Barish's tracing of theatricality's ties to deceit, falsehood, and trickery in *The Antitheatrical Prejudice* similarly argues that representation is frequently characterized as inferior to the real. Barish suggests that a favouring of the real is now entrenched in Western metaphysics in such a way that "the concept of appearance cannot be regarded as philosophically (or morally) neutral; the suspicion that some form of deception is being worked is never very far away."[27] This valuing of the real is also found in Erving Goffman's writing, here cited by David Wiles: "that we all have frontstage and backstage modes of behaving is symptomatic of a modern devaluing of public life in favour of a more authentic private domestic life." This concept from *The Presentation of Self in Everyday Life* suggests a sharp demarcation between a lesser, public, fictive presentation of the self and a preferred, authentic, private self.[28]

Interestingly, just as imitations may be suspiciously viewed as being less-than-truthful reproductions that invade the real world, intrusions of the real into the representational can, arguably, be equally anxiety inducing. Marvin Carlson, in his monograph tracing the antecedents of theatre of the real throughout Western theatre history, describes how Plotinus drew on Plato –somewhat incorrectly – in the third century CE to argue that art can bypass the everyday and directly access the ideal real.[29] Carlson traces this general viewpoint into Romanticism, which characterizes "the romantic dramatist and the romantic actor as inspired geniuses, whose work imitated not surface reality, but the visions into the heart of nature gained by these geniuses within their own sensitive psyches."[30] Everyday reality, or objective reality, is troublesome, distracting, or limited in this instance.

The popularization of the proscenium arch and the accompanying enforcement of stringent audience etiquette in Western theatre also provides an example of a strict delineation between the real and the representational, in which the real world threatens representation.[31] This style of theatre architecture suggests that the intrusion of the real world into the fiction of a play can be highly disruptive. In terms of audience behaviour, audience members are inherently poised to both audibly and visually disappear in the silent darkness of a dimmed auditorium. Transgressions of this boundary result in removal from the theatre, other patrons' scolding, and general disapproval; the "magic" of the performance is broken or lost. Theatre's situation is such that it must manipulate and manage the real world using the tools of closed spaces, framing devices, and audience etiquette in order to build or sustain the fictive. This is in part related to the foundations of realism, which, as Roberta Barker and Kim Solga write in their introduction to *New Canadian Realisms*, in strictest terms "refers to the development in late nineteenth-century Europe of a genre of theatre dedicated to the direct mirroring of everyday life."[32] Realism relies upon signification at its core; that is, it does not put actual reality on stage but rather represents it through detailed and accurate re-creation. The illusion is that of a "walled-off (by a fourth wall) fictional totality"[33] that is thus vulnerable to any irruptions of the real world that might destroy the illusion.

This is where the genre of theatre of the real is a disruptive intervention into real/representation binarism: the genre of theatre of the real puts pressure on, and often self-consciously draws attention to, the debates between the real and fictive that Carlson, Barish, and others highlight simply because it aims to bring the real onto the stage, to put reality into the representation. In theatre of the real, rather than transforming real things into their fictional counterparts, "the real-world material employed in the creation of theatricality passes through fiction almost unaltered."[34] That is, theatre of the real uses as its raw material real events, real words, real spaces, real bodies, etc. that are not transformed into fictional representations but instead perform as themselves. Including documentary theatre, verbatim theatre, reality-based theatre, theatre-of-fact, theatre of witness, tribunal theatre, non-fiction theatre, war and battle re-enactments, autobiographical theatre and more, theatre of the real is that which "claim[s] specific relationships with events in the real world."[35] Carlson, in his very fittingly titled *Shattering Hamlet's Mirror*, refers to theatre of the real as an art form that necessarily catalyzed a major shift in the practical and phenomenological world: the rise of the genre marks a turning away from the centrality of mimesis that has been at the heart of theatre.

This increasing interest in bringing the real onstage is such that, Carlson writes, the history of "twentieth-century art (and of twentieth-century politics) has been dominated by a search for the real, for authenticity."[36] Referring to historical precedents, Bert O. States similarly suggests that "When stage imagery was freed of its servitude in mimetic signification, the one-to-one relationship between the sign and its signification, the theaters of Brecht, Meyerhold, Artaud, Wilder, the Absurdists, and Grotowski, among countless others, became possible."[37] This was important, Melanie Binette writes, because during the decade associated with the rise of Nazism and war propaganda, alienation and illusion were closely intertwined in political life. Hence, for both Bertolt Brecht and Antonin Artaud, the disruption of the illusions in the theatre auditorium had the potential to teach audience members how to also break with illusions in real life.[38] In addition to Brecht and Artaud's invocations of the real, Carlson's text charts a sweeping range of examples that indicate theatre's changing relationship to reality. From the *Living Newspapers* of the 1930s Federal Theatre Project in the United States and their use of real news items staged within, at times, a highly aesthetic, non-realist form to more contemporary high-profile verbatim works like *The Laramie Project* by Moises Kaufman and Anna Deavere-Smith's *Fires in the Mirror* and *Twilight: Los Angeles, 1992*, his impressive documentation of examples of theatre of the real all point to an increasing interest among theatre artists in subverting or otherwise blurring the delineation between the real and representation throughout Western theatre history. Referencing these twentieth-century theatremakers alongside the works of more recent artists and scholars in this book provokes a consideration of what might have prompted this resurgence or, indeed, whether the contemporary turn to the real is simply a continuation of these earlier modernist impulses. States argues, "One could define the history of theater – especially where we find it overthrowing its own traditions – as a progressive colonization of the real world."[39] In saying this, he points to a continuous development in which the real and the theatrical collide.

Although the real remains one half of theatre's persistent binary of fiction/reality, it is therefore clear that such a binary may no longer be stable nor productive for performance forms that utilize irruptions of the real. Carlson sums up the current state of the field in the closing to his introduction of *Shattering Hamlet's Mirror*:

> Theatre has not rejected the ideas of mimesis and the real, but it has moved those terms out of the realm of verifiable objectivity and into the realm where the theatre actually takes place, within the infinitely complex and variable scene of human perception and understanding. Here the traditional contrasted binary of the two terms becomes a constantly shifting field of differing relationships.[40]

As Carlson indicates, where theatre – and realness – really occur is "within the infinitely complex and variable scene of human perception and understanding," pointing to the necessary contingency, multiplicity, and instability that persist in any discussion of realness, especially as regards audience perception.

Thus, though "the real" has a long lineage, with reality being the essential reference point for ontological, epistemological, and ethical existence, an essential definition of the "real" is still lacking, and it remains a profoundly complex and volatile word.[41] Funk, Huber, and Groß sum up that "the only essence that postmodern thinking seems to accept is the fundamental gap between reality and its symbolic representation in language, images, or ideas,"[42] although the size, nature, and effect of that gap remain very much still up for debate. Sutton, Brind, and McKenzie agree: whether referring to "Realism (an art historical category) or 'the Real' (a philosophical construct), it is evident ... that neither is going to oblige us by falling tidily into a unified or stable definition. They are both inventions that have already been reinvented many times over."[43] The essentially contested and constructed nature of the real in philosophical discourse is reflected in my use of the term *real-ish-ness* to denote experiences of the apparently real produced, perceived, and/or felt by the audience within the given time and space of a performance. None of my arguments in this text are intended to confidently denote what is or is not "real" but instead play in realms of what I call "real-ish" by highlighting perceptions, feelings, or qualifications of realness.

As Marvin Carlson quotes in *Performance: A Critical Introduction*, following W.B. Gallie's *Philosophy and the Historical Understanding*, "Recognition of a given concept as essentially contested implies recognition of rival uses of it ... as not only logically possible and humanly 'likely', but as of permanent potential critical value to one's own use or interpretation."[44] The data of this study accordingly do not support a tidy one-to-one relationship wherein one form of theatre invokes one kind of realness. It is not the case that the audiences of historical re-enactment articulated only authenticity or that audiences of documentary theatre highlighted only truthfulness when asked about realness; they also variously invoked familiarity, liveness, relatability, facticity, credibility, emotion, intimacy, immediacy, sensory experience, and more. The term "real" was used flexibly by both the audiences and theatrical creators I interviewed, and I reflect that flexibility in the ways I similarly use the term throughout this book. This points to the complexity of the concept and frustrates any easily generalizable findings but also importantly demonstrates the wide array of language and ideas that individuals consider to be instantiations of the real: this is of particular relevance to wider social discussions about realness vis-à-vis fake news, truthiness, and more. In their work on documentary theatre, Alison Forsyth and Chris Megson reject defining theatre of the real, instead deciding to "probe the utility and viability of these terms [including documentary and verbatim theatre]."[45] The aim of this book, similarly, is not to define "the real" but to engage more broadly with notions of what might be received as real – or real-ish – in the context of performance.

FEELING

> AUD 2g: And realism never *feels real*. Because it's so ... people don't really talk in that way.
> AUD 2a: Because it's such an artifice.
> AUD 2g: Yeah, realism is false.[46]

In this interview excerpt the audience member articulates how important feeling is to an assessment of realness: realism just doesn't "feel real." Indeed, "feeling real" was a recurrent theme throughout my audience interviews in which affect, emotion, and feeling were frequently used as a barometer of realness. Within this text, I understand affect and emotion to be closely linked and to both fall under the wider concept of feeling. Following Erin Hurley's *Theatre & Feeling*, affects are unconscious bodily responses to stimuli or "immediate, uncontrollable, skin-level registration of a change to our environment."[47] I also borrow from Carl Plantinga, who helpfully articulates affect as "felt bodily states."[48] In the theatre, audiences may gasp, cringe, laugh, weep, or get goosebumps as they react affectively to what they view. Emotions, says Hurley, "name our sensate, bodily experience in a way that at once organises it and makes it legible to ourselves and consonant with others' experiences or emotional lives."[49] Plantinga similarly acknowledges the necessary reflection involved in assigning emotions, which he describes as requiring "a higher degree of cognitive processing" than affects.[50] Peta Tait lays out this cognitive processing in her description of emotions as "feelings and bodily sensations in the present (momentary), which are linked to previously experienced (remembered) voluntary and involuntary patterns of responses and a cognitive system of interpreting these."[51] We may, in other words, recognize affects as fitting particular emotions: getting teary eyed indicates we've watched a sad play, for instance.

Several scholars have noted the importance of feeling, emotion, and affect in theatre and performance: Hurley writes that it is "the affect-producing machine of theatre [that] lets us know that we are (by letting us feel that we are here)"[52] and that theatre's "solicitation, management, and display of feelings ... is the most important aspect of theatre's cultural work."[53] Most relevant to this work, scholars have also connected ideas of realness to affect. Julia Walker describes theatre as offering "an experience of the world as registered within our body's viscera in the form of an affective engagement that is very much in the moment and real."[54] Media scholar John Durham Peters, in his analysis of witnessing and audience in media, suggests that the body is a last bastion of the authentic and real, an entity that is used in broadcast media as "a criterion of truth and truthfulness."[55] Taken together, these comments suggest that there is something in the embodied, affective experience of theatre that impacts perceptual realness of theatrical effect. After all, as audience members, our bodies have real responses – visceral, affective – to what occurs onstage. A racing heart, teary eyes, goosebumps, or even boredom-induced sleep: such bodily experiences are real embodied responses that are experienced as such.

This is, in some ways, an extension of philosophical arguments that claim sensory experience as lived reality. Documentary filmmaker Lennaart Van Oldenborgh explains: "In lieu of a discussion of various philosophical discourses of the real, most writers on documentary practice appear to plump for an everyday definition of the real as perceptual, lived reality, without making this explicit."[56] Accordingly, even if poststructuralist theory argues that reality may be composed entirely of signifiers, the body – the sensory system being the means through which we experience the world around us – is the "thinnest" or most minimal layer of mediation between ourselves and observable reality. Antonin Artaud's writings on the importance of thorough sensory materiality to create a "real" experience are apt in this context: "We want to make out of the theatre a believable reality which gives the heart and the senses that kind of concrete bit which all true sensation requires."[57] Jacques Derrida, in his writings on Artaud's Theatre of Cruelty, further describes Artaud's work as being "not a *representation*" but "life itself, in the extent to which life is unrepresentable."[58] Rather than representing something using signs, textual or otherwise, Artaud desires some more immediate method of communication that bypasses representation, instead using the real body's sensory experience.

Furthermore, in a society where Photoshop, Instagram filters, deepfakes, and other forms of visual doctoring are commonplace, computing and human interaction scholar Michael Smyth suggests that the maxim "seeing is believing" may be replaced by the notion that "it is touch that determines reality."[59] The comment may seem obvious in a world of increasingly sophisticated virtual technology in which "[t]echnologies of virtualization have, in this sense, replaced the corporeal or 'hard' world with an objectless or 'soft' one."[60] In immersive theatre, hard materiality is accordingly a major part of what generates the genre's aura of realness, an idea further explored in chapter 5. Nicola Shaughnessy writes: "If 'authenticity' is attributed to this 'body' of work (and bodies at work), it is not a result of mimesis, but emerges from the spectator's felt response to the experience of liveness, being in a shared space and being affected by the haptic, visceral qualities of work which can 'touch' them (sometimes literally)."[61] I argue, following these scholars, that perceptions of realness, or at least the linked ideas of authenticity and liveness as articulated by Shaughnessy and Auslander, depend substantially on the feeling body.

The relational dimensions of affect are also important to note in this study of audience perception of realness. Patricia Ticineto Clough conceives of affect as the "power to affect and be affected,"[62] highlighting how affect (both any particular affect like disgust, surprise, etc. and affect as a class of psycho-physiological response) takes two: two bodies or objects passing forces in an encounter. In this case, a theatrical performance and all its affecting strategies acts upon the recipient body of the spectator to create an affective relation. The affecting and affected bodies are, in some ways, co-constituted and engaged in a continual feedback loop: as Caroline Heim has articulated, for instance, the affective response of an audience to a performance impacts the performers in turn.[63] This also means that, by virtue of its real embodied effects on an audience member (e.g., causing them to cry), a performance may come to feel increasingly real to that audience member. This affective circuit suggests a mutually reinforcing sense of realness and is discussed further in chapter 6 in terms of affective labour.

I also draw on the social cultural theories of Lauren Berlant and Eve Kosofsky Sedgwick, who consider affect to be, in Hurley's words, "socially readable."[64] In other words, affect also has a social purpose: it puts our feelings on display in the way that it makes us, for example, unintentionally gasp, grimace, or attend to danger in noticeable and interpretable ways for those around us. Nicholas Ridout in "The Vibratorium Electrified" describes the vibratory dimensions activated by theatrical performances that enable an exchange and circulation of energy or affect among the various actor and audience bodies present.[65] Teresa Brennan similarly describes how affect passes amongst crowds and groups, generating an atmosphere in a room[66] such that affect is "a social thing."[67] This suggests the importance of the audience as a collective, impacting each other just as much as the theatrical event impacts each individual. Melissa Gregg and Gregory J. Seigworth usefully articulate the ways in which affect operates in circulation:

> Affect arises in the midst of *in-between-ness*: in the capacities to act and be acted upon. Affect is an impingement or extrusion of a momentary or sometimes more sustained state of relations *as well as* the passages (and the duration of passage) of forces or intensities. That is, affect is found in those intensities that pass body to body (human, non-human, part-body and otherwise), in those resonances that circulate about, between, and sometimes stick to

bodies and worlds, *and* in the very passages or variations between these intensities and resonances themselves.[68]

If affects are a series of forces that are in-between bodies, within bodies, and between bodies and the world, then affect as experienced through the spectator's body in relation to other spectator and performer bodies can have a powerful impact on felt realness.

Each genre of theatre of the real considered in this text draws out affective bodily responses of some kind, offering a kind of realness in and through the soma of the spectator. These responses, after all, are real: they actually happen (hearts race, tears well up). The realness of the affective response during a show may then be reinforced or, perhaps invited to be perceived as such, by the real elements onstage: verbatim text, historical fact, site-specificity, etc. This suggests that realness can be mutually confirming through its affective engagements, especially when co-constituted by a multitude of bodies who, as a collective audience, are feeling together.

AUDIENCES

Though there are a multitude of competing, contested, and convoluted explorations of the "real," and how it might be felt in performance, there is one characteristic that is essentially undisputed: Van Oldenborgh states that "Quite aside from the *truth* of an image, 'realness' does have a great effect on its reception; it changes the way the image *performs on the viewer*. One could call this the special effect of the real."[69] If realness undeniably has an effect on its viewers, who are these viewers? What exactly do they perceive of as this "special effect of the real"? The third and final core concept of this book concerns audiences and spectatorship. In centring audience research, I explore the work done to the audience and done by the audience in relation to the perceived realness of the performance.

My analysis of audience members and the role of the (necessarily polyvalent) audience avoids neuropsychological analysis in favour of affective and phenomenological analysis to consider what audiences perceive realness to be, as well as why and how they perceive it to be thus. This focus on audience reception serves in part to help ameliorate the general scarcity of scholarly research on audiences in theatre and performance studies – despite the foundational role of the audience in performance.[70] Helen Freshwater describes a lack of empirical audience research in theatre and, as a result, a deeply limited research perspective: "theatre scholars seem to be more comfortable making strong assertions about theatre's unique influence and impact on the audiences than gathering and assessing the evidence which might support these claims."[71] Instead of speaking to "ordinary audience members," Freshwater goes on, scholars tend to draw on their own experiences or the opinions of reviewers and largely ignore other spectators.[72] This is despite the fact that audience research has a decades-long history in other fields including fan studies and media studies. Freshwater writes that "whereas researchers working on television and film engage with audiences through surveys, in-depth interviews, and ethnographic research, almost no one in theatre studies seems to be interested in exploring what actual audience members make of a performance."[73] Part of the reason for the lack of sustained attention may be the many challenges of actually conducting audience research; data collection is frequently labour intensive, requiring research ethics board approval, coordination of interviews or survey distribution to a relatively small sample size at in-person performances, and partnership with theatre companies or arts institutions. In additional to these practical, ethical, and logistical challenges of data collection, Kirsty Sedgman also points to barriers in the form of ideological concerns about audience research related to how the audience is typically characterized: audience members are either dismissed as non-experts whose perspectives are therefore of little value, or they are limited to the role of capitalist consumer whose only valuable contribution relates to what they will be willing to pay for.

As pertains to the first characterization of audiences as non-expert, there is a perception that somehow audience research might dangerously destabilize or disrupt perceived hierarchies around expertise. Writing on conducting audience research during what she characterizes as an "anti-expert age" Sedgman asks, "In a political climate beleaguered by efforts to delegitimize expertise, what are the implications for a research tradition that seeks to understand cultural value from a range of diverse perspectives?"[74] Her question suggests that the inclusion of multiple audience voices might inadvertently reinforce anti-expert rhetoric. Liz Tomlin alternately describes a "sense of protectionism over the 'ineffable' nature of the art object and the desire to hold onto the expertise of the professional critic or scholar who alone is qualified to appreciate it," a belief that has the effect of de-valuing the non-expert perspective of audience members.[75] This is a misreading of much audience research, which does not aim to find equivalence between the perspectives of the expert and non-expert but to study, as Sedgman goes on, "how people from different subject positions and social locations actively make sense of things by drawing on varying 'cultural reference points, political beliefs, sexual preferences, personal histories, and immediate preoccupations.'"[76] Especially when considering an idea as fraught as realness, or "the real," it is undeniably paramount to consider the implications of allowing for a multiplicity and foregoing perceived singular objectivity. Importantly, I do not aim to vault the position of the audience beyond the level of expert. I consider audiences as experts in being audiences: I aim at studying not what the essential meaning of a performance is but how audiences are approaching, negotiating, and analyzing it, embracing diverse systems of knowledge.

Turning to the second characterization of the audience as capitalist market force, this perception likely stems from the tendency for audience research to occur in marketing and development, rather than scholarly, contexts. Within her formative *Theatre Audiences*, Susan Bennett suggests that the majority of audience research has occurred outside the academic realm.[77] This, Janelle Reinelt suggests, feeds into a perception that audience research is synonymous with market research or "ratings games that are at the heart of commercial ventures within consumer-based capitalism" and therefore of limited value to scholars.[78] And yet, as M. NourbeSe Philip articulates in her piece "Who's Listening? Artists, Audiences, and Language," audience and market can be two very distinct things, the latter subject to hegemonic, capitalist, often exclusionary values that might threaten the community and relationality inherent in audiences.[79] My attempts here are not to generate market research or popularity ratings that will simply "give audiences what they want," ascribe success or quality, or offer some means of best instrumentalizing theatre for profit.[80] Instead, following Sedgman and Martin Barker, my emphasis is on epistemological considerations: how do audiences come to understand what they view?[81] How do they value and perceive? What hermeneutics are at play? And what methods of framing and interpretation are at play? If we wish to know how productions are being felt, perceived, and valued by those that attend them, we must engage with audiences. These ideological characterizations of audiences as dismissively non-expert or mere capitalist pawns deeply underestimate the utility and value of audience research.

Encouragingly, there are signs of a growing interest in audience research methods. While theatre and performance studies generally resisted audience methodologies up until the 2010s,[82] the launch of the Centre for Spectatorship and Audience Research in 2016, and the International Network for Audience Research in the Performing Arts (iNARPA) in 2017 suggest a growing interest in what empirical audience research may offer to theatre and performance studies. Matthew Reason's important work on children's experiences of theatre (2010), Jennifer Radbourne, Hilary Glow, and Katya Johanson's collection of audience studies in the performing arts (2013), Willmar Sauter's work on audience engagement (2000), Janelle Reinelt's project on UK spectators (2014), Sedgman's investigation of audiences at the National Theatre Wales (2016), Caroline Heim's work on audience talkbacks (2016) and actor–audience relations (2020), Ben Walmsley's study of audience engagement (2019), Dani Snyder-Young's work on spectatorship in relation to white supremacy (2020), and Matt Omasta's work on theatre for young people (2011), among others, have also all made important contributions to this emergent field. And yet, as Walmsley cautions, "audience research remains a fractured discipline" that is scattered and atomized, lacking coherence and rigour."[83] Reason and Sedgman, in their special issue of *Participations* on audience research likewise write that "The gap [of audience research] may not be absolute ... but nonetheless there has certainly been a *feeling* of absence ... a sense that until recently empirical research in theatre studies has largely consisted of sporadic pockets of activity, rather than something fully integrated into the subject area as a whole."[84] This book comes, therefore, at an important moment of expansion and consolidation of the field of theatre audience research, and aims to productively engage with extant work while also developing original theoretical analysis and methods.

In total, I interviewed seventy audience members (see table 1.1, following) across three productions.[85]

At each of the performances I attended, I made an announcement either shortly before the show started or after the show finished (as desired by the theatre artists producing the show). In the announcement I introduced myself and the project and invited audience members to approach me if they were interested in being involved. I usually remained in the theatre space itself since, in each case, the unique style of show precluded a traditional lobby. As audience members approached me, I provided them with a letter of information and

Table 1.1
Overview of interviews conducted and data collected

Production title	Company and location	Dates of performances attended	Number of audience members interviewed	Name and position of artistic personnel interviewed
Good Fences	Downstage, Calgary, Alberta, Canada	25, 27, 28 March 2015	10	Ellen Close, artistic producer (until 2017) and artistic director (from 2017) Simon Mallett, artistic director (until 2017) Col Cseke, actor (group interview)
Trinity Pageant	Rising Tide Theatre, Trinity, Newfoundland, Canada	20, 24, 27, 31 August 2016	23	Donna Butt, artistic director (individual interview)
TomorrowLove™	Outside the March, Toronto, Ontario, Canada	1, 2, 3, 4 (evening and matinee) December 2016	37	Michelle Yagi, producer (individual interview) Mitchell Cushman, artistic director (individual interview)
An Enemy of the People	Tarragon Theatre, Toronto, Ontario, Canada	22 October 2014; 15, 17 October 2015	Attended post-show talkbacks	Maria Milisavljevic, translator (via email)

consent form. Consenting audience members were then interviewed in two ways: semi-structured group interviews or semi-structured individual interviews. The composition and size of interview groups depended on audience members' preferences: I invited participants to be interviewed in the groups they approached me in, or to be interviewed individually. This resulted in interview group sizes ranging from one to eight, and lengths of interviews ranging from five to twenty minutes.

These brief interviews were intended to extend the theatre-going experience as organically as possible – offering a space for conversation about the performance immediately following that performance, in the same physical space. I spoke to audience members in a church hall while the actors put away the set at one show and huddled under a balcony after a particularly memorable outdoor performance in the rain at another. This follows Kathleen Gallagher, Christine Balt, and Lindsay Valve's description of "guerrilla-style" audience research that allows for "emplaced processes of collective meaning-making" to unfold.[86] For many of the productions I attended, this meant that some of the experience of the show seemed to linger: the benefits of this method were the ability to capture affect as audience members immediately "came off" a performance and to explore the social dynamics of the audience in the same site in which they were previously spectating. In this way, traces of the performance were acting to extend the audience member's experiences "in situ."

Participating audience members were typically asked the following key questions: What did you find important, unique, or valuable about this show, if anything? What did you find real about this performance, and is realness important to you as an audience member? I followed these up with a number of optional additional queries, including

> How do feel about the performance? What words would you use to describe yourself/your emotions at this point?
> How would you describe the performance?
> What did you find valuable about the experience?
> What did you know about the show prior to attending? Have you seen other theatre before?
> Would you describe this show as more or less real than other theatre you have seen before? How does it differ from other shows in terms of acting style? Set and settings? The position and role of the audience?

How would you describe realness in theatre? What makes a theatre production real? How would you define the word real? Is there anything else you would like to add?

No identifying data were gathered from participants, and it is important to highlight that this audience research is neither sociological nor demographic. These questions, instead, largely followed the practice of "guided introspection." This method is described by Melanie Wallendorf and Merrie Brucks as a method in which "people other than the researcher are asked to introspect or think aloud about themselves and their actions [and in this case also their experiences, emotional states, and heuristic models], and their introspections are recorded as data."[87] This method was most apt given my interest in how audiences processed and understood their own experiences of a show's felt realness.

The interviews were audio recorded, then transcribed and analyzed using basic coding techniques for discursive analysis: I created a variety of codes that were descriptive, values-based, and *in vivo* (i.e., taken from the words of the interviewees themselves). I used these to code the interviews in order to study patterns, contradictions, and emergent themes from which I might develop theory. For instance, in coding the interviews related to *Good Fences*, a production about the oil and gas industry in Alberta, an emergent metaphor around the notion of "both sides" in response to my questions about realness became evident: several audience members remarked on some version of the idea that the play was balanced, which in turn spurred my investigation of how the idea of political balance might be related to felt realness. As another example, the analysis of interviews related to my immersive theatre case study suggested the importance of not only what is said in interviews but also those moments when language and description is elusive. The pauses, hesitations, jumbled syntax, "hmms" and "uhhs" and all sorts of extra-discursive data from this series of interviews revealed the deeply affective experience the audience members had as they struggled to put their experience to words.

The data garnered from my audience interviews thus largely led my theorizing; the kinds and frequency of certain phrases, terms, or other patterns, and the descriptions of experiences of realness (or the lack thereof) provided the impetus in each case for analysis of particular production elements and consideration of particular theoretical lenses. Ben Walmsley cites Celia J. Orona in his project on audience perception of cultural value to argue that grounded theory is useful in audience studies for its "flexible and reflexive process of introspection, intuition and rumination."[88] This was particularly true of my investigation of the multifaceted idea of realness, which I pondered over often simultaneously with the audience members I spoke to. At the same time, I also approached the topic with a certainty of scope, scale, and direction and a determination of pre-existing theoretical study. I thus consider my methodology not to be strictly grounded theory but describe it more accurately as "audience-led" research: my inquiry and examination of each production theoretically was led by the audience data I gathered. Like Walmsley, I aim to engage in "thinking with" audiences, who are not only sources of data but also possess knowledge bases, skills, and complementary perspectives.[89] This framework offers a model for audience research that marries the multiple perspectives of the audience with the singular expertise of a researcher, allowing for a spacious co-creation of analytical possibility.

In addition to the audience members I interviewed, I also had the opportunity to interview the artists and creators of the shows under study. I found these interviews highly useful as a means for me to try to examine the performances for evidence of what the creators and performers suggested their intent or hope was. It must be stated that, as a result, I developed relationships with many of the artists, and in this text, I work to best represent that relationship in an incisive but ultimately respectful way. Their generosity and openness to my research demands a kind of reciprocity alongside criticality and distance. In many cases what I experienced, in combination with the audiences' voices, added to or supported the creators' words. At other times, I felt a distinct disagreement with some of what the artists said.

These instances of disagreement served to further my conviction that elements of realness can be read and unread differently by different bodies at different times. This raises the question: what happens when what the creators think of as real and what the audience thinks of as real do not align? This query seems to be a productive rather than a problematic one. I found it to be illuminating when my perceptions of what was real about a show contrasted with what the creator or the audience (or both) thought was real. I do not consider these contradictions between artist intent and audience reception to be failings or necessary points of criticism that I, as researcher, should highlight.

Instead, such moments were productive insofar as they provide opportunities to consider what assumptions we make about what others will find to be real or not and what truths about experience those assumptions might reveal. Might our understandings of the real need to be adapted to relate to contemporary concerns, multiple audience members with a concordant multiplicity of life experiences, backgrounds, and intersectional identities, and several possible understandings?

Finally, while this book is not a work of autoethnography, it is necessarily informed by my subjective experience as a fellow audience member attending the productions I examine herein. Debate as to what constitutes ethnographic practice within audience research is lively, and many audience researchers describe their work as ethnographically inspired, or using ethnographic approaches, even as the work they do typically does not satisfy traditional ideas of ethnography. As Sedgman writes, "the real point behind this argument seems to be less about the relevance of the term 'ethnographic' per se as it is about the need to study how the relationship between cultural engagement and lived experience is negotiated in practice."[90] Ien Ang corroborates this view and argues that "scrutinizing ... audiences is not an innocent practice. It does not take place in a social and political vacuum."[91] In this case, there are a variety of contextual factors to note: the fact that most interviews occurred in groups composed of both strangers and theatregoing companions; interviews usually took place in the space of the performance immediately after its conclusion; all interviews were conducted by me (a white cis woman in her mid-twenties), and in almost all cases I had also watched the show and thus was also imbued with all the affective and other traces of the performance; and the majority of this research was initially conducted as part of my doctoral thesis. These aspects necessarily colour the audiences' responses to my interview questions, as well as my subsequent analysis. Sedgman, following Kim Schrøder, Kirsten Drotner, Stephen Kline, and Catherine Murray's *Researching Audiences*, calls for self-reflexivity in audience research: "threading through findings a critical consideration of how the knowledge generated may have been inflected by (1) the conditions under which discourse is first captured and then analysed and (2) the communicative conditions of research itself."[92] I have therefore attempted to demarcate when I am describing my own meaning-making of a particular performance or audience response.

I follow Sedgman's lead and describe my work as simply empirical audience research – not to suggest scientific validity or objectivity by using the term empirical but to denote that my analysis is based on data gathered directly from audience members rather than speculative claims about an imagined or generalized audience. Indeed, my work is necessarily far from objective and it suffers from several limitations: a relatively small sample size, a dependence on auditory communication, and self-selection bias, to name just a few. As Katya Johanson and Hilary Glow suggest, cited by Walmsley, "qualitative audience research is plagued by a whole host of ethical and methodological challenges, including vested interests of evaluators and commissioners of evaluation, a defensive tendency towards advocacy rather that objective evaluation, the lack of sufficiently affective language to describe artistic experiences; audiences' sense of responsibility for their own cultural experiences, their tendency to empathise with audience researchers, and their conflation of cultural value with other socio-political values."[93] But, as Schrøder et al. put it "the methods available may not be perfect, but there is no alternative – except ignorance."[94] To best attempt to overcome some of the challenges of qualitative research, I use a combination of methods: firsthand experience as an audience member myself, observation of and interviews with fellow audience members, and interviews with artists to explore the dramaturgical, scenographic, and other means by which contemporary performances might come to feel real.

REAL-ISH-NESS

This text necessarily builds upon the work of other scholars who investigate theatre's realness. While Jenn Stephenson's analysis of theatre of the real in *Productive Insecurity: Perils and Products of Theatres of the Real* draws out the impossibility of the real in theatrical performances that promise it and the resultant insecurity, I argue here that spectatorial belief structures, as constituted by perception and affect, can actually construct a kind of realness. My aim is to investigate how spectators come to perceive realness in response to theatrical productions that invoke – and provoke – real experiences. This is a question that Natalie Alvarez also engages with in her study of immersive experiences related to cultural differences. Her experiences in a mock Afghan village used as training ground for soldiers, as part of a simulated terrorist cell, and participating in a staged border crossing between California and Mexico demonstrate how embodied immersions can "*produce* the realities they ostensibly merely emulate" for those participating.[95]

If performance experiences, then, can not only (re)present the real onstage but also construct it, understanding how performance does so from the perspective of audiences and spectators themselves is paramount for a better understanding not only of realness in theatre but also potentially realness more broadly. I thus offer *real-ish-ness*, or the sense of realness produced, perceived, and/or felt by the audience within a performance, as a product of audience reception that combines cognitive understanding, sensory perception, and affective relation. Each chapter considers these aspects by drawing together the case study's initial status as a conceptual object of realness (i.e., its categorization as documentary, participatory, historical, or immersive theatre; that is to say its status as a form of theatre of the real), the experience of time and space created in the production, and finally the affective engagement of the spectator in that time and space.

Importantly, the case studies for this book were chosen because they engage with different forms of the real in their content, spanning documentary performance, participatory theatre, historical re-enactment, and immersive theatre. In particular, the contemporary performances considered in this book "ride the line" between the real/fictive worlds. It is the particular in-betweenness or, to use Patrick Duggan's term in *Trauma-Tragedy: Symptoms of Contemporary Performance*, "mimetic shimmering" afforded by these examples that results in a pervasive undecidability in determining what is reality and what is representation.[96] In *Good Fences*, audiences hear a discussion about Alberta's real-world reliance on oil staged on a highly theatrical, representational set. In *An Enemy of the People*, real audience members participate in a staged debate that invites both real-world political discussion and fictional storyline. In the Trinity Pageant, audiences learn about Newfoundland's real historic buildings through imagined tales. In *TomorrowLove™*, audiences engage with very real emotions and relationship building while they watch entirely fictional, futuristic stories. All four productions blur any neat division between the real and the representational: they present real-world issues, times, spaces, affects, and sensations within, amongst, or alongside the fictional. These productions allow for a diverse understanding of how theatres of the real produce perceptions and feelings of realness.

Chapter 2 "'Everything is True, Some Things are Scripted': Documentary Practice and the Presentation of Multiple Truths" focuses on documentary theatre-making practices. It begins by looking at an aesthetics of the amateur and the deliberate scripting of uncertainty or error in Downstage theatre company's *Good Fences*. This is a piece of theatre about the contentious relationship between the oil and gas and ranching industries in Alberta, Canada, which typically exist within political silos or echo chambers. The presentation of multiple, conflicting times and spaces suggests the necessary multiplicity of perspectives when it comes to the very fraught issue of the oil and gas industry. In this way, the show's constant renegotiation of what is real, what appears real, and what might become real demands a constant renegotiation of one's political position while watching the play.

Chapter 3, "Talking to, at, and with Audiences: The Politics of Participation," considers how *An Enemy of the People* (Schaubühne/Tarragon Theatre) engages its audiences in active political discussion. The show uses a fourth-wall-breaking town hall to encourage audiences to voice opinions, but the relationship of that town hall to the real world and the play world remains obscured, such that the role of the audience as simultaneously real/fictive threatens the efficacy of their participation. Using theories of relationality, politics, and audience participation, the ethics and effects of this means of generating audience participation are explored.

Chapter 4, "'You Will Long Remember': The Nostalgic Real in Sight-Specific Historical Re-enactment," focuses on historical re-enactment and site-specific performance. It uses the example of the Newfoundland-based Trinity Pageant to consider how historical re-enactment both uses and produces cultural identity by employing real past, real space, and real intended future gains for the tourism industry. The temporal blending at work in this production specifically locates a concern that spans both past and future – the survival of real Newfoundland culture. And, it explores this concern in the very geographical region it is dedicated to preserving. This artistic practice encourages a blurring of past, present, and future and both the real and the fictional. The resulting construction of a national identity is ultimately based on both the real and the mythical and prompts a careful consideration of the ethics, risks, and limitations of such an alchemy.

Chapter 5, "Constructing Immersive Experiences for 'Real' Engagement," takes as its focus immersive practices in theatre. I first highlight the operation of time and space in what might be considered generic immersive structure. This structure can be found in the expansive worlds that audiences encounter in productions, especially those created by the well-known British company, Punchdrunk, which are crafted for independent spectatorial exploration. The chapter proceeds through analyses of spatial configuration and personalization using Toronto-based theatre company Outside the March's *TomorrowLove™* as a case study to argue that immersive theatre employs sensation and proprioception as "real" engagement that in turn generates perceived "realness."

Finally, chapter 6, "Immersion and Exertion: Audiences, Feeling-Labour, and the Production of Real-ish-ness" investigates the emotional investment and audience labour necessary in participatory and immersive theatre. Most specifically, I focus on the labour required of audiences to make their experience explicitly more real. I investigate the relationship between realness and affect, as well as the ways in which they may be combined to make an experience both feel real and produce real feelings. The chapter argues that an audience's emotional investment in a performance generates its own kind of felt realness.

Throughout all chapters, primary research conducted with theatre makers and audience members allows for a thorough, multivalent consideration of notions of the "real" from a variety of affective and phenomenological perspectives. As theatre of the real, the productions considered in this book blur any neat division between the real and the representational: they present real-world issues, use real-world spaces, and provoke real sensations within, amongst, or alongside the fictional in various manifestations. In doing so, they achieve at least two things: they playfully invoke spectators' perception of time, space, and reality, and they cultivate a group of theatregoers who experience an affective experience of realness. Rather than argue for a particular definition of realness, I suggest throughout that contemporary performance realness stems from a local, immediate, and intimate engagement on the part of the spectator. The case studies included here make use of particular space(s) and time(s) that encourage a felt realness or affective real, one which moves to create relationships between and among audience members, site, and performers. The realness that is used and performed by these companies is thus less reliant on absolute facticity, veracity, or need for verifiable source material and more on the perceived realness of the performance from the perspective of the audience experiencing space, time, and affect. That is, the performances examined are ones that exist as a product of the real source material but also unfurl as real products in their own right – because of the ways in which they engage spectators' perceptions and feelings. It is precisely this real-ish-ness – the result of the felt immediacy, intimacy, and nearness that spectators experience – that allows for an examination of the construction, destruction, and valuation of the real both within the theatre, and also beyond.

2

"Everything is True, Some Things are Scripted"
Documentary Practice and the Presentation of Multiple Truths

"Everything is true, some things are scripted, and some things are not," quips Artistic Producer Ellen Close in response to an audience member's question about the extent to which *Good Fences* – the theatrical production examined in this chapter – is real. Produced by Downstage theatre company, *Good Fences* examines the real-world relationship between the oil and gas and ranching industries in Alberta, Canada through a fictionalized storyline about an oil executive whose new home is the location of a proposed pipeline. The talkbacks for the performances I attended during the show's 2015 "Community Tour" invariably addressed questions of the show's realness: audience members consistently asked about what was real, how much was real, and how the actors "really feel" about the issues presented. The audience members' questions stem not only from the show's aforementioned engagement with real-world issues, but also from its creation process: it was based on interviews with ranchers and oil workers conducted by the Downstage Creation Ensemble of Braden Griffiths, Ellen Close, Col Cseke, Simon Mallett, Ethan Cole, Anton de Groot, and Nicola Elson. Though the show uses these interviews with real-world individuals, however, the creators do not classify it as verbatim or documentary theatre. Further, although the cast members play themselves at various moments in the show and describe their actual experience of creating the show, they also do not perceive the play to be autobiographical. As Close explained, "There's nothing verbatim in the show, and it's not documentary theatre, and actually everything is quite carefully fictionalized from – taken a step or two from real people that we met."[1] As both of Close's quotes above demonstrate, the company desires to shift the conversation away from a strict true/false or real/not-real binary to generate a more expansive definition of realness: The show can be true and authentic at the same time that is scripted and fabricated. It can both be about the artists themselves and their process, and carefully fictionalized. Close's response to the audiences' eager desire to know what in the play was "really real," and what was not, speaks to the slippery nature of the real, which gets caught somewhere between objective ontology and subjective experience.

The story in *Good Fences* follows Devon MacIntyre, an executive at an oil and gas company whose family purchases land in a ranching community in the Southern foothills outside of Calgary in Alberta, Canada. Shortly after Devon moves into his new home, another oil and gas company reveals plans to build a sour gas pipeline through his new property. This leads Devon to convene with his new neighbours, including Caroline Stewart, a rancher whose family has lived on the land for generations, and Garrett Shaw, whose wife's multiple sclerosis seems to be aggravated by sour gas leakage. Devon soon finds himself going head-to-head with a land surface agent from the oil and gas company and facing consequences from his own employer for acting out. He ends up in a deeply complex situation where livelihoods in both the ranching and oil and gas industries are threatened. Interspersed within this fictional storyline, the performers – as themselves – frequently break the fourth wall to describe their process of creating the piece, recall personal memories, and comment on the action.

Good Fences operates with a sense of realness that is difficult to pin down; it oscillates between feeling fictional and feeling more akin to documentary or autobiographical work. However, it is precisely this suspended or withheld nature of the real in *Good Fences* that, I argue, contributes to its feeling real. By preserving space for contradiction and multiplicity, the play's conclusion is, ironically, inconclusive – much in the same way conclusions are rarely tidily resolved in the real world. The show finishes without revealing to the audience whether the main character, Devon, eventually capitulates to the oil and gas company in order to save his job or sticks with the ranching community to defend the land and prevent the pipeline from being built. Instead, the cast and crew end each performance with a talkback, turning from the fictional story-world out to the real-world. In these talkbacks, Close answers questions and encourages conversation between individual audience members. The other actors sit in the audience and respond to questions as needed, which range from comments about the accuracy of the depiction of the ranching community, to technical questions about the oil extraction process, to requests for the show to travel to other communities. By self-consciously attempting to resist classification and conclusion, *Good Fences* manages to engage with several "reals" that contribute to an overall affective real, (i.e., something that feels real but is paradoxically unresolved, fragmentary, unstable, and entirely subjective). This real-ishness aptly reflects the fragmentation and indefinability of the real cultivated by the performance. Even the creators' resistance to classifying the show as documentary theatre highlights the importance of leaving space for different interpretations over what might be considered real within the performance and, more broadly, in the real-world politics in which it also engages. Prompted by interviews with audience members in which notions of balance and the presence of "both sides" were pointed to as producing a sense of realness, this chapter considers how a real-world partisan issue, staged in such a way as to forefront multiplicity, instability, and multiple truths, can actually come to produce a strong sense of felt realness for audiences, with important implications for the production of political belief structures in the real-world.

LOCATING THE REAL

While its creators do not consider *Good Fences* to be a piece of documentary theatre, the working style of Downstage theatre company, and this show in particular, do make use of some conventional documentary practices. Alan Filewod, for instance, details the unique thrust of Canadian documentary theatre as having an emphasis on "collective creation and the transformation of historical or community experience into art."[2] Downstage often works using a collective creation ensemble model to make "theatre that creates meaningful conversations around social issues." They produce performances that are inventive, relevant, accessible, and local and almost always include a talkback after the performance in which the audience can discuss the show with its creators and performers.[3] Filewod goes on to suggest that historical Canadian documentary theatre shows were largely "intended originally for audiences who had a special interest in the subject but little familiarity with the theatre. In most cases, the original audience brought their own experience to an understanding of the performance."[4] This is also true of *Good Fences* which locates both its real-world audience and its story content in Alberta. In touring to various communities in the province, this meant audiences could be expected to arrive with a special interest in and knowledge about the oil and gas industry examined in the show.

In fact, day-to-day life in Alberta is almost inextricably bound up with the oil and gas industry. Alberta is widely regarded as "the energy province" or the "Texas of Canada," known for its oil industry (it is the third largest crude oil reserve in the world[5]) and generally politically conservative jurisdiction.[6] As one might expect in an economy so dominated by one industry, life in the province is tied to the rise and fall of oil prices, including theatre.[7] During "boom" cycles, this can mean increased disposable income for the population to spend on theatre, and increased funding and sponsorship opportunities for the arts. *Good Fences* premiered, for instance, in 2012 at a festival titled the "Enbridge playRites Festival of New Canadian Plays" – Enbridge being a major owner and operator of several oil and gas pipelines in the province, which the performers highlight during the performance.[8] During "bust" cycles, however, the opposite situation occurs, resulting in a fairly volatile economy.

Alberta's economy also provides inspiration for *Good Fences*'s content, which explores the long-standing conflict between the oil and gas and ranching industries. Close cites a murder in which an oil executive was shot and killed by a rancher as prompting the creation of the show.[9] The incident she refers to took place in October 1998, when Eifion Wyn (Wayne) Roberts, a farmer from a small town north of Calgary called Bowden, shot and killed Patrick Kent, the vice-president of the oil and gas company called KB Resources. Court records state that Roberts fired five shots at Kent as the culmination of a long-standing dispute over possible contamination from a KB Resources well that was on Roberts' ranching property.[10]

Articles about the trial illustrate the deeply entrenched animosity between the oil and gas and ranching industries in Alberta. In an article describing the creation of a fund to support the Roberts family, farmer Bill Pankiw says that he "doesn't know Roberts from a 'bucket of bolts' but knows the frustration farmers feel when dealing with oil companies."[11] Memorably, Roberts himself stated that he believed the only reason he was charged with first-degree murder was because he killed the vice-president of an oil company: "Money from the oil companies lines the provincial coffers," he said. "If it was [just my] neighbour you would've charged me with manslaughter."[12] Comments such as these are emblematic of widespread tensions between the two industries over issues of public health and safety, environmental concerns, and economic benefit.

In their interview with me, Close and Mallett described how the initial impulse for the show also came from reading a true-crime novel by Andrew Nikiforus called *Saboteurs: Wiebo Ludwig's War Against Big Oil*. The novel is based on the story of Wiebo Ludwig, the leader of the Trickle Creek Christian community in rural Alberta who was convicted of sabotaging oil and gas wells that he believed were responsible for poisoning his community and causing miscarriages and still-births. Wiebo Ludwig's story inspired not only Andrew Nikiforuk's book, but also a National Film Board documentary called *Wiebo's War*, a musical from Ghost River Theatre in Calgary titled *An Eye for an Eye*, and a 2017 production at the Tarragon Theatre in Toronto, *Peace River Country* by Maria Milisavljevic. The volatile situation created by conflicts between the oil and gas industry and the ranching community is apparently appealing for artists looking to dramatize conflicts that are locally relevant. The different perspectives and possible readings of the characters and incidents in both Ludwig and Roberts' cases invite strong and aggressive partisan opinions, characterized by the epithets used to refer to Ludwig as "eco-warrior" on the one side and "industry-terrorist" on the other.[13]

Dramatizing such provocative issues poses a real risk of creating increasingly entrenched partisan opinions. Nowhere is this truer than in Alberta, where local audience members of *Good Fences* likely frequently wrestle with the oil and gas industry in their real lives. A show based on a series of deeply divisive real issues could easily produce that same divisiveness among audience members. After all, are audience members attending theatrical productions to have their own views reaffirmed, or are they attending in order to have their views potentially challenged? The latter is, arguably, the less-likely reason for attendance.

This question has wide-reaching implications well beyond theatre attendance that are worth considering: in the world of online media, fears of creating political silos and echo chambers wherein users only ever encounter opinions similar to their own and therefore become deeply entrenched in radical viewpoints or hyper-partisan perspectives have been widespread.[14] As Rachel Botsman writes, the internet amplifies homophily, the tendency to associate and connect with people similar to us, in terms of ethnicity, age, gender, education, political affiliation, religion, and occupation.[15] This is because social media sites in particular have made it easy to identify and align oneself with particular users and therefore particular viewpoints: "recent analyses of Facebook feeds and Twitter networks reveal that their user's informational input is being radically filtered, that users are being exposed largely to arguments and views with which they already agree."[16] If, as I suggest, our tendency is to drift towards media that affirms currently held opinions, there is a danger that, as Botsman goes on to say, we end up in "loud and polarizing echo chambers with less space for constructive disagreement, debate or enlightenment."[17]

C. Thi Nguyen examines the dangers of becoming inculcated in such single-sided discourse. He differentiates between epistemic bubbles and echo chambers, defining epistemic bubbles as "social epistemic structure[s] in which other relevant voices have been left out, perhaps accidentally" and, the arguably more dangerous, echo chambers as "social epistemic structure[s] from which other relevant voices have been actively excluded and discredited."[18] This is an important distinction to make because it makes clear how people can become deeply entrenched in an epistemic structure vis-à-vis an echo chamber: it is not only that a person doesn't encounter contradictory evidence due to a highly curated Facebook page or YouTube algorithm[19] but that counter-evidence has been already, pre-emptively discredited.[20] As Botsman quotes from Barack Obama's farewell speech in January 2017 "we become so secure in our bubbles that we accept only information, whether true or not, that fits our opinions."[21]

Given their desire to produce theatre that creates meaningful conversation, this is precisely what the creators of *Good Fences* wish to avoid. To avoid creating outright divisiveness, the show deliberately avoids offering a partisan argument or aligning with one side or the other. Such alignment might prompt audience members to have vehement reactions, in either agreement or disagreement, that would only further entrench their current perspectives. As former artistic director Mallett articulated in an interview, the company's interest in the dramatic potential of the piece had more to do with the relationship as a whole rather than any one perspective: "[we were interested in] the relationship as a whole [as opposed to choosing one side or the other] and we sort of identified the lack of positive communication as one of the sort of barriers to mutually beneficial relationships."[22] The focus, then, of *Good Fences* is not on taking one position or another to convince would-be audience members but on considering the larger situation in which these two sides have developed and how they might speak to each other: a kind of meta-examination of how such opinions are formed.

In *Good Fences*, audiences watch as the characters encounter various information and perspectives that both confirm and challenge their previously held beliefs. For instance, the character Devon is a firm supporter of the oil and gas industry as the play opens because he is vice president of an oil company. His perspective shifts after meeting his neighbours and learning about a rival company's plans for a sour gas pipeline. Even his stalwart ranching neighbour, Caroline Stewart, has a complex position on oil and gas. In theory she is opposed, but her younger brother works on a nearby drill, and this complicates the way she views the industry. Garret and Pat Shaw, two other ranchers, display two other shifting attitudes towards the oil and gas industry: Both desperately need the money the construction of the sour gas pipeline would bring them, but they are suspicious of the dangers of sour gas.

This is not to say that audience members attending *Good Fences* are not suspicious about the show's political position as regards oil and gas. I myself questioned whether it was possible for the Downstage ensemble members to have a neutral stance after having done so much research. Accordingly, instead of maintaining a kind of constructed objectivity, the performers in *Good Fences* actually reveal their own biases or changing opinions about the oil or ranching industries as the show progresses. The actors frequently address the audience in asides that effectively reveal the structures of creating the play, and also the structures of the actors' beliefs about oil and gas. These revelations play like slips in the script or otherwise unscripted interruptions. For instance, at one point in the show Ellen Close addresses her own attempt at achieving neutrality when she describes how the company tried to talk to people who had several different perspectives:

> Okay, sure, [I'm] an opinionated person, uh, I definitely came in with my own opinions about that pipeline. And you know I had thought a lot about how I should really try to stay open to whatever he [an oil and gas company land surface agent] might say, but that experience made me realize that I initially probably wasn't open in a real way, because I was really surprised by how compelling and, and charismatic and generous I found him, that I walked out of the meeting with a completely different, um, perspective on that project than I entered with.[23]

In this way, the production refuses to present a single side or view, but at the same time it does not attempt objectivity and reveals biases and opinions.

Part of Nguyen's argument about the dangers of echo chambers is, notably, that so-called neutral or objective information does not actually disrupt them: "the route to undoing their influence is not through direct exposure to supposedly neutral facts and information; those sources have been pre-emptively undermined."[24] Facts and truths actually (and perhaps worryingly) hold relatively little weight when it comes to political issues: A 2016 Buzzfeed analysis of social media posts concluded that "The best way to attract and grow an audience for political content on the world's biggest social network is to eschew factual reporting and instead play to partisan biases using false or misleading information that simply tells people what they want to hear."[25] Importantly, then, instead of attempting any kind of neutrality, *Good Fences* tries to subvert a binary framework by instead suggesting the possibility of more nuanced opinions and examining the construction of such opinions: The piece takes as its dramatic arc not a singular event that explicitly produces partisanship but rather a series of constantly shifting perspectives and developing opinions. Moments of staged disagreement and conflict between the characters and actors about the oil and gas industry and the show's creation process are what actually prompted the audience question referred to in this chapter's introduction about the extent to which the play was "real." The audience member was specifically interested in how many of the "fights" in the show were real.

In this way, *Good Fences* remains very tied to a specific, local issue and its relationship to place; however, it manages to do so in a way that doesn't proselytize. Instead, the company's careful curation of space and time creates an encounter for audience members that is immediate, local, and inviting. This means that it feels real but doesn't necessarily invite real-world partisanship. This allows the production to offer a space that is neither a self-reinforcing echo chamber nor supposedly neutral ground, but one that allows for continually shifting perspectives that are distinct from, or outside of, the day-to-day reality of entrenched opinion.

THE AMATEUR AESTHETIC

One of the most important design features of the 2015 tour of *Good Fences* is that it was specifically designed for real-world spaces like community halls, churches, and gyms, rather than for theatres. Performing a piece about Alberta, in Alberta, might suggest that the already held beliefs of the audience members would merely be reinforced by performing the show in such a "real" space. If the audience members already hold beliefs about the contentious oil and gas industry, then watching *Good Fences* staged in spaces like community centres and church halls would seem to invite them to carry their real-world opinion with them into the performance. This is not to say that spectators would fail to fully suspend their disbelief or engage with the performance in a space outside of a theatre. Rather, that performing a piece about an issue that audience members may engage with on a day-to-day basis needs to take into account that audience members will enter day-to-day spaces with already established opinions. Audience members, in their lives outside the theatre, may have even met to discuss these issues in the very same spaces now used for the performance. Take, for instance, the mounting of the production in the Longview Community Hall in 2013. This site is a real-world space in which residents meet to discuss community concerns. More significantly still, it was the location for the theatre company's initial research interviews during the creation process. As such, performing the play in real-world spaces like this one could cause audiences to feel more polarized about the issue. They may be more quickly reminded of the real-world debates on the same issue because those debates have occurred in those very spaces.

However, these real-world spaces offer a significant advantage for *Good Fences* and its creators' ambitions to avoid partisan presentation. The non-theatrical nature of the spaces of performance, in this case, invites the audience to enter into a place suffused with an "amateur aesthetic" in which the absence of experts and the potential for failure, change, and adaptation encourage an exploration and openness on the part of the audience. That is, performing professional theatre in non-theatrical spaces requires adjustment, flexibility, and makeshift solutions as companies must confront such atypical challenges as where to place the lights or how arrange the chairs. These are challenges amateur productions or community theatre often face, performing in makeshift theatres in churches, gymnasiums, lunchrooms, and meeting halls, but that professional productions in union houses do not usually have to address. Through its carefully tailored aesthetic style, I argue that the production purposefully and consciously makes use of a kind of amateur aesthetic in spaces primed for discussion and community involvement. In this way, *Good Fences* manages to use space as a means of lowering rather than heightening the partisan nature of its content.

Helen Nicholson, Nadine Holdsworth, and Jane Milling argue that amateur theatre is in its ascendancy in the twenty-first century.[26] As part of this trend, Holdsworth, Milling, and Nicholson point to the presence of "impersonations of amateurishness by professional artists as a cultural imaginary of the amateur."[27] This is what the professional theatre artists of Downstage are doing in order to generate a precise tone for their performance and audiences, and their "stylistic amateurism" is evident from the outset of the performance. The design of the show is simple, composed of a limited set-up of a light blue back drop and a variety of portable set pieces including a barbed-wire fence, table, chairs, and boxes. The set pieces are moved on and offstage to indicate changes in location, as the story moves from Devon's house, to Caroline's farm, and so forth, coupled with some very basic lighting changes afforded by the use of a few front of house and backstage lights. There is no real backstage, so the actors not currently performing sit off to the side, changing costume or taking a sip of water, usually completely visible. The play begins with an actor saying something along the lines of, "I guess we should get started" or making the outright declaration, "This is the beginning of our play." At one performance, the artistic director at the time, Simon Mallett, had the job of controlling the house lights. This required him, somewhat awkwardly, to walk in front of the audience in order to flick a switch on the other side of the room. This signalled the start of the show and he jokingly acknowledged this as "a very high-tech opening." Such actions appear amateur because they contravene many of the accepted rules of theatre: they acknowledge the "eventness" of the event.

This performance style continues throughout the show, refusing to provide the illusion theatre so often creates, instead offering only the flimsiest of fourth walls during narrative moments and otherwise relying entirely on direct address. Of course, these self-referential actions are neither exclusively amateur nor necessarily amateur at all: Brechtian theatre, metatheatre, and a great deal of professional and avant-garde theatre within and beyond Western convention is similarly staged. In this case, however, the site of performance has a unique impact: this style is facilitated, or perhaps demanded, by the constraints of the spaces themselves. If the light switch for the room happens to be on the other side of the stage, there is no real alternative to Mallett's inelegant stage cross. It is also important to note that these actions are conscious, practiced decisions by the company. While not explicitly rehearsed, things like starting the show with a flip of a light switch or an announcement are not barriers to be overcome but rather are conscious decisions that invoke a particular kind of relaxed amateurism in the production.

Holdsworth, Milling, and Nicholson's description of the impact of space on amateur performance is particularly noteworthy here: "The space of the local amateur theatre can serve as one manifestation of the 'physical fabric' that constitutes a plethora of community spaces that invite and facilitate community groups to congregate, which might also include local libraries, community centres, and church meeting halls and many amateur theatre spaces also play host to other cultural activities."[28] The multi-use, multi-function physical fabric of community spaces to which Holdsworth, Milling, and Nicholson refer illuminates the connections between space, community, and amateurism. The theatrical production of *Good Fences*, by being staged in community spaces like the Arbour Lake Community Centre and the Unitarian Church of Calgary, subverts the expected characteristics of what a show produced by a professional theatre company would look like. Downstage has a permanent home in the Arts Commons building in downtown Calgary, a professional venue that boasts 400,000 square feet of purpose-built arts space and comprises a full city block. I do not make the above observations in order to promote an amateur/professional binary. Instead, I make them to suggest the utility of generating occasions that increase the "visibility of community involvement in making theatre"[29] by actually staging the play in community venues that highlight their multi-use "physical fabric." *Good Fences* clearly works in spaces that are not explicitly designed for it nor even tailored for theatrical productions. Instead, as a touring production, it situated itself in community centres and churches: spaces wherein discussion, debate, listening, and communal activity regularly occur.

Performing in community-based spaces highlighted a number of mundane challenges for Downstage that further suffused the production with an amateur aesthetic. In the Parkdale Community Association building an outlet for the lights had to be shared with a microwave in another room which caused the stage lights to flicker anytime someone next door wanted to heat up some food; every time this happened, the shared use – the multi-purpose nature of the space – had to be acknowledged. Performing in these spaces also resulted in the use of a number of conventional metatheatrical tactics: audience members could clearly see the lights and the stage manager controlling them, all the actors remained onstage for the duration of the performance, and the actors deliberately and directly acknowledged the audience members. These actions, necessitated by the physical space which offered no proscenium arch and no backstage or offstage space out of sight of the audience, served to create conceptual space within the narrative. The aesthetic style of the piece clearly reveals the essential duality of theatre by making visible both the real-world mechanisms – the costuming, the acting, the research – and the fictions that they appear to produce, offering insight into the construction of such illusions. This ability to see both the real and the performance follows Bert O. States's "binocular vision," in which semiotics suggests "everything is something else" while phenomenology dictates that "everything is nothing but itself" in a kind of constant oscillation between the character and actor, oil rig and its actual composition as several stacked boxes.[30] The doubling process of theatre reception that States outlines parallels what the audience is asked to do for the content of *Good Fences*: They must hold differing viewpoints and oscillate between them. It is a necessity in watching *Good Fences* to balance, hold, or maintain a multiplicity of times, spaces, and opinions as the actors perform as different characters, as versions of themselves, and both forwards through the story and backwards in recollecting the devising process. For example, the audience watched the character Devon consider a number of options: join his neighbouring ranchers in their opposition of the proposed sour gas pipeline, side with the oil and gas company to preserve his job, or just leave the area altogether. At the same time, the audience watched Braden Griffiths, the actor, change his costume. The storyline, then, was continually expanded and punctured by such moments of metatheatre; the theatrical frame was unstable, or at the very least porous, as audiences watched both the performance and the preparation for performance.

This production style and framing arguably facilitates the audience's reception of the show's content. While the show's openness to various opinions can be seen in its attempts to offer a balanced storyline as content, one that moves between Caroline the rancher, Jamie the oil and gas land agent, Garret and his wife who are suffering financially, and Devon the wealthy oil and gas executive, the amateur aesthetic provides an additional model for openness and generosity in frame. For instance, the apparent informality of the beginning of the show invites the audience to engage in the topic in a similarly informal way. Because the show begins tentatively, and in a way that states outright from the beginning that it is relaxed and casual, for the audience there is less need to raise their guard against a potentially biased show.[31] This is crucial given the play's potentially inflammatory and complex topic. It means that the audience is essentially primed not for agreement or disagreement but for tolerance by virtue of the opening: they must make concessions for the space not being designed for this production. The audience is implicitly required to "go with the flow" when the lights are disrupted by someone microwaving in the other room or as people wander into the church without realizing a play is occurring. Further, the constant challenging of the dominant storyline about Devon and his changing relationship to oil and gas – it is interrupted by the actors interjecting to talk about the show, by the space itself malfunctioning, etc. – moves toward diminishing polarized views and opening up discussion by discouraging any singular dominant voice. The communal nature of the space demonstrates to the audience that unpreparedness and interruptions are acceptable; there is no single view being presented and any view may be interrupted.

This may in turn encourage audiences to approach the content of what is discussed in the show with the same degree of flexibility they allow for the theatrical frame it is contained within. In other words, audience members are asked, by virtue of the unstable frame of the piece, to allow for intrusion of contradictory, surprising, or complicating material that may either challenge or reinforce their previously held beliefs about the oil and gas industry. As one returning audience member articulated: "I came into it [with] a sort of bias thinking sort of pro-rancher, anti-gas and each time I see it I see that it is a balance. That there's not a single perspective. And try as I might, I still don't see that. So, I actually find that valuable that it's, that it's both sides."[32] We can hear in the audience member's description their recognition that the show presents multiple perspectives. In particular, the audience member provides compelling evidence of the show's ability to convincingly present several different viewpoints through the acknowledgement of their own bias "coming in" and subsequent inability to see only one perspective as the show progressed. Just as the show's storyline manages to allow for contradicting opinions, the real space does the same: It is a practical, multi-purpose space with no backstage and difficult sightlines and yet within it we experience a fictional world. In other words, its pragmatism upsets theatrical illusion even while it facilitates a fiction.

The constant breaking of the fourth wall, including those times when the space malfunctions or otherwise draws attention to its non-theatrical nature results in frequent disruptions. Close described the utility of this aesthetic approach:

> For me, too, there's something about not knowing whether it's scripted or improvised that is disarming for an audience in a way that's useful for a topic in which people can come in a bit armed. "Ok, let's see what they're going to do with this. Are they going to mess it up?" And there's something someone said last night, like, "Do you guys know what you're doing?" off the top ... But there is something, I don't know, I think there's something nice and deliberately disarming about that. 'Cause then hopefully we do show that we do know what we're doing in terms of like the level of preparation and some of the stagecraft.[33]

As Close elucidates above, the amateur aesthetic has a particular function and purpose: it disarms the audience. And while she recognizes the utility of this function, she nevertheless hopes that ultimately the audience realizes the company's competence at stagecraft and accepts the basic industry knowledge they impart.

The actors in *Good Fences* are indeed all professional performers, but they also deliberately stage themselves as non-experts in this show. Audience members watch them slip in and out of roles and costumes, take water breaks, and appear to backtrack, change their minds and make mistakes. As an example, as part of his opening address to the audience, actor Braden Griffiths states, "Behind us was Col, driving his truck with Ellen, and Nicky was with me and the rancher. Of course, that's not Nicky, that's Carly [gesturing to fellow performer Carly McKee], but you're playing the role she originally played, so ... I'm getting off topic. Ellen was also less pregnant than she is now, which might be confusing because her character isn't pregnant. Anyway." Griffiths corrects himself in his meandering, somewhat confusing description of the research he conducted before the show's premiere. He backtracks before returning to the main story he was trying to tell about visiting a rancher. Similarly, a small argument occurs over the (mis)-pronunciation of a word when actor Col Cseke, in an aside, describes his experience visiting a farmer:

COL: And he did so with all of like, maybe twelve seconds of instructions whispered into my ear as a bleating calf was drug towards us –
ELLEN: It wasn't bleeding.
COL: No, bleating, with a "t," bleating.
ELLEN: Oh, I thought you said it was bleeding.
CARLY: I heard bleeding too.
COL: Okay, this *noisy* calf was being drug towards us

The actors are able to revise, rewrite, or correct themselves as they perform mistakes and errors.

Other scholars have written about the performance of non-actors[34] and examples abound in the world of theatre. German company Rimini Protokoll famously uses "experts of the everyday" in their productions, while Ravi Jain's *A Brimful of Asha* charmed Canadian audiences by starring Jain's untrained, non-actor mother. *Good Fences* is not about the performance of non-actors but rather raises the question of what other productive instantiations of the non-expert may be invited by such a performance style. While we might characterize a non-actor to be one who disrupts the usual constraints, definitions, and qualities with which we describe the role of actor, in the case of *Good Fences*, non-expert performance can potentially also invite audiences to be non-expert on the subject of the oil and gas industry. Just as the actors appear non-expert in their sometimes-confusing delivery, audience members may be liberated to feel similarly unsure of, or oscillating in, their expertise about issues relevant to Albertans. The style thus extends an invitation to the audience to allow for change, adaptation, and apparent lack of knowledge. The cast, for instance, take the time to define all industry and ranching terms they use and describe what oil wells, pipelines, ranching properties, etc. look like and how they function. This is not done to convey that all present lack such knowledge; instead, it suggests to everyone in the room that they can take on roles as amateur residents of Alberta, newly invited to re-evaluate their relationship to the oil and gas industry. As Nicholson, Milling, and Holdsworth argue, quoting Rugoff, "we are all amateurs" in some aspects of life, suggesting that the boundaries between expert and non-expert are not fixed binaries but instead "networks of connection."[35]

To a large degree, *Good Fences* appears to function as a catalyst for a balanced talkback following each performance: The fictional world acts as a common reference point for all to refer to that is distanced from the real world. Since multiple sides are set-up and portrayed in the show, expressions about all angles of relationship with the oil and gas industry are welcomed in the post-show discussion. As Close and Mallett articulated in an interview:

> CLOSE: So for me I think the value of the show is that we have these shared resources that belong to Albertans and the way that they are handled is really important to the future of the province, but it's not something we normally have a vast discussion about in the province, outside of this really charged political realm, where it's not ok to even sometimes have a nuanced opinion. Early on, this is diverging from a couple of sentences, but early on we thought, why bother to make a show about this because like there's nothing to be done about the relationship anyway, or you like having hospitals, don't you? You like having schools, don't you? There's this very heightened rhetoric of, if you like all the niceties of modern life than you must support the oil and gas industry without question, without being able to have a nuanced discussion of like, "Ok well I could support the industry but question regulation" or "I could –" you know, there's a million different ways to think about the interaction between the two industries outside of oil and gas is necessary in a way or sort of, our province is perfect, or we have to shut down all of this type of energy production and shift to something else, and –
>
> MALLETT (interjecting): Well, I think the lens is a willful ignorance in terms of a lot of people, in terms of you know, the specifics of processes and what happens, and I think the main part of the value of the show is, obviously the conversation that results, but I think it's equipping people to have the conversation, too in a way that other than that which any of us would have been equipped to have such a conversation prior to the creating of the show and I think that, while it's certainly not – there were some people who were factors that could be brought into the equation, in terms of government regulation and other elements –
>
> CLOSE (interjecting): Indigenous perspective –
>
> MALLETT: Yes, and other types of extraction. I think that the show sort of gets to the fundamental core conflict and then does enough sort of explanation and then equips people to have a conversation that's being carried out and forward, hopefully in a

way that can be productive to the way that they encounter it elsewhere in their lives. 'Cause I think what we all learned was, when you have that sort of heightened awareness of how prevalent elements of these industries are around you, it can change – it does change the way you observe your surroundings.[36]

This extended dialogue makes at least two important points. First, it demonstrates that the play aims to disarm its audience members and then equip them for a talkback by inviting members to approach the topic as non-experts. Second, it establishes that such an approach might "change the way you observe your surroundings" by encouraging audience members to re-imagine and re-articulate their relationship to place. This second point is particularly underscored by the company's use of community centres, which may themselves be contested sites. Community centres may be funded by the oil and gas industry but may also house meetings about the same industry's negative effect on the environment and Indigenous communities. Thus, while the amateur feel of *Good Fences* may prime disarmed audiences for the reception of new knowledge or perspectives, the multi-use sites, as well as the multi-perspective interjections of the actors, help to illustrate the necessary multiplicity and complexity of the real world. As Close articulated above, the real world "can make it sometimes feel impossible to have a nuanced opinion," but *Good Fences* forefronts the necessity of such complexity to accurately represent the reality of the situation.

The community hall, with its limited aesthetic possibilities – a "flaw" that the company members of *Good Fences* deliberately exploit to their advantage – foregrounds the extraneous real world. This aesthetic is actually what crafts a more real experience for audiences insofar as it remains open to the realities of the external frame in which it is presented. The openness of the space also contributes to an amateur aesthetic that invites audiences to remain open to current industry concerns and conflicts; the amateur invokes multiplicity and contradiction and not only invites the audience to be non-experts but asks them to reconsider their stances, to be unsure or insecure about their social/political selves in "real" contexts. All of these factors combine to convincingly generate a sense of realness. Audience members in a post-show talkback following the 28 March 2015 performance accordingly commented on how, in this show, "theatre ceases to become theatre and actually becomes life" and that it was "refreshing to see how life and theatre intertwined." Their comments point to the impression of realness, partially cultivated by the very real performance sites Downstage theatre company utilized.

THE OPERATION OF UNCERTAIN TIME

"It could have been today's paper," exclaimed one audience member in a post-show talkback following the 28 March 2015 performance of *Good Fences*. The comment is an apt representation of how *Good Fences* moves temporally. The show's quality of being "of the now" is provocative in terms of the perceptual realness it emanates: the show feels presciently relevant to contemporary concerns. This sense of immediacy is coupled with the production's ability to synchronously stage past, present, and future, and its capacity to constantly shift and respond to "the times," updating and changing the script as necessary for each subsequent tour in 2012, 2013, and 2015. In many ways, the show is *too* repeatable; conflicts between oil workers and ranchers are all too common, as are mediatized accounts and productions of those conflicts as described in the first section of this chapter. *Good Fences*'s repeated runs exhibit that the company has an ability to face its own indeterminacy and contingency by actively responding to, reinterpreting, and restaging its theatrical creation. This all has the effect of producing a kind of self-conscious multiplicity of times. In this section, I make thorough use of David Ian Rabey's *Theatre, Time, and Temporality: Melting Clocks and Snapped Elastics* to argue that the presentation and perception of time in *Good Fences* both relies upon and invokes a kind of allowance for temporal multiplicity that contributes to its perceptual realness. That the production invites a validation of the subjective underscores the multiplicities inherent in reality, resulting in a more persuasive sense of realness for audiences.

To begin, it is worth quoting at length an excerpt from one of the audience interviews I conducted:

> AUD 2b: So I know the actors in this have a real proclivity for creating real theatre, speaking to real issues, current issues, and their ability to uh evolve the story as things change. Which they've also done over the last three or four years.
>
> KJ: *What's the importance of it being real? Or is it important?*
>
> AUD 2b: Yeah, well yeah it's important! I mean for me, I mean what it is, as opposed to watching a play let's say, Edward Albee's play *Who's Afraid of Virginia Woolf?* Which is going to be produced you

know forty years ago and will be produced forty years from now, [*Good Fences*] is a play that can only exist in the moment. You know. And if they do it six months from now it will evolve again. And so, that's what makes it – it, it's – it has beauty in that. It's transitory theatre. Transitory art. Yeah, yeah. It just moves and grows and it evolves. And so, me, I could come and see this play a year from now and if they continued to do it, and it would be different. And I will still derive enjoyment from it and go "Oh they did that differently, and this differently, and now there's that issue differently." Because things will evolve differently. There will be new perspectives, new regulations that they need to address, new stories that they may look at. So I feel any theatre like this is always good.

AUD 2a: Yeah.

AUD 2b: I mean, there's the traditional theatre of the story yadda, yadda, yadda, but there's also a big need for this. And we wish shows like this had a bigger audience. You know where you could do this in front of 150 people on a night like tonight where it would be fantastic, um you know art speaks to issues that news agents don't or news don't, or other people don't. Before people write a story you know ten years down the road. But this is now, this is happening now, this is current, and that's true.[37]

The final words of the audience member, "this is now, this is happening now, this is current, and that's true" underscore the "in the moment" quality of the show and interestingly also tie it to notions of truthfulness vis-à-vis the impression of immediacy. The audience member identifies that *Good Fences* points directly to a specific moment in time. Paradoxically, the audience member's comments regarding the show's continual changes and adjustments in subsequent productions also suggest the show is not limited to a specific point in time, instead indicating its fluidity and reflexivity. The comments thus underscore how *Good Fences*'s relationship with time is flexible: It operates both in the moment and in several possible moments.

The story structure of *Good Fences* also negates temporal singularity. The performance follows a narrative, sequential storyline but it is frequently interrupted by actors breaking the fourth wall to recall and divulge information either about their research process or themselves that add multiple other time frames. At one point, Col Cseke, one of the performers, talks about his and fellow actor Ellen Close's upcoming summer baby shower, pointing towards a future event in the "real world." In addition to this gesture towards the future, Cseke and Close also speak about their past experiences attending meetings at the Longview Community Hall. The present is also perceptible when the limiting aspects of the space become apparent: lights flicker, it becomes evident there aren't enough chairs for the audience, or members of the public randomly wander into the hall. These are just some of the "upsurges of the real"[38] experienced at the performances I attended and display the many possible times referenced: future, past, and present.

Downstage's research-based creation method is of course also necessarily multi-temporal: It includes data-gathering, interviewing, and research trips (past action), presentation of that information in the theatre (present action), and problem-solving or deliberation as the audience and performers consider what's next (future action). In fact, the show's lack of resolution clearly indicates several possible futures. Instead of a satisfying denouement, the performances conclude with an audience talkback that often revolves around possible future actions for the audience members. As one audience member articulated,

> I think it's tremendously valuable, uh, it educates people on um some of the issues on the subject that might be controversial or that you might need to draw peoples' awareness to. And I hope that possibly one of the questions that could be asked at the end of such a presentation as this, a dramatic presentation as this, is what can we do about this situation? What are some positive things we can do? So, as I said in the discussion after the play, rather than just bringing forward the problem, a lot of us care a lot about it, some of us are realizing that our, the survival of human species is really threatened. We're not, it's not just polar bears that are endangered species. I think this is becoming sort of a, a widespread awareness across our country and, and many countries I'd say, but let's not just talk about the problem or the situation and say what can we do and maybe try and put that, put that forward as a question.[39]

The multi-temporal nature of the production, with its multiple pasts, presents, and potential futures requires a more expansive model for comprehending time than linearity.

French philosopher Gaston Bachelard usefully characterizes time as pluralistic and dialectical rather than single, linear, or absolute. He suggests an understanding of time in which two dimensions – continuous and discontinuous – are delineated by significance: "continuous as possibility" and "discontinuous as being."[40] David Ian Rabey develops this concept by pointing to the ways in which we may, "in a given instant, decide either something is happening or nothing is happening: a value judgement of significance, based on temporal duality rather than unity, and on a subjective definition of function."[41] When this conceptualization is applied to *Good Fences*, the production still resists categorization: moments from the story-world may be conceived of as discontinuous insofar as the audience is very aware of the pre-determination of the script. We know, in other words, that Braden Griffiths-as-Devon the oil VP has a predetermined storyline. However, the character's trajectory may simultaneously fluctuate and appear continuous as a consequence of upsurges from the real world (e.g., if a cast member decides to interject or, as noted above, if the multi-use nature of the space results in an unplanned interruption). At all times, then, there are many possible moments.

Bachelard's description of time's multidimensional density, or what Rabey calls a "pluralistic spectrum of lacunae,"[42] is also useful for understanding how time operates in *Good Fences* to create an affective real or a feeling of realness. Bachelard builds on philosopher Richard Hönigswald's concepts of immanent or vertical time (subjective time) and transitive or horizontal time (objective time, as demarcated by the world at large) to define reality as the site of agreement between these two axes.[43] In this way, reality is "a superimposition of transitive (horizontal, objective) time on immanent (vertical, subjective) time, in ways that are deemed mutually confirming, congruent and hence 'give an impression of objectivity.'"[44] If, as according to Bachelard, the agreement or confluence between these two "times" – one objective, the other subjective – gives us the perception of reality, then this means that there are multiple possible meeting points, depending upon where subjective time intersects with objective time. In other words, if we imagine running a single objective time in one direction, there is the potential for multiple subjective time vectors that intersect with this objective time. Such a scenario allows for multiple conceptions of realness or at least multiple possibilities for what feels real. What does this mean, however, if – as in *Good Fences* – the determining line of objective time remains hidden? *Good Fences* moves in and out of story world, metatheatrical world, and real world; they all operate on their own "times." Other forms of time are also at play, creating even more possible intersections in *Good Fences*: the timeline of the relevant news reports from which the company drew material; the time of legislative process, implied in the potential for legal action between the ranchers and the oil workers in the play; and even the time of the economic market based on the oil and gas industry's operations in the real world affecting attendance numbers and funding for the production. In the absence of any marker of one objective, transitive time we have several possible immanent times that, without intersection, all remain potentially real.

As a consequence, *Good Fences* has no objective authority. In her book, *Timescapes of Modernity: The Environment and Invisible Hazards*, Barbara Adam articulates the potential of a timescape perspective. While she is writing specifically about environmental hazards and the human propensity to factor out future implications in modern industrial decision-making, her call for a more plural, speculative understanding of time is relevant here, not least because of the related environmental impacts of the oil and gas industry. She writes that a timescape

> allows us to move from single and dualistic approaches and abstract, functional perspectives to knowledge that emphasizes inclusiveness, connectivity, and implication. It promotes understanding that acknowledges the relativity of position and framework of observation whilst stressing our inescapable implication in the subject matter and acknowledging personal and collective responsibility. It explicitly incorporates absences, latencies and immanent forces, thus helping to move away from the futile insistence on proof and certainty for situations characterized by indeterminacy time-lags of unspecified durations and open dispersal in time and space.[45]

Good Fences demands this kind of timescape perspective: much of the show's perception of time is affective. The actors describe the importance of their past research experiences and anticipate exciting future moments like Col and Ellen's impending baby shower, emphasizing the fluidity of time(s) represented onstage.[46] *Good Fences* also constantly switches between timelines. The show moves from the fictionalized narrative about a rancher and oil executive, to moments wherein the cast discuss their process of creating the show, to clear references to the "here and now" of the space (e.g., gesturing to the lights). The open ending of the show in which we don't know how the characters will proceed also leaves the implications of investing or divesting from the industry open and indeterminate but still very much present.

Moreover, the company is constantly revising the script for each new performance: As previously mentioned, at one point in the 2015 production, the actor Col Cseke – in one of the many moments of direct audience address – breaks character to announce that he and fellow actor Ellen Close, who is his wife in real life, will invite one of their interview subjects from the creation process to their upcoming baby shower. He appears to make the decision spontaneously, without first consulting Close, but it is nevertheless based on a past interaction with that rancher. Moreover, it will affect a future event: "I haven't told you this yet – or you," Cseke says to Close and, in a unique moment, also to Close's parents who were in the audience that night. Close responds to Cseke, "Are you asking me right now?" She then, in a reprimanding tone, adds, "We'll talk – we'll talk about it later." In the original production in 2012 Cseke broke out of character to stage an argument with Close, but in this version the argument was about inviting an interview subject to their wedding, not a baby shower. As this suggests, the impact of time passing is literally written into the show as it adapts and adjusts to the current realities of performers who are now married and expecting a baby. It simultaneously operates within the confines of the timeline of the fictitious script and creates its own record of events and sequence of performance related to the real world.

I would like to pause here to more closely examine Ellen's above-quoted query, "Are you asking me right now?" and how even this simple line plays with temporal perception. For this consideration, I draw on the concepts of chronos and kairos, as they are defined by theatre artist Anne Bogart: "*Chronos* is measured time. *Kairos* is unbound and unmeasured time ... the difference between chronos and kairos is the difference between time and timing ... chronos is a particular way of understanding time by the clock. *Chronos* is chronology ... Kairos, on the other hand, is timing or opportunity."[47] What is Close specifically referring to with her line, "right now"? Is she just referring to this particular, sequential moment in the script, or is it meant to distinguish itself from those other times Close has asked the same question? In other words, is her query, "right now?", falling into chronos, a chronological order of time (in this case the line happening repeatedly night after night), or into kairos, a moment of affective timing in which meaning might be made (a consequential decision might be made)? The ambiguity of these two potential times, invited by Close's singular response of "right now?" overlap and meet, rendering ambiguous the phrase's "real-world" status. Is this "right now?" different from tomorrow's "right now?" If so, in what ways? *Good Fences* is thus active in its use of time, taking advantage of real time(s) and fictional time(s) to create moments of suspension in which choice and turning point, among other elements, are presented but ultimately unresolved. As Close articulates it, "We'll talk about this later."

One of Rabey's more provocative ideas is to think of theatre as a quantum art: "Quantum physics *admits* the principles of temporality, relativity and reflectivity: the very terms that theatre deals in, even more actively and variously than poetry, in its physicalized interactive reorientations, and intersubjective emergences in materialized expression."[48] *Good Fences* seems to celebrate and intensify rather than shy away from notions of time's relativity. We see this demonstrated not only in Close's "right now?" but also through subtle disagreements between the performers and the consequent highlighting of subjective time. For example, in an extended discussion over the timing of community meetings about land stewardship that the company attended as part of their research process, one of the actors, Braden Griffiths, explains that they learned about the community meetings online. Close steps in to correct him, positing that they actually learned about them from one of their first contacts. Close then rebuts Griffiths's remark that they then attended the community meeting "about a week later" by indicating that, no, "it was the next day." The two performers appear to have very different understandings of timing.

While the differentiated timeline in the example above seems to underscore the importance of dialogue in forming one's personal perspective and interrogating one's subjective experience, there remains the question of whether two contradictory times can coexist nevertheless. Rabey quotes Valtteri Arstila and Dan Lloyd who suggest that subjective time can be replaced by subjective *times*: "the psychology and phenomenology of subjective time [could] rest on mechanisms that operate at different scales, but that overlap at their edges."[49] These overlapping temporalities clearly reinforce the subjective but not in a way that diminishes the subjective as inferior to a "factual" objective. Instead, the co-existence of several subjective *times* substantiates the claim that affective time and affective truth exist. Griffiths' perception that the meetings were later than Close thinks they were points to a particular affective relationship with the events: the meeting *felt* later. Close's perception suggests a different, though equally valid, sense of time and relationship to the events Griffiths talks about. The combined presentation of both times, at the same theatrical time, thus eradicates any potential singularity of "truth"; both timelines are a kind of felt truth that is at once both relational and adequate. The resolution of a dominant timeline is simply not necessary; it is acceptable for the purposes of this show to have these two different relationships to time.

Theatre scholar Jerzy Limon suggests that theatre is an art form that needs "the articulation of at least two different modes of perceiving reality."[50] He continues, "time in performance becomes split: it is the real time of the performer, who is a live human being, and the created fictional time of the figure (which may occasionally seem to overlap). In fact, we are dealing with not only split time, but also with two presents: one is the present time of the live performer and the audience, the other is the present time of the fictional world, which might be labelled *agreed or transferred present.*"[51] When we apply this concept to *Good Fences*, we understand time in a number of senses. A dizzying layering of times occurs: there is the time of the fictitious characters the actors are playing (i.e., Devon the oil VP); the time of their "real" character selves that are also performing scripted material under the guise of their real selves (Braden Griffiths as Braden); the time of those "real" character selves' memories of creating the show (Braden Griffiths re-enacting past Braden); and finally the actual real time of the real actors (Braden Griffiths) and the audience. Limon is describing multiple possible presents that require attending to by the audience and are coloured by different affects. Intensifying and thickening Limon's description, Rabey notes that theatre "is distinctively *intersubjective* in its form, thematic concerns and effects, which are manifested through different frames of foregrounded subjective time – and through considered and resonant estrangements of linear time."[52] The audience does not need to believe or disbelieve any particular time as true or untrue when watching a performance. Times may exist simultaneously as we watch both actor and character (or, as in *Good Fences*, actor, actor-as-past-self, actor-as-character, and character) present a multiplied temporal structure that refuses a singular or dominant truth but is nevertheless key to the theatrical experience.

To continue an analysis of the presentation of multiple character/actor selves and its effect on perceived realness, when the distance between character and actor becomes precipitously small – as in the case of Cseke and Close considering invitations to their baby shower – it is difficult to determine the realness of the characters' interaction. Close is visibly pregnant, and thus her pregnancy is true. It is also true that Close and Cseke are married and that they are having a baby shower. Is it true that they might invite one of their interviewees? An audience member may not be aware of the extent to which these perceived truths are actually true. I, after all, only know about the truth of the pregnancy and the marriage because of my time spent with the company over the course of my research. An audience member may question whether the pregnancy is just a costume piece. Every truth, then, even the really true, is debatable and open to interpretation. Jenn Stephenson writes, "When the innate ontological distinction between the character-I and the performed-I is compressed to near identity, this similarity is disconcertingly not the source of epistemological stability we hope for. Instead ... this radical compression generates more doubt about what is 'true.'"[53]

Stephenson suggests, however, that uncertainty in temporal presentation can be a politically generative aspect of post-dramatic theatre of the real.[54] The result is "productive insecurity," a phrase she borrows from Ulrike Garde and Meg Mumford. In a play that deals with a highly charged subject matter, such as *Good Fences*, the lack of truth-telling inherent in productive insecurity may be a useful destabilization. Given the highly politicized oil and gas industry in Alberta, where different truths are spun by disparate groups, an encouragement to consider one's subjective perspective may in fact be welcome. The truths, or facts, about the oil and gas industry can at times be vastly different, divided along partisan lines. Consider, for instance, the politicization of the terms "oil sands" and "tar sands." The latter is associated with the environmentalist cause and implies a kind of dirty pollution. The former, associated more with the industry itself, implies a kind of specific utility. Neither term is technically correct. The sands are, in actuality, bituminous.

In the face of overwhelmingly unreliable information, it becomes clearer why the multiple truths Downstage invites in *Good Fences* are actually favourable to the audience and feel real despite their instability: At the very least they invite conversation, dialogue, and relationality. Although the actors appear to disagree with each other about timelines, they continue to perform together, articulate their concerns, and listen to each other. What they are doing, in fact, is *sharing* time: Braden Griffiths, at one point, abruptly stops talking to the audience and says to another actor, "You tell this. I talk a lot at other times." This sharing of time is possible, in part, because of theatre's ability to use synchronous time in which everyone experiences the performance at the same time, face-to-face: synchronous interactions "rely on all participants being present and engaged at the same time."[55] By contrast, social media generally uses asynchronous time, in which comments appear one after the other, or emails follow one after another: My time follows your time; it is not "our time." Christian Crumlish and Erin Malone articulate that: "Public conversations in forums and streams, like Twitter, are often asynchronous and take place over extended periods of time. Individuals can be online at different times, participating in the conversation when it is convenient. Comments on a blog post which all refer to a single starting object are generally very easy to follow and can drift in and out of activity over a long period of time."[56] In the case of the aforementioned concerns surrounding political silos and echo chambers online, sites like Reddit, Facebook, and Twitter allow for commenters to assert their own opinions, one after another, without affecting the original post. The forum does not require individuals to relate to one another or engage simultaneously.

Theatre offers a necessarily more engaged kind of exchange. For example, Close ended one of the talkbacks that I attended for *Good Fences* by describing how an audience member had approached her at the end of a previous talkback, pushed a piece of paper into her hand, and left abruptly. On the paper, the audience member revealed that she was the wife of the man whose murder had prompted the initial creation of the show. This interesting anecdote has at least two functions. First, it points to the real-world implications of the show and highlights the ability of someone so closely tied to one particular side of the argument to approach and engage with viewpoints potentially divergent to her own. Second, it demonstrates to the audience the very necessity of their being present; that is, it underscores their ability to affect future shows and actually alter the original script. This woman's individual story has now become a part of the show's wider story. The audience member irrevocably altered *Good Fences* and further complicated the story by "sharing time" with the performers.

Stephenson writes that "the affective lessons of productive insecurity teach us that we need to abandon core assumptions ... not to be so certain in our conclusions, or even in our ability to assert conclusions at all."[57] She continues, "Productive insecurity arising out of the essential undecidability of reality-based performance thus has the potential to generate a more hesitant, thoughtful, open, and inquisitive attitude in the audience."[58] In the case of *Good Fences*, I would suggest this hesitant, thoughtful, inquisitive attitude is explicitly modelled by the actors who take turns with time, disagree about time, and generally demonstrate their lack of surety about how time functions. As Rabey argues, "Theatre's manifestations of temporal *inconsistency* demonstrate a plurality of claims on human consciousness, and human dealings. These effects mitigate any sense of a single, exclusive, ideological authority or perspective, often establishing one frame of reference in order to qualify or interrogate it by the introduction of another (which makes it a powerful medium for ethical enquiry, investigation and speculation)."[59] The actors in *Good Fences* do just that. This promotion of an open-minded recognition of multiple possible times, ones that exist concurrently with subjective time, suggests to audiences that their own perceptions are welcome within the space of the performance – but so are those of others. As it is presented in *Good Fences*, time, is shared, destabilized, and questioned.

The making visible of the different frames or heuristics by which the performers make sense of their process, as suggested by their different perceptions of time, echoes what Hans-Thies Lehmann calls in his analysis of post-dramatic theatre the implicit, self-aware politics of perception required by theatre due to its use of signs: "the mutual implication of actors and spectators in the theatrical production of images ... make[s] visible the broken thread between personal experience and perception. Such an experience would be not only aesthetic but therein at the same time ethico-political."[60] The presentation of a multitude of times produces a kind of temporal relationship that is predicated on an "ethico-political" engagement. What facilitates this is the performed flexibility with which the actors approach this temporal relationship; they come to it in ways that reinforce the inevitable effect of personal experience on perception. The politics of the timescape in *Good Fences* are not associated with a particular political slant or side. Instead, they encourage an ethico-political relationship with the other, the contradictory, or the discordant by recognizing the necessary multiplicity of personal perceptions. We might ask, then, what is the effect created by moments in *Good Fences* when the actors disagree over how something either happened (past) or should happen (future)? Should they invite the rancher to their baby shower? Did the meeting occur one week or one day following their finding out about it? Patricia Schroeder says that playwrights, in investigating how events relate to each other, must decide what the past actually entails, suggesting that the past is sometimes "not entirely a sequence of objective facts but a matter of recollection and interpretation," and if so, if any one "interpretation is more valid ... if all viewpoints contain elements of truth and fantasy, and if those seemingly factual prior events are objectifiable at all."[61] As I suggest here, time is inherently made relative to the individual. We experience time in *Good Fences* in relation to our own experience of it. Consequently, *Good Fences* promotes a recognition of multiple possible readings of time and highlights one's highly subjective, highly personal concept of it, both within and beyond the world of the play.

Good Fences is also full of fragmentation and, as I have frequently noted, it often breaks the fourth wall with disruptions. In one moment, audiences watch a scene in which Braden-as-Devon the oil executive, meets with a colleague in the bar, and in the next audiences see him step out of his role to address the audience directly about what it was like, as himself, to conduct interviews with ranchers in Longview, Alberta. In another instance, Ellen Close begins to describe herself: "I'm an overthinker, I'm–" but she is cut off by fellow actor Carly McKee who dryly offers the descriptor, "Opinionated." Close reacts, saying of McKee that "She's been working with us for like a week and a half." She is referring to the fact that McKee is filling in for Nicola Elson, who helped write the roles McKee is now performing and who first played those same roles. Breaks like this in the narrative flow that provide verifiable information contribute to an overall sense of disruption and, consequently, add to the show's realness. As an audience member described when asked about what seemed real in the show, "And so when they say okay 'This is Ellen' and they're talking about [Ellen], I'm like 'I know Ellen' you know so it means you relate. So I liked that. I liked the sort of bouncing back and forth between the show and the real people."[62] Not only do the interjections feel real, in other words, but they also reveal real details about the cast members and their process of creation.

In *Great Reckonings in Little Rooms*, States suggests that "a play plucks human experience from time and offers an aesthetic completion to a process we know to be endless ... [and] imitates the timely in order to remove it from time, to give time a shape."[63] Rabey echoes his remarks: "the audience at a theatre event engages with the proceedings with an enhanced expectation and sense of experiential *finitude* and duration."[64] I would argue that these remarks actually run contrary to what happens in *Good Fences*. While the show still "plucks human experience from time," rather than offering a closed system for aesthetic contemplation, the shape *Good Fences* creates remains open. *Good Fences* eschews an ending in any temporal sense of the word, instead moving to layer and even disfigure time by presenting multiple temporalities in and out of sequence. Consequently, it does not formalize boundaries between staged and real, between past and future; rather, it disrupts them. We may have a moment between rancher characters in the fictional storyline, or in fictional time, that is quickly followed by a breaking of the fourth wall for an actor to address us, in real time, about a past or future event. Actor Col Cseke, for instance, describes in one of the play's direct address moments how,

> Four years ago a rancher we met while researching asked Ellen and I, we're married, he asked us to come to his branding, we missed his call and at the time I felt like we missed out on a, literally, once in a lifetime opportunity.

This remark contains within it several different impressions of time that require unpacking: there is the gesture towards feeling disappointed four years in the past because of the impression of the invitation being a once-in-a-lifetime opportunity. The perception of a missed opportunity illustrates a particular relationship to temporal dimensions that is coloured by personal affect and perspective. Indeed, Cseke follows his remark with information about going to a branding the following year. So, in this case, the once-in-a-lifetime opportunity is purely subjective and not objective and ends up not being a missed chance. Rather, the audience quickly finds out that Cseke was offered a kind of "standing invitation" to the annual branding, such that it is something he might attend in future. Cseke's relation of this episode demonstrates how much the play's content relies on personal perspective – what felt to Cseke like a once-in-lifetime opportunity was, actually, not – and celebrates open endings. Cseke may or may not continue to attend the rancher's event. There is no sense of finitude or delimited future; time remains open and personal.

Theatre scholar Matthew Wagner notes that time in theatre is frequently "not so much the destruction of one form of time (the clock) in favour of another (or, as it might be tempting to think, in favour of a kind of 'no time,' an atemporality); rather they make manifest the juxtaposition of differing temporal schemes. They point up temporal dissonance as a key constitutive element of theatrical time ... it restructures and redefines 'now.'"[65] While he focuses his analysis mostly on Shakespeare, his statement implies a kind of chiastic time that resonates with what Downstage presents in *Good Fences*. The company melds the past (interviews), the present (onstage performance), and the future (implied events such as Ellen and Col's baby shower and Ellen's giving birth). As such, "the now" is not so much "this moment" or "this second" as it is a relational time that is dependent on the people and bodies present, how they might have interacted in the past, and how they might interact in the future. This time is neither heralded as better than other times nor suggested to be especially problematic. Instead, this time is portrayed as adequate for the purposes of this particular time and place; the time "restructures and redefines 'now'" in order for the audience to competently understand the production. Maybe, then, theatre is the *ideal* form for forum; it plays with and operates on at least a duality of perspectives. By its very nature it asks audience members to moderate their perceptual experience by acknowledging its subjectivity. *Good Fences* is thus active in its presentation of contradictory opinions and perspectives, challenging audience members' perception of the veracity of their opinions.

FUTURE-HAUNTING AND THE SPECTRE OF POSSIBILITY

In addition to the heightened focus on the individual affect that colours temporal perspective, *Good Fences* makes use of several prospective times, each of which point to elusive futures. As opposed to the perceived facticity of the past and the sensorially confirmable present, the future remains entirely intangible. The show's plot does not include a resolution. By the time the show ends, audiences are uncertain what Devon's future looks like or whether the proposed sour gas pipeline will be laid on his land. Similarly, in the metatheatrical world, the audience does not learn whether actors Close and Cseke will actually invite any of the play's interview subjects to their baby shower.

These uncertainties mirror not only the uncertain and unstable multiple times of the play that I considered earlier but also reflect the ambivalences of audience members who are invested in future of the oil and gas industry. The economic and environmental uncertainties staged in *Good Fences* may inform or reinforce the audience's ontological uncertainty as regards the veracity of the actors'/characters' representations. If the future of the oil and gas industry in Alberta is uncertain, so too might be the audience's perception of the extent to which the actors' or characters' futures are singularly determined. These multiple uncertainties do not impede the affective real-ish-ness of *Good Fences*; they may actually be advantageous insofar as they drive the play to achieve a level of productive insecurity. Stephenson asks, "How do we move forward (or really in any direction) in a world of pervasive uncertainty?"[66] The necessary indeterminacy of the future as an explicit temporal concept in *Good Fences* becomes contingent or implicated: *Good Fences*, and the real-world post-show discussion, is haunted by the future. This looming pervasiveness contributes to the play's affective realness.

Anthropologist John MacAloon broadly calls cultural performance "occasions in which as a culture or society we reflect upon and define ourselves, dramatize our collective myths and history, present ourselves with alternatives and eventually change in some ways,"[67] a common idea applied to theatre and theatre history. It is particularly the notion of alternatives that is significant to this case study. I suggest here the idea of a simultaneous co-presence of multiple futures. Rather than imagining futures using the popular metaphor of a pathway with several possible ways forward, I want to consider the assembling of a presentation of simultaneous alternatives that are not necessarily in front of or behind us. Instead, they are an alternative to the present; that is, they are a positioning that is essentially *beside*, not *forward from*.

What if, for instance, the plot line of *Good Fences* took place in the real world simultaneously with its performance in the story world? Maybe it is, considering the scale of the conflict between the oil and gas and ranching industries: Two stories – the same stories – unfold at once. Two presents happening simultaneously do not suggest forward movement, instead adumbrating flexible movement in a single moment. This is where the notion of haunting becomes useful: The several possible futures to the fictional and real storylines of *Good Fences* are "present" in the immediate experience as ghostly or imagined possibility. Consider a ghost haunting a room. The ghost is not a physical presence, but it is nevertheless ostensibly *felt*. That felt presence, in this case, suggests future possibilities that are uncertain or that loom, pregnant with possibility. These possible futures also exist in the present insofar as they are indicated and ruminated on. Nevertheless, they are not fully present in the present; they are not experienced sensorially or "really." The equally plausible possibilities such a scenario generates makes for a particularly affective experience for audiences that, while not "real," does have real affect. They are a further example of real-ish-ness: They are really plausible, and their implications for the real world are potentially real.

One of the most interesting aspects of the 2015 tour of *Good Fences* that might help to further explicate the notion of future haunting concerns the actors' performative bodies. Actor Ellen Close, as noted, was visibly pregnant. As performance scholar Susan Bennett writes, "The singularity of autobiographical subject, author, and performer can hardly fail to create, as I have suggested, an over-investment of spectatorial response in corporeal evidence against which we might better understand the narrative, by sifting through its more or less fictive truths."[68] Stephenson likewise describes the ways in which a body may act as an archive of real past experience: "This body is a body that in turn has given birth, emigrated to Canada, undergone gender reassignment surgery, been raped, survived genocide."[69] Past bodily experiences may be visible through scars, trauma, or body alteration. In the example of Close, we may assign a higher degree of realness to Cseke's contemplation of their future baby shower because we can see that she is pregnant. In this case, however, the "body as archive" of past events becomes instead "body as medium," telling or predicting future events: Close will have a baby. Stephenson describes Bennett's view of the chiastic relationship of the subject body to the protagonist body as one not only reaching into the past but also into the future insofar as the body is evidence of construction of identity.[70] In other words, the presence onstage of bodies as evidentiary of both past and future events is also in the process of building a particular identity.

As another example, the absence of one of the original creators necessitated a casting change. As mentioned earlier, in the 2015 production, Calgary-based actor Carly McKee performed the roles originated by Nicola Elson. McKee's body – as "other than," having been absent during the show's creation – was specifically acknowledged in the 2015 production. She is introduced as "Not Nicky." This moment is simultaneously both highly theatrical and very real. By drawing attention to and using the tools of the theatre to highlight, script, and otherwise control the presentation of the "unreal" body of Carly as a substitution for the "real" body of Nicky (the originating actress), the moment feels both intimate and distanced. We are both further from the original show's contributor and closer to the real-life actress of Carly. In other words, the company is not pretending she *is* Nicky, even while defining her in relation to Nicky. Insofar as the identity-building process it implies, this substitution of bodies is also a kind of "body-as-medium," predicting the future: Who or how might roles be played in future performances if another original actor is absent? What if someone needs to replace Carly, who needed to replace Nicky?

Ellen Close's pregnancy is also a potential indicator of a future absence: Nicola Elson, we are told, is absent from the performance because she has a newborn baby. Close's pregnancy thus might also indicate her future absence in a run of the show. By being dependent on the semi-autobiographical nature of the creators-as-actors, the way in which *Good Fences* may be produced in future is as precarious and unstable as the plot. At the time of writing this case study in 2022, the show has not been re-produced since 2015. And, with no published script, it still "belongs" to the original actors. Consequently, the show is inextricably linked with the real bodies that created it. Deviations from those real bodies must be attended to, even while those departures from the original point to future uncertainties and instabilities. The very realness of the bodies and their potential real effects on the future of the show create a destabilized potential real: it might happen.

The final spectre of possibility comes from the audience themselves when they are invited to engage in group reflection through a talkback. They draw on their own pasts and presents to reflect on several possible futures. Their actions in the real world with regard to oil and gas in Alberta may prompt any one of several different outcomes, each of them having wide-ranging effects on the province. Will they leave the performance determined to protest the industry? Will they be committed to better understanding how oil wells work? Will they grow more accepting of the ways the oil and gas industry supports Alberta? At the talkback following the 25 March 2015 performance, one audience member described how all the young men he grew up with west of Calgary "had oil wells going in their backyards." Another asked "What can we do about [improving relations between the oil and gas and ranching industries]?" Yet another remarked, "Maybe now when we drive out [to rural areas] we'll say we know what that is [referring to oil extraction sites]." Through these comments, audience members gesture both forwards and backwards in time to create this kind of thick time. They simultaneously illustrate uncertainty through words like "maybe" and through open-ended questions. Just as the play's plot remains unresolved, with several different potential outcomes, so too do the audience's real-world actions open up space for several possible futures. In the absence of certainty, multiplicity exists, not only in the fiction of the story, but in the real world as well.[71]

MAKING TIME AND SPACE FOR CONVERSATION

Downstage theatre company's mandate is to produce theatre "that creates conversation." As former artistic director Simon Mallett articulated in an interview with me, that conversation is in continuous evolution, changing according to the climate one finds oneself in.[72] A related challenge for the company is to create a theatrical experience that is able to sustain relevant conversation in an ever-changing environment. How can the company evolve and adapt so as to make space for debate and discourse? I argue that the company's engagement with a multi-use space – one that generates an amateur aesthetic – combined with the show's multiple and contingent temporal dimensions, encourages audience members and actors to respond to, dialogue with, and relate to each other in continually evolving fashion.

Theatre is, after all, an inherently relational meeting place, in which the co-presence of actor and audience is considered fundamental. Further, if we consider that space and time are dynamically responsive to the acts and bodies within it, and bodies and acts are responsive to space and time,[73] then the behaviour of others and mutability of experience imply that what is at work in any given place is really others at work. In other words, the time and space one finds oneself in are contingent upon the acts of oneself and one's "neighbours," to use *Good Fences*'s titular metaphor.

For example, following the time I spent with the artists on tour, I found myself reflecting on their generosity. I also found myself considering how their acts of generosity affected my own reading, interpretation, and analysis of the play. In other words, the chiastic meeting of time and space that I found myself in, at Red Deer College, the Unitarian Church, and the Parkdale Community Association attending *Good Fences* and getting to know the Downstage collective, is both evidence of pre-existing social relations and generates its own social relations as a result. The implied reverberations illuminate the limitations of the lesson: More than good fences are needed for good neighbour relations; it all depends on who those neighbours are or who you are with. Mallett also articulated the importance of considering relationality in conjunction with effect:

> I don't know that the effect needs to be specifically articulated because I think even at this point, three years after completing the show, I still don't necessarily have a clear idea of my relationship to the conflict. It's fluid and so constantly changing subjects, too, with whatever specific conflict you're talking to, but I do think that in terms of more engaged citizenry as it relates to – that is an effect that has the potential for wider-spread implications and further dissemination and discussion and so, fulfilling that role in that way, that is the effect of the show rather than necessarily the creation of an online petition to collect signatures.[74]

Mallett's description of the show as fluid and constantly changing, as well as his delineation of his relationship to the show, echoes the necessarily open and dynamic nature of the production itself. Indeed, the show becomes more effective through "dissemination and discussion" than through any kind of stable, tangible, or measurable marker of "effect." It is thus not just the human interactions that invoke a kind of relationality but the spatial-temporal dimensions as well. Helen Nicholson writes on applied theatre and the intersections between the affective and social turns in theatre (citing Thompson 2009 and Jackson 2011, respectively). In these writings, she notes that there is "an attempt to capture the political implications of a relational ontology for applied theatre, in which it is recognised that pathways to social agency are created not only through overthrowing structures of power but also biopolitically, in performative flows and rhythms of human and non-human interaction, and the spatial, temporal and material habits of everyday life."[75] The perceived effect of the *Good Fences* then might be seen in the relationality between bodies of peoples as they discuss and consider the show but also the ways in which the spatial, temporal biopolitics of the play craft their own relational web.

Of particular note for *Good Fences* in terms of relationality is the use of conflict and staged argument. The divergent perspectives and opinions highlighted in moments of conflict in the show make possible a kind of relationship: a relationality between two opposing sides. After all conflict may be a "negative" form of relationship, but it is a relationship nonetheless. These conflicts are frequently presented in the fourth wall breaks of the show: the actors perform as themselves to describe the process of creating the show directly to the audience. In one such instance, actor Braden Griffiths remarks on his loyalty to the ranching community, saying he "felt like we were their troupe." Col Cseke quickly retorts, "You felt [that]." "If that was your experience, great," Cseke continues, "that wasn't my experience so it can't be our experience." "We don't have to talk about this now," responds Griffiths. While Griffiths identified strongly with the ranching community, Cseke apparently did not. Such instances underscore the highly individuated perspectives from which the show is built. There is no consensual "we" even from within the same unified artwork. Another example occurs when Griffiths describes driving with a rancher in rural Alberta while he was conducting research. The rancher allegedly made fun of Cseke's truck by calling it a "toy truck." Cseke appears taken aback and slightly offended: "You never told me this before," he says to Griffiths. Such a discrepancy demonstrates the fickleness of facts and the unreliability of the "truth" such that even reality is subject to individual perspective and therefore invokes conflict.

What is most interesting about these conflicts is the way in which they are characterized by the Downstage team. The moments in which the narrative storyline is disrupted by breaks in the fourth wall are what the Downstage company calls "invitations": moments in which the actors, as themselves and not as their characters, speak to the audience. They "invite" the audience into the process as they recount the making of the play. In an interview, Mallett described the company's rationale for this term:

> We framed them as invitations in that sense of invitations we were issued and accepted throughout the course of our creation process that crafted our experience, partially as a lead-up to an invitation to the audience to do the same with us, to accept our invitation, and also to question, to drive through where we get to that narrative if you will, which is, given the invitations that are accepted, what are our allegiances as a result of the invitations

and the generosity of people that they granted us, so what are our responsibilities to them in the telling of their stories?[76]

Close and Mallett described the impetus for these invitations as being the result of their realization that presenting impartial work was inconceivable; they spoke of the "impossibility of doing something unbiased."[77] Mallett's description is pressingly close to my own navigation of Downstage's invitation extended to me, to be allowed to accompany them on their community tour and write about them in this book; what are my responsibilities and allegiances to Downstage? How has this invitation resulted in a biased perception of the work (and displayed the impossibility of an unbiased one)? Nevertheless, Close and Mallett articulate their desire for audiences with wide-ranging opinions to see that the work is balanced, that it is open to multiple perspectives and opinions. The implication is that audiences feel invited, and therefore comfortable, to share different opinions in the post-show discussion. As Close explained,

> And for me those sections are actually, for me personally, they're the most important, the most important factor of them is that it's actually impossible to create a piece that is going to be perceived by everyone to be balanced or unbiased. And so, by painting some of the complexity of like, this is what artists go through in trying to create something that's reasonably balanced and complex, helps the audience have a more nuanced understanding of what we were trying to do … and that helps often for there to be richer conversations after the show, rather than people just trying to suss out, "what's their slant?" and "are they trying to tell me x or y?" and it's always been interesting, the discussions that people will pull out different things depending on their background or their political slant or their experience … it's an interesting interpretation that, no matter what we put in place, you can't tell whether or not a character is telling the truth.[78]

Close's comments, particularly about avoiding having audiences attempt to "suss out" a slant or bias follows the kind of indirect or negative pedagogy that Carl Lavery advocates for in his analysis of the political potential of environmental theatre. Theatre that makes use of a negative pedagogy "hesitates to prescribe a 'strong meaning' and willingly opens itself to further interpretation and dialogue."[79] To extend this analysis of *Good Fences*'s negative pedagogy, we might use the term "weak theatre," following Gianni Vattimo's term "weak thought."[80] Lavery writes, "To appropriate Vattimo's terminology, the point of 'weak performance' is not so much to do as to 'undo', to impose a certain limit on the possibilities of theatre, to trouble notions of mastery and intentionality, to remain hypothetical and suspensive."[81] There is much in *Good Fences* of such indirectness, variability, and presentation of the non-expert. The many characters offer differing perspectives of the oil and gas and ranching industries, further multiplied by the actors' character personas who offer meta-commentary on the process of creating the show, and the variety of audience responses in the post-show talkback. The effect is one of bringing perspectives together to incite conversation, which, following Nicholas Ridout's *Passionate Amateurs: Theatre, Communism and Love* confirms that theatre is "a real place, where real people go to work, and where their work takes the form of 'conversation.'"[82] It was the moments of staged conflict, after all, that prompted the audience question referred to in this chapter's introduction about the extent to which the play was "real." As noted, the audience member was specifically interested in how many of the "fights" in the show were real. Although these moments of disruption or disjuncture are repeated, night after night, many audience members described them as feeling unscripted and unplanned. This points to the affective sense of real such moments of disjuncture cultivate, even in the absence of being "really real" by impersonating a "real place, where real people go to work" and converse.

In an interview with Mallett, I asked specifically about the staged arguments within the show:

KJ: *You talked about a blurring. "Is this real or is this scripted?" What's important about that?*

MALLETT: I think when we first did the show, we had a similar argument between Braden and myself, but all of those were framed as these sort of documentary recordings that took place in the past. Although we were acting out a script, the argument that we say took place in the past, to me there's a real difference between the audience's relationship to kind of a scripted argument where they understand – they're listening to the nature of the argument as you would with any other scripted piece of material versus a sense of, how to articulate – I think there's a liveliness to it, which I feel is still present in terms of us not being settled and satisfied with where we sit in relationship to the material, and to the nature of the arguments that are taking place. I do think that there's value in the audience experiencing ... in bringing them into that place with us in a way that is more jarring and unsettling and therefore I feel more provocative, to use that term, in terms of provoking an immediate need to actually, for an audience member to find a side in that and to rectify the situation for themselves.[83]

Mallett's remarks echo Paul Heritage's description of "impossible encounters"[84] in that *Good Fences* brings together people who may not usually move in the same circles and invites them into dialogue. While one's inclination may be to assume that "impossible encounters" necessarily imply two people or perspectives coming from vastly different cultures or geographical locations, social scientist and geographer Doreen Massey maintains that localism can harbour impossible encounters too. Massey refers to "strangers without,"[85] a term that applied and community-based theatre scholar Jan Cohen-Cruz picks up on to describe as, "not abstract and distant but rather concretely present in the everyday, material reality of our lives."[86] Indeed, some of the audience members I interviewed perceived the central issue in *Good Fences* to be one of not-in-my-backyard-ism (nimbyism). The literal geographical range of the work is thus very local, though the highly divergent viewpoints are conceptually much further apart.

> AUD 5b: I think it was real. And as [AUD 5a] says, it shows uh that it's ongoing and every day. And the Not in My Backyard that comes a couple times in the play, there, it's a tough choice to make between the oilfield – you know you have to have it – make your footprint as they said in the play to uh Garrett or go farm somewhere else.
> KJ: *Get away from it.*
> AUD 5b: There isn't anywhere else.
> AUD 5a: [repeating] ... there isn't anywhere else.[87]

As the audience members articulate, "There isn't anywhere else," pointing to the relatively small geographical scope being considered in the production, even while it harbours two highly divergent opinions on oil and gas. Cohen-Cruz writes of community-based performance, it problematizes an easy definition of the local as "lived experience" by bringing elements of the local that we *don't* see to the here and now. I wonder if it's not so much the *global* that people reject as part of their immediate lives, and hence avoid responsibility for but *anywhere* with which they avoid making a relationship. That is, we are spared a bad conscience for ignorance of "global" conditions in which people produce the coffee and sugar, and extract the milk, that we unthinkingly consume. But in fact "the global," in this sense, stands for unseen and unknown conditions in any geographical location that are distant in terms of our consciousness of them.[88]

This provocative idea clarifies the potential effect of *Good Fences* to encourage people to see versions of the "here-and-now" that are different from their own. It may be rare to see characters within the same fictional world disagree about common events. It is more unlikely for audience members to see creative partners disagree about aspects of their creative process. However, having these instances on full display in *Good Fences* and, additionally, offering an audience talkback demonstrate the company's desire to make room for multiple possible revelations of "unseen and unknown conditions" as regards the oil and gas industry that may be contradictory or strange to what an individual might previously believe.

In one talkback in Red Deer audience members spoke of their varied relationships to the oil and gas industry: some of them were currently working or had previously worked in the oilfield, some were staunchly against oil extraction and its devastating environmental effects, and many had a complex relationship to the industry as, for instance, beneficiaries of scholarships from oil companies. Regardless, they were encouraged to make their own experiences visible to each other. As Mallett described,

> I feel as though we are getting to a point where the kind of experience we are able to offer an audience is becoming desirable beyond just the content of the show itself. I think the opportunity to engage and connect with others who you otherwise wouldn't engage with is appealing to a certain portion of the audience and an experience that I think they value.[89]

While the potential for conflict may, as an affective experience, seem to discourage relationality, Barbara Schaffer Bacon, Cheryl L. Yuen, and

Pam Korza from the Animating Democracy program for civic engagement through arts and culture in the United States write that reciprocity in community-based performance requires "two or more parties with differing viewpoints working toward common understanding in an open-ended, face-to-face discussion."[90] Youth culture scholar Jacqueline Kennelly similarly writes that "The need for this recognition of plurality is an ethical one, in that a truly democratic public sphere cannot exist without it. The problem is that an individual may not even realize that he or she is missing plurality in his or her life until confronted with it."[91] In this way, the presence of scripted conflict between the actors brings into view the kind of varying perspectives present in the real-world politics of modern-day Alberta. It encourages plurality, using it to foster discussion, in turn, in the talkback in which the audience members are able to speak as their real selves.

It is key to this argument connecting multiplicity with perceived realness to highlight that in these moments of staged conflicts the actors are using their real names and referencing real events. In doing so, they appear to be truth-tellers not just in the show but also in the real world. In response to my question about things that may have contributed to the show's realness, an audience member described

> the monologues ... Sort of breaking the fourth wall and saying you know this is what we did and this is how we felt ... even though it is scripted they did say, there are real things that I know that they you know went through when they were doing the research for it.[92]

Another audience member described how the similar break in character in the talkback wherein the actors appear as themselves contributed to the realness: "Uh I feel like this – as far as a lot of theatre goes – I feel like this is very real. Like they talked about in the talkback they've created three shows, the ensemble together and yeah they said it's very real."[93] Rather than the usual operation of autobiographical theatre in which the ontological difference between actor, playwright, and character is elided into a single identity, the realness in this example is grounded in the clearly established and differentiated bodies of the actor, playwright, and character. Thus, rather than the perceptual collapsing of the actual world (inhabited by the audience) and the fictional or play world (of the characters) – Jenn Stephenson calls these world[a] and world[b][94] – the reality effect in this case comes from a clear and maintained delineation between the two. After having seen the show in near identical iterations several times, the artistic effect of their soothsaying – the sense that they were spontaneously speaking truths – had disappeared. However, during my first experience with *Good Fences*, I was fairly convinced that these were real conflicts between the actors. As I later learned, they were indeed *based* on real conflicts. As such, they were actually possibly more real than I had come to perceive them to be. Cseke and Griffiths are not really having this argument about the truck for the first time; Cseke is not hearing about his truck being called a toy for the first time, even if he protests that he is. But, in the other aforementioned conflict about Griffiths and Cseke feeling like they were on the ranchers' team, Mallett revealed that the conflict was not actually between those two men but rather between himself and Cseke. The conflict therefore is a re-telling of a real conflict – and the way it is presented, it feels real – even if it belongs to a different real person who is not performing onstage. As one audience member described in response to my question about moments in the show that felt real, "You know I liked the little snippets in between even though they're staged and you know and you get that, but it still lends a little bit to the process that they went through while they were making the play."[95] Mallett is worth quoting at length here:

> I think that the realness of the journey of the artist in the creating of the show and including that story within the piece, I do think it opens the door and invites people to engage with and express their own relationship to the material in a way that I think would go beyond what a purely narrative-based approach would. And it's why there are a number of points that we discussed both in the original production and – well, I think, we discussed whether it was a worthwhile component to add to what we were doing, and I think in a way, what I mentioned before about a sort of burgeoning understanding and knowledge base is an experience that audiences often undergo when they're watching the shows. Sometimes they bring – what we've heard on this tour is like, that they bring a certain component to that perspective that perhaps they don't understand it from the other side, for example, and so I think that the reflection of the realness of us being able to share stories that are based in truth and based on real experiences that we really, really had, even though sometimes the voices of the experience sometimes are displaced because originally there were seven of us

and now there are only four, and so, in fact, what Braden was advocating for was putting on my experience, but I'm not there to talk about it anymore, so it kind of gets taken on in another voice, and so ... but yeah, so, for me, the element of realness and the ability to sort of take down that fourth wall and connect with audiences is different. I think ... they are invitations to engage with the work in a different way that I think enhances the impact of the show.[96]

The complex real-ish-ness of the staged arguments operates in multiple times (past, present, future): The conflicts are real insofar as they did occur in the past; they *feel* real in their unfolding in the present because of the metatheatrical circumstances under which they are aired; finally, they seem to have a real effect on the future insofar as they prompt real audience discussion. Audience members confirmed the ways in which the show invites real personal reflection:

AUD 2b: I think, I think the play's important because it's illustrative of, of the whole issue of – and it relates to not just agriculture versus oil and gas especially as it relates to Southern Alberta but as one of the other people – it relates to community issues and to the government ... when I watch a play like this – so, where's the truth? Is it a truth in that these people are being NIMBYs "I don't want it in my backyard," or is there a bigger thing of uh "we're all in this society together and you have – there is a cost and part of the cost is producing energy." And there is, there is a, there is a cost. Or do you just say "Okay shut everything down." Which is what some people want to do, you know, like is that really practical or rational. And so I, living in Alberta we are, you know, our bread is buttered by the oil and gas industry. You know this is all ... [gesturing around the theatre space] a result of the oil and gas industry. Do you bite the hand that feeds you? Or do you come up with alternative thoughts and processes, which um, which help generate solutions to these issues that they talk about in a play like this.[97]

AUD 1: ... what I found valuable was it showed both sides of a situation.

KJ: *Yeah?*

AUD 1: Of something that's happening in our society, in our world that um people have differing views and see how they come together. And sometimes you're, you see faults on both sides, you see good things on both sides and sort of compromises we make in day-to-day life. And um I'm going to admit, I myself with other topics, like um, whatever. But I mean GMO foods whether people believe it or not you put a lot of emotional energy into it and its good to see a different perspective. You know, do people feel like you do and agree with your stance, or are people a little more moderate or – and what are the good and bad points from the other side of the discussion?[98]

These interviews are not only indicative of the personal political reflection *Good Fences* invites; they also underscore the lack of consensus that was made visible among the audience members. The individuals quoted here suggest multiple perspectives and opinions even as they articulate their own personal opinion, full of changes of topic and self-interruption. They are not so much advocating a single perspective as they are demonstrating that they are aware that opinions will necessarily conflict. This is key to the piece as a reflection of real-world politics: Following Chantal Mouffe's *Agonistics: Thinking the World Politically*, Liz Tomlin figures "'the political' as the inevitable and interminable eruption of conflicting desires within a society in which consensus would (indeed must) never be achieved."[99] This requires a resistance of antagonism, wherein one identity is perceived to threaten another identity, and rather an encouragement of agonism: "an acknowledgement and validation of opposing positions that are held and fought for within democratic structures."[100] These quotes offer a somewhat optimistic or idealized version of real-world politics, but given my earlier contemplation of Nguyen's echo chambers and epistemic bubbles in contemporary politics, bear further consideration. The play, as a meeting place, is able to hold multiple, contradicting views. This is unlike the limited perspective of epistemic bubbles, and the purposefully self-insulating and self-limiting echo chambers frequently found in social media discourse. In an age of post-truth, pervasive fake news and rampant misinformation spread online, *Good Fences*'s ability to act as a porous and fluid site of exchange, rather than a closed and insulating "bubble" or "chamber" is important to consider – however limited in scope and scale it may be.

Interestingly, many audience members of *Good Fences* suggested in their interviews that this maintenance of "both sides" and the staging of disagreement contributed to the show's perceptual realness. In one of my most memorable interviews – and the shortest I conducted, topping out at just under one minute – a man approached me after I'd finished interviewing other audience members and told me he had something to say.

> AUD 4: Ok, so uh you just said do you appreciate the realness?
> KJ: *Yeah.*
> AUD 4: And uh yeah the answer is yeah. Too often uh in, in plays that are dealing with these kinds of themes they come down, to be a political statement one way or another. This was good that they kept it to the real situation.
> KJ: *Yeah.*
> AUD 4: And uh tried to portray the various points of view and things that happened.
> KJ: *Right. The complexities.*
> AUD 4: The complexities, yeah. So yes, I did appreciate the realness.[101]

This may be because the show created a potent affective experience that was predicated on building relationality and relationships between and amongst audience and performer. Applied theatre scholar Julie Salverson points to the potential empathic and political power invested in staged argument: "Theatre as an art form has the political potential to hold contradictory material – including the 'me' and the 'not me' – without insisting on its truth or resolution."[102] For Salverson, an ethical engagement in storytelling also means continually resisting the tendency to tell "one … story" and responding instead to how particular people live their multiple positionings.[103] In other words, situating multiple perspectives or possibilities within a single work requires that audiences (and characters) relate to an "other" who may have a different experience, perspective, or opinion. I characterize this as a comfortable conflict. It is not, after all, that real-world groups with staunchly held partisan beliefs – like extreme right wing Facebook groups or QAnon forums – don't think that there are others in the world with differing opinions but rather that they cannot comfortably accommodate the presence of contradictory perspectives and so dismiss and discredit them as fake news or media manipulation. An audience member described how, conversely, *Good Fences* managed to contain difference without suppressing it, which resulted in an increased perception of realness (rather than a forced dismissal of alternate viewpoints as fake):

> Sort of breaking the fourth wall and saying you know this is what we did and this is how we felt, it's good to hear the performers uh talk about that because um it, it shows that they, that it took all the angles into consideration. They had no set ideas. They wanted to make something balanced. And they all, even though it is scripted they did say, there are real things that I know that they, you know, went through when they were doing the uh, the research for it.[104]

Performer Col Cseke echoed the same sentiment:

> I think to me the question of realness, is, and this kind of goes back to all of the questions you've asked us, is I think the effect is humanizing. A topic that is almost always talked about as a commodity or as political policy, and now increasingly environmental impact, but very rarely the human impact, and so I think putting it onto us as creators really reinforces, "This is a creation of individuals from Calgary" and puts it into a human scale, that I think allows for more – my hope is that it allows for more empathy towards a topic that is usually very either policy-driven or economically-driven as a commodity.[105]

Hans-Thies Lehmann suggests that post-dramatic theatre, of which theatre of the real is one particular form, has not given up on relating to the world. Instead, it no longer represents the world as a surveyable whole: "'World' does not mean the walled-off (by a fourth wall) fictional totality, but a world open to its audience, an essentially possible world, pregnant with potentiality."[106] It is the multitude of spaces, times, and perspectives a production allows for that can best facilitate its realness: multiplicity generates reality effects. While *Good Fences* is paradoxically locally focused and temporally respondent to the politics of the here and now, the invitation for conversation, both literally as in the use of the talkback and generally in its refusal of resolution or position, invites multiplicity and a general sense of real discussion. The show fittingly ends on a speculative note: we don't know how the fictional storyline finishes, and because of *Good Fences*'s reworkings and subsequent tours involving cast replacements, even the meta-story of the performers remains perpetually unwritten. There is an overarching suspension and invitation to the audience to participate in the post-show discussion, actively bringing their real-life experience and political ideas to reflect on the performance.

To put it differently, even in a piece that obviously revolves around a particular certain time and space, namely Alberta in the 2010s, *Good Fences* presents many possible perspectives. The company's capacity to recognize the opportunities for discussion that a show with this degree of divergence offers, and its refusal to present itself as a neat whole, is what actually asserts the show's realness. As Stephenson writes, "Perhaps the most influential reality effect arises from the confluence of all these stratagems. Over and above the sense of a nonfictional encounter momentarily created by these specific practices, they also operate cumulatively to cast a reality aura over the remainder of the performance, producing a wholesale reframing of objects and behaviors that might ordinarily have been read as fictional under other circumstances, but now project a sense of being really real."[107] In the case of *Good Fences*, it is the continued presence of several contradicting and conflicting elements of reality that create this atmosphere of reality, or real-ish-ness, for audience members. One example is when audiences are jarred out of the moment of the play world and into the reality of the real word because the performance space is also a community hall and someone needs to use the microwave. Another is when an actor breaks out of his or her character. In moments like these, the play shows it is able to maintain multiplicity. Even the refusal of the show's creators to label their play (refuting any claims that it is verbatim, documentary, or site-responsive) shows that the play maintains a kind of multifaceted ontology that, by its very refusal to be wholeheartedly classified as theatre of real, thus becomes more real.

Carol Martin contends that when a theatre company welcomes multiplicity into their production, theatre of the real has significant potential to "invite contemplation of the ways in which stories are told."[108] She likens this kind of theatre to "a form of Brechtian distancing that asks spectators to simultaneously understand the theatrical, the real, and the simulated, each as its own form of truth."[109] This staging of contradiction – a suspension within disagreement – results in the audience perceiving a show (in this case, *Good Fences*) as balanced and, therefore, real – or at least real-ish. The diverse opinions and perspectives the actors, and actors-as-characters, present reflect the varied opinions held by humans in the real world. *Good Fences* takes a partisan issue and reframes it conceptually to examine multiple belief structures and the development of political opinion itself; an examination that is presciently relevant to broader debates about truth, fact, and trust in contemporary politics. Perhaps an audience comment written on a post-it note after watching the show was the most apt: "Great perspectives from both sides of the fence."

3

Talking to, at, and with Audiences
The Politics of Participation

While Downstage's *Good Fences* from the previous chapter invites audiences to participate in a post-performance talkback, Tarragon Theatre's production of the Schaubühne's *An Enemy of the People* takes a different tack in order to engage audiences in political discussion. Like *Good Fences*, *An Enemy of the People* centres on environmental issues and the economic impacts on industry. Rather than wait until the end of the performance, however, *An Enemy of the People* invites audiences to actively participate in a town-hall during the show itself. In this version of Henrik Ibsen's original text, the central plot issue remains the same: the storyline focuses on the potential contamination of an unnamed town's therapeutic natural baths. What makes this production unique is that after being presented with this economic-environmental issue, the fourth wall is broken and the audience is encouraged to respond to the arguments made by the characters, one of whom advocates shutting the baths to prevent illness, and one who wishes to keep them open to stave off an economic downturn. The discussion that results is wide-ranging; on the evenings I attended, my fellow audience members raised not only questions of pollution in the fictional baths but also introduced real-world issues like the local Toronto mayoral election and Canadian national politics. There is a distinctly complicated real-ish-ness in this dramaturgical innovation: Is the audience in this production meant to "play" a citizen of the fictional small-town? Or be their "real" selves? Are they meant to speak to the fictional issue in the play, of the contaminated town baths? Or to the issues of the "here and now" in the real-world?

The desire to actively involve real audience members in the overall creation of the theatre experience – whether through participation during the show itself or as active discussants in the reflective sensemaking processes afterwards – prompts pressing questions about the audience's involvement in "making real." *An Enemy of the People*'s unique dramaturgical strategy offers a means of analyzing the effect of audience participation, specifically in terms of the audience's ability to contribute "real" opinions, concerns, and feelings vis-à-vis their participation and the perceived effect and valuation of that participation. Using *Good Fences* as a counterpoint, I focus on *An Enemy of the People* to put forth a series of provocations about the nature and role of audience participation in what I am terming "politi-real theatre" or "politicized theatre of the real." I use this term to refer to theatre that takes political issues as content and combines that with aspects of reality in framing, whether as documentary, participatory, or community-based. In this chapter, I assess how such a form might generate experiences of real-ish-ness: an audience's felt perceptions of realness.

This form is critically in need of consideration given a larger trend toward upgrading the creative role of the audience. Gareth White memorably begins his book on the subject of audience participation with the line, "There are few things in the theatre that are more despised than audience participation." And yet, he goes on to say, its popularity has continued to increase.[1] Post-show discussions in which the audience may ask questions of the actors or otherwise engage in conversation about the show – as seen in *Good Fences* – have similarly proliferated, at least in North America.[2] This is occurring, perhaps, in response to the suggestion that contemporary audiences play a less contributory role than they have in the past. Caroline Heim cites theatrical shifts in the twentieth century resulting in

> the disempowerment of the theatre audience, the decline in audience sovereignty, and the change from active to passive spectatorship. Due to changes in theatre architecture, the rise in power of arts professionals, changes in audience demographics, and the rise of a commodity culture, contemporary audience contribution has been largely relegated to laughter and applause.[3]

This perceived de-activation of theatre audiences over time is regarded as problematic and connects with the pervasive notion that, as Matthew Reason writes, "an active audience is good, a passive audience bad."[4] Jacques Rancière's important text *The Emancipated Spectator* describes the two beliefs underlying this idea: "the spectator is held before an appearance in a state of ignorance ... the spectator remains immobile in her seat, passive. To be a spectator is to be separated from both the capacity to know and the power to act."[5] A spectator is perceived to be, essentially, incapacitated. As Rancière articulates, "Theatre accuses itself of rendering spectators passive and thereby betraying its essence as community action. It consequently assigns itself the mission of reversing its effects and expiating its sins by restoring to spectators ownership of their consciousness and their activity."[6] But this valuation is highly simplified. Rancière himself vouches for a re-valuing of the act of viewing, in which apparently passive processes of selection, interpretation, connection, acceptance, or negation are actually active actions from audiences.[7] Audiences, he says, are already active insofar as they are "individuals plotting their own paths in the forest of things, acts and signs that confront or surround them."[8] And yet, the idea that being an apparently passive spectator is a bad thing "has stuck fast and resonates widely."[9] Complicating this valuation is the implicit connection between theatrical and political activity. In her book on theatre audiences, Helen Freshwater connects the desire for active spectatorship to political action when she describes "one of the most cherished orthodoxies in theatre studies: the belief in a connection between audience participation and political empowerment."[10] In performances that deliberately include political issues, the apparent stakes of audience participation are arguably even higher since an apparently non-participatory audience would seem to suggest a non-participatory citizenry. In other words, the perceived participation of the audience in politi-real theatre like *An Enemy of the People* can feel as if it is indicative of broader ideals of democracy, civic engagement, and citizenship in the real world.

In this chapter, my conception of theatre's relationship to the political is necessarily broad; Joe Kelleher advocates for a wide-ranging definition of politics in his examination of not only political theatre but also the more general relationship between theatricality and politics. He uses Stefan Collini's definition of politics as "the important, inescapable, and difficult attempt to determine relations of power in a given space."[11] The audience participation in the town-hall scene of *An Enemy of the People* is, accordingly, the focus of my analysis because it is a moment in which the power of the audience potentially shifts: they are encouraged to speak up and directly impact the performance. Speaking to the juncture of audience participation, politics, and theatre that occurs in this moment, Assistant Director David Jansen writes in his program notes that, "In examining the relationship between the individual and the body politic, the slippery nature of truth, lies, pragmatism, and how politics works both privately and publicly, the play stages the theatricality of political discourse brilliantly."[12] Using audience data in the form of observation and attendance at performances and talkbacks, as well as archival footage of *An Enemy of the People*, I am here interested not so much in the theatricality of political discourse but in the politic of theatrical participation and the kinds of real produced therein. As theatre scholar Carl Lavery writes,

> It is incumbent on practitioners and scholars to reflect, rigorously, on how theatre works as a medium, while at the same time remaining vigilant with respect to its supposed efficacy … assuming, in advance, that theatre actually has the capacity to achieve something, a premise that not everyone might be willing to accept. For many activists, for instance, theatre's politics are vicarious and rhetorical – they can only gesture towards the "real" rather than impacting on it.[13]

The stakes of inviting or producing realness in theatre that takes politics as its subject, then, are high. Can such examples of politicized theatre of the real have real-world impact by virtue of the participation of real audience members in political discussion? Or, if they can only ever "gesture" to the real, to what end are audiences invited to participate?

PLAYING POLITICS AMIDST BLURRED BOUNDARIES

The production of *An Enemy of the People* under consideration in this chapter has a multifaceted origin. While the play text of *An Enemy of the People* was originally written in 1882 by Norwegian playwright Henrik Ibsen, the production staged in Toronto at Tarragon Theatre used a modern-day version adapted by Florian Borchmeyer and translated into English by Maria Milisavljevic.[14] This Toronto production was itself based on an earlier production of Borchmeyer's script staged in Berlin at the Schaubühne in 2012, directed by Thomas Ostermeier and for which Borchmeyer was dramaturg. Tarragon Theatre essentially bought the production from the Schaubühne (including the staging, blocking, design, etc.) and enlisted international playwright-in-residence Milisavljevic to complete the translation to English, which she attempted to do as faithfully as possible by transcribing video recordings of the Schaubühne production. As per Tarragon Theatre's usual programming, talkbacks followed several nights of performance, allowing audiences to reflect not only on the show itself but also their participation in it. The show was very popular with audiences; after its initial run in 2014, it was reprogrammed again in the following season.

The storyline remains much the same as Ibsen's original, though there are several updates to modernize the production: language and idioms are revised for the twenty-first century, some of the characters are in an indie rock band (who at one point sing David Bowie's "Changes"), and the stage design is more suggestive than realistic, with a simple but effective design in which the walls were covered in black chalkboard paint. The plot follows Doctor Stockmann who believes that the local therapeutic baths, which are a promising economic stimulant for the town, are being contaminated by pollution and are unsafe. The doctor plans to reveal this by releasing their[15] findings in the local paper. Doctor Stockmann's brother Peter, however, happens to be a town councillor and vehemently opposes releasing the findings, citing the disastrous economic impacts of closing the baths for the town. Peter persuasively points out not only the immediate financial implications of closing the baths but also the reputational damage for future years. Doctor Stockmann refuses to be swayed and eventually becomes convinced of broad corruption in local politics and persistent media manipulation. While Doctor Stockmann initially has allies, including Hovstad who edits the local press, these allies disband when it becomes clear that the financial burden will hit the town's citizens hardest: without the income from the baths, there will be less funding for schools and other local infrastructure. Doctor Stockmann makes notes in chalk on the walls throughout the play until eventually the entire set is literally whitewashed when the doctor is silenced; the other characters use water balloons and paint rollers filled with white paint to cover the black walls.

The most radical adaptation from Borchmeyer turns a town hall scene in the fourth act into a fourth-wall-breaking participatory discussion. This scene is when the conflict about closing the baths comes to a head, but it also reveals Doctor Stockmann's increasing disillusionment with contemporary society. In his version, Borchmeyer replaces Doctor Stockmann's speech with sections from a twenty-first-century French anarchist manifesto touching on individualism, consumerism, and corruption.[16] The house lights come up and the actors solicit audience members to weigh in on the debate over whether the baths of the show's unnamed town are contaminated and what action is warranted. Some audience members gamely responded "in character" as citizens of the small fictional town. One spectator, for instance, stated that they would be "taking their business out of this town and setting up elsewhere!" at the performance I attended on 22 October 2014. Other audience members stayed firmly within the real world and brought up modern-day politics like the 2014 Toronto mayoral election or 2015 Canadian federal election. As is obvious from these different audience responses, it isn't immediately clear who the audience are meant to be in the town-hall, and as a result, what they are meant to contribute. As one audience member put it, "we can speak what we're thinking as ourselves or we can take up sympathies of townspeople that we may not share,"[17] pointing to the variety of positions audience members might take.

For some critics, this offered an exciting range of possibility: Christopher Hoile for instance writes that,

> Ostermeier and Borchmeyer's best idea is to have the audience represent the citizens in the town hall meeting that Stockman calls. Directors have done this before but this time Rose via Ostermeier actually encourages audience members to speak out in response to what characters say. This is both exciting and slightly dangerous since we can't know how off-kilter the audience's remarks will be.

In undated archival footage of a performance from 2014, one audience member brings up a local nuclear project that he was able to get his community to mobilize against: he is invoking a real-world experience in his response to the fiction. An actor interrupts and asks him, "Sir, can I just ask, with what you just said, how would you like the community to proceed? What is your recommendation?" "For this [community] here?" the audience member asks, gesturing to the stage. "Yeah, considering the baths" the actor responds, apparently steering the audience member back to the fictional world and away from his real-life experience with the nuclear project. Another audience member later in the same performance completely avoids the real world, and states, "The crisis is the baths. If we don't solve it, our town is still doomed," confidently jumping into the fictional role of local townsperson and referring to "our town." This back and forth between real-world and fictional-world politics creates delightfully complicated moments. The actors have to choose whether to respond as fictional characters and feign ignorance of the real-world or step out of the fiction into their real-world selves and respond knowingly. In the talkback on 17 October 2015, two actors discussed the complicated nature of this interplay. As one put it, "We started in Norway [but] it got a little complicated if things like Walkerton [an *E. coli* outbreak in the town of Walkerton in 2000 that contaminated local drinking water]"[18] came up. It was not, in other words, immediately clear what world(s) were at play and what the desired audience response was; to play in the fiction or to invoke real-world comparisons.

One might move to quickly point out how this blurring of times and spaces is similar to that in *Good Fences*, but there is a distinction to be made between *multiple* times and spaces as in *Good Fences* and *indeterminate* time and space as in *An Enemy of the People*. In the latter, the fictive frame is neither clearly broken nor maintained but relentlessly obscured. The actors in *An Enemy of the People* are not clearly stepping out of role and addressing the audience as "themselves." This is unlike in *Good Fences* where the strategy created a complex but ultimately distinguishable break between character, actor-character, and actor. Neither is it always clear in *An Enemy of the People* whether audience members are speaking their own, real, personal opinions or also taking on a character during the scene. Further, space(s) and time(s) that are relevant to and/or welcome in the discussion are also difficult to determine: does the play want audience members to reference Rob Ford's real Toronto mayoral candidacy? Or stick to the fictional Norwegian baths? This murkiness is evident in the script. Take, for instance, these lines from beginning of the town hall:

> STOCKMANN (to the audience): Good evening. I'm very sorry. We had to improvise on this. Could we have the lights up in the theatre, please? (House lights up.) Thank you. Apologies for the location, but this won't take long.[19]

The character clearly breaks the fourth wall and directly addresses the audience. The audience and performers are really gathered in a theatre, so the line asking for the lights up in the theatre seems to be a gesture towards realness. The house lights do indeed come up. But, is the character referring to *this* real theatre, Tarragon Theatre in Toronto? Or a different, fictional theatre in the story world? The apology for the location seems to suggest that the performance is still within the fiction. Why would the actor apologize to the audience for the relatively comfortable, well-equipped Tarragon Theatre mainspace? Rather than a presentation of multiplicity, there is a presentation of indeterminacy and a resultant ontological collapse. This is not, in other words, a layering or intertwining of the real and the fictive, both of which imply the presence of borders or boundaries even as they become blurred. Instead, we might think of this as murky or shimmery dramaturgy, wherein the effect is one of squinting through the fiction at what are possibly bits of the real.

In addition to the in-character responses as townspeople, and invocation of real-world political references, there was also a third kind of audience remark that I am particularly interested in as it relates to this lack of border between real and fiction: a metatheatrical gesture to Ibsen and the original text, or theatre more broadly. An actor described in a talkback that "sometimes someone will mention Ibsen, which is actually terrible. Someone yesterday said, 'I hope Ibsen is listening' and you go … 'He's not a character?'"[20] In another talkback this discussion returned: "It's really awkward in the town hall when people yell out references to Ibsen … like, 'Ibsen would be proud!' and I don't know what to say to that, 'Who is this Ibsen?'"[21] Translator Milisavljevic also recalls one performance where a gentleman left the theatre mid-performance, shouting "this is not Ibsen!"[22] This response, of gesturing to Ibsen to variously indict the adaptation or applaud it, is notable because it suggests a move to re-establish the boundary between the fiction and the real. By deliberately referring to the original playwright, audience members offer a kind of frame that creates distance between the real and fictive: This – the play – is a fiction, written a long time ago by Ibsen, and I, the audience member referring to Ibsen, am real. In the archival footage of the 2014 production, an audience member suggests that in order to save the town economically, it should "Diversify, how about local theatre?" another metatheatrical gesture that elicits much laughter in the moment and might be an example of what theatre critic Richard Ouzounian referred to as the audience distancing itself from the show through laughter.[23] Whether such remarks ultimately serve to reinforce the boundary of the fiction of the play world or highlight the realness of the audience (or both) is unclear, but suffice it to say that the metatheatrical referencing served as a kind of border-reinforcement between fictive and real worlds that were increasingly hard to delineate.

TORONTO, NORWAY: THE INVITATION TO LOCALIZE

The pervasive indeterminacy at play in the show is due in part to the (ab)sense of place. While *Good Fences* is unquestionably tied to a specific place and its politics of land, resources, and industry, the "place-ness" of *An Enemy of the People* is less definite: is this a Norwegian town or Toronto or a non-specific proxy town? Are we all assembled in a fictive-world theatre or a real-world theatre during the town hall? A consideration of place is particularly important given the sense of "local issues" present both in the fiction of the script and in the real-world references made by audiences to events impacting modern-day Canadian citizens. In a video lecture series posted to YouTube, the Tarragon Theatre production's Assistant Director David Jansen responds to a question from an audience member asking how current local events influenced the production by stating, "Not so much in current events of neoliberalism and how that affects our behavior, but definitely discussions of how much political agency and politics fit in, and then in terms of particular events like Walkerton, the oil sands, all of those issues."[24] His reference to specific, Canadian environmental issues is interesting in its declared localness. Many of the more favourable reviews cite such recent, local political events as increasing the relevancy (and thus overall strength) of the production, specifically because of references made to events like the *E. coli* outbreak in Walkerton, Ontario: "I was skeptical how this participatory section would work in buttoned-down Toronto. Well, perhaps it's because of the wild mayoral race to succeed Rob Ford – or the obvious resonances of the play given wider Canadian debates about the oil sands and the dysfunctional Parliament – but the crowd got engaged and enraged and didn't even wait for permission."[25]

Translator Milisavljevic and director of the Toronto staging Richard Rose were very interested in the show being deliberately about Toronto and Canada, but they were limited in being able to make any actual changes to the Schaubühne script. Steering the audience towards local conversations was instead promoted in the unscripted town hall; Milisavljevic cites actor Rick Roberts, who played Peter Stockmann in both the 2014 and 2015 productions as being particularly gifted at steering the conversation towards the local Toronto context.[26] Interestingly, Milisavljevic and Rose went on in 2016 to create their own version of *An Enemy of the People* for Saint John Theatre Company in New Brunswick that became highly specific in its references to local events, including Indigenous and environmental issues, after consultation with local arts councils and local elders. Comparing the scripts for the Tarragon production and the Saint John production, the difference in the declared "place" of performance is apparent: while the Schaubühne script does not offer any setting, the latter includes some sense of place in the setting, "Present. A beach town in Canada."[27] The desire for local contextualization, then, was certainly present but was not actually in the script itself.

This is in large part due to the international touring of the Schaubühne production. While I focus specifically on the Toronto production that I had access to, the Schaubühne production and script has an extensive performance history in Germany and globally. Each production, however, does offer some sense of localness due to the varied audience response and degree of participation in the town hall. Toronto theatre critic Ouzounian writes that "From all reports, in Germany, England, Quebec and New York the atmosphere was heated, the engagement passionate and the end result exciting."[28] In China the production was shut down after reportedly inciting an impassioned audience response during the town hall scene, with some audience members invoking comparisons to local issues of censorship in the People's Republic of China.[29] In a meta-democratic (or pseudo-democratic) moment, a performance of the touring Schaubühne production at the Moscow Art Theatre involved the audience rushing the stage. The actor playing Doctor Stockmann put the question of continuing to Act V to a public vote, proceeding only when the audience voted in the affirmative.[30] Theatre critic Ouzounian uses these reports from other locales to somewhat criticize the Toronto production: "Here in Toronto, at least at the performance I attended, the cast members suddenly started playing clichés instead of people, the audience distanced itself with laughter, the few participants responding with jokey attempts at rhetoric ... Good Lord did I not like it."[31] His comments suggest a more temperate audience response. Thus, despite its portability and global touring history, *An Enemy of the People* does manage in some ways to offer a sense of the local or, at least, insight into relational mores and local cultural dynamics. Theatre production is indelibly linked with the place of performance; the norms and understandings of how theatre means are necessarily cultural and social, as is audience behaviour.[32] To invoke political engagement, or apparent political engagement, alongside theatre spectatorship only seems to intensify this sense of locality.

To return to Collini's definition of politics as "the important, inescapable, and difficult attempt to determine relations of power in a given space,"[33] the emphasis on a given space is vital. Contexts necessarily shift power relations, including the relations between a local audience and the production they are attending. In his program notes for the Toronto production, Jansen fittingly writes that, "theatre, as an art form of presence and the present tense, makes particularly forceful demands on its translations. They must adhere to the profoundly local nature of all theatre. If all theatre is local so is all politics."[34] While *Good Fences* is well aware of the entrenched and pervasive politics of its local audiences, the transported story of *An Enemy of the People* from Berlin to Toronto concerning a possible Norwegian town did not necessarily have the same intimate awareness of its audience. This is not to suggest that theatre cannot be presented effectively out of its original context or that broad notions of late capitalism are not felt globally; rather, theatre must be presciently aware of its various contexts and the norms and ideas operating within them. This is especially true if, as in *An Enemy of the People*, ideological or political labour in the form of audience participation is to be asked of those audience members present within them.

Spectators are, after all, always already imbricated in their own ideologies and worlds.[35] Theatre therefore must be aware of the effects of the dramaturgical strategies by which it invites audiences, with their contingent ideologies and worlds, into the play worlds presented. In his writing on the concept of ideology, Slavoj Žižek warns of the "inherent impossibility of isolating a reality whose consistency is not maintained by ideological mechanisms, a reality that does not disintegrate the moment we subtract from it its ideological component."[36] If we transpose this to notions of theatrical worlds, play worlds likewise must be maintained by particular ideologies. In building the world of the play, productions must take into account the not-so-autonomous subjects of the audience and their ideologies. If the Canadian federal election was on the political mind of the spectators in attendance at Tarragon, as suggested by attempts to draw it into the story, the question is then whether the created world of the performance was able to accept the pre-existing ideology of its spectators. Even beyond questions of to what end the realities of the spectators are being invited into the production and whether the production can accommodate them, we can also ask how the invitation to participate itself functions to generate a sense of realness – or not.

PERCEPTIONS OF POWER: MAJORITARIAN, MINORITARIAN, AND ABSTAINING AUDIENCES

Audience members were generally curious about the invitation to participate, and often asked questions about the intent of the town hall scene during post-show talkbacks. In one talkback I attended, an audience member asked directly what the purpose of the town hall scene was. An actor responded that there is a town hall in the original script, and so opening it up to the audience was an obvious choice since "they [the audience] were right there." The actor went on to suggest that the town hall scene puts the issues "in the audience's lap" and essentially generates some "allegiances or intellectual discordances" that the audience is meant to wrestle with.[37] This phrasing from the actor describes an interesting offer: in audience participation there is, to use White's term, generally a kind of invitation issued that audiences may or may not take up. White articulates the conditions that must be met in order for the invitation to be accepted: if the audience does not understand the participation being asked, or have the skills or resources to do so, the participation will not work.[38] If the issues are placed "in the audience's lap," as the actor suggests, it is implied that it is incumbent on the audience to take up the mantle of discussion – but whether the audiences fully understood the nature of the participation is somewhat debatable given the varied responses garnered. This lack of clarity was also reflected in the audience member in the talkback pushing further, asking whether there was "any goal in bringing that discussion? [Were you] pushing people's thinking in a certain particular direction ... were you guiding to a certain idea or just letting it formulate?" The same actor responded that the discussion is "partly" guided by the audience and that the actors respond from their character's point of view – "I don't know if it's anything more than that." The actor then clarified that the performers "do try to guide it into the issues ... sometimes we do try to steer it into issues of democracy." As an example, the actor described how both times they did the show (in both 2014 and 2015) there were political elections happening. The actor suggested that people appeared to enjoy the game of shutting down a politician who wasn't really listening to the will of the people – perhaps something the audience weren't able to do in real life but could in the context of the show.

This second vein of questioning from the audience about leading the discussion in a particular direction is interesting in that it points to a suspicion of bias, much as Close described audiences of *Good Fences* trying to "suss" out a bias in their work. In *An Enemy of the People* there are actually clear sides in the script, and the immediate lead-up to the audience participation in the fourth act suggests that sides must be chosen by the audience. Aslaksen, publisher of the local press, and Peter Stockmann, the town councillor, put pressure on the assembled audience to respond to Doctor Stockmann's speech by asking audience members to publicly declare their stance by raising their hands and stating their reasons:

> ASLAKSEN (to the audience): ... Who of you agrees with Doctor Stockmann here? And now let's do a cross check – What do you think? Can everyone who agrees with Doctor Stockmann please raise their hand. See. Doctor Stockmann, you offer no alternative. What you say sounds good. But it doesn't get us anywhere. One of you who raised their hand: can you tell us why you would support him.
> (Actors take audience responses and questions.)

There is very quickly an invocation of two clear sides: are you with the doctor or against them? The actual questions are slightly more complicated; do you think the baths should be shut down, or do you think they should be kept open? Do you think the doctor's perspectives on the corruption and individualism of modern society are correct? Or do you think they're overblown and extremist? Despite the nuance possible, the script and actors emphasize only an either/or binary. There is also a sense of urgency, and a strong emphasis on "making up your mind" so as to drive towards an unambiguous conclusion.

> COUNCILLOR: All of you. You gotta make a decision now. Do you want to be able to send your kids to Kindergarten tomorrow? When you drive to work, do you want to drive on streets that are safe? Who wants to go to the Baths? Do you want to be able to sit here tomorrow? Do you want to have a theatre? Make up your mind now![39]

As a result of this insistence on binarism, there is also a definitive "winner" in the debate. While *Good Fences* provoked fairly balanced debate in its inclusion and presentation of the opposing interests of oil and gas and ranching, when it comes to the two sides in the town hall of *An Enemy of the People* there is a decisive victor. In the original Ibsen text, the townspeople populating the fictional town hall turn quickly against Doctor Stockmann, with the crowd ultimately declaring the doctor the eponymous "enemy of the people" and threatening to "break his windows! Duck him in the fjord!"[40] In the Tarragon production, the scale seemed to be weighted entirely in the other direction, such that audiences were almost unanimously allied with Doctor Stockmann. An audience member in the 17 October 2015 talkback actually asked Rick Roberts, the actor playing Peter Stockmann, whether he ever managed to actually get an audience on his side, describing how "obviously you're portraying a negative character – or – maybe it's not very obvious? But it feels like the audience tends to gravitate towards supporting the Doctor." Roberts replied that he didn't recall the audience being on his side at all in the 2014 run of the show, though there were a few times in the 2015 run where it did happen and the actors "stood there with [their] jaws open" while some people spoke up to say Doctor Stockmann's speech was going too far and was too extremist. "It will come out occasionally but it doesn't last very long and as soon as we start to agree with that person … people get riled up again" concluded Roberts. His suggestion is that the audience is, generally, on the side of the doctor. Corroborating this perception, in the archival footage of the 2014 production, a majority of the crowd raise their hands and cheer to signal their support of Doctor Stockmann after Aslaksen asks who agrees with the doctor. In response, Aslaksen laughs and says, "Well, I'm sure that wasn't everybody … I'm sure that there are people out there who think Doctor Stockmann is going, well to put it mildly, a little too far in his rhetoric and that they – " "No!" an audience member unequivocally interrupts. Aslaksen's invitation to the audience to participate in the town hall emphasizes various perspectives: "We need to discuss this," he says, "any questions – if you're pro or con, for or against this – questions, comments, that's why we're here tonight. Big decisions to make, and we need to hear from you." Despite this, the audience, for the most part, appears to unilaterally support Doctor Stockmann.

Reviewers remarked on the propensity of the audience to side with Doctor Stockmann and use it to evaluate the production overall. Eric Emin Wood describes that

It's likely you won't see the townspeople turning against Doctor Stockmann either, because the show casts you – yes, *you*, and the rest of the audience – as the townspeople. Instead of the long, frequently interrupted monologue of the original play, Doctor Tommi Stockmann[41] only gets far enough to say that last year's tourists became sick because the town's hot springs are contaminated, which her brother [Peter] interrupts by asking if that's a good reason to shutter the town's economy for two years and put everyone's livelihood at stake. They wait for you to respond, and the evening's 20-minute improvisational highlight begins. By the time you read this in print, Canada's next government will have been chosen, but my guess – and, judging from the program notes, Tarragon's – is that the recent election will have made the audience particularly sympathetic to a cause echoing the 21st-century scientists who have been prevented by government officials from releasing inconvenient information about Walkerton's water quality, or the environmental impacts of fracking, or building a pipeline, or climate change. I expect those audience members will then be more likely to confront Peter than Tommi, as ours did. (Though I'll admit, the reverse would have made for even more riveting theatre).[42]

Emin Wood's final parenthetical note about what might make for more "riveting" theatre is interesting, not the least because it suggests how clearly the audience was on the side of Doctor Stockmann. Critic J. Kelly Nestruck echoes his perception of an audience preference for Doctor Stockmann in his review: "The Tarragon audience, however, was clearly on Thomas's side – and it took certain plants in the crowd to go on the attack, in a way that sees this town hall turn messy (literally, and thrillingly)."[43] The suspicion of audience plants (which came up in more than one review; see also Cushman 2014) who would speak up against Doctor Stockmann is notable. There were in fact no audience plants, so presumably there were some audience members who spoke up against Doctor Stockmann during the show Nestruck attended. Nestruck's inability to believe that such audience members were expressing their real views and were not characters planted in the audience speaks to the "unbelievability" of the political position implied by opposing Doctor Stockmann. The interplay between the expectations of fiction (Emin Wood's suggestion that more audience members opposed to Doctor Stockmann would make for better theatre and Nestruck's presumption of the use of audience plants as a device to further the fictional plot) and the apparent reality of the actual audience response points to the complex real-ish-ness or lack thereof being produced in the act of inviting the audience to participate. In other words, the real world was presumed to offer poor fictive mileage (it wouldn't make for a good story), while the really real was dismissed as fictive (there's no way real audience members would speak up against Doctor Stockmann and those who did must be plants).

I return to the idea of a murky dramaturgy of the real to further analyze this apparently unilateral mobilizing in favour of Doctor Stockmann. Without the clear delineation of real-world discussion and fictional plotline, a persistent lack of clarity remains for the audience about whether to voice one's real opinion, most especially if it appears it will derail the fictional world. This line between real and fictive plays into narrative building. In *Good Fences*, there is no singular protagonist upon which to hinge or complete the story. The deliberate unfinishing and lack of a conclusion firmly leaves the story in the hands of the audience, who can continue the conversation in the post-show discussion. It is not that *Good Fences* refuses narrative, closure, or bias. In fact, the show is entirely teleological and orchestrated, even more scripted and contrived than *An Enemy of the People*, which does include a truly unscripted and improvised town hall. In *An Enemy of the People*, however, there is closure, outcome, and a perceived "right" side in the plot. Even though Doctor Stockmann does veer into extremist views, calling for the extermination of those "in charge" and later declaring "let it be destroyed, let everybody be wiped out!"[44] they are clearly the protagonist of the story. Narratively speaking, the audience may feel, in part, compelled to support the apparent protagonist in order to bring the story to its assumed conclusion.

In discussing the effect of open-ended conclusions, it should be noted that Borchmeyer's adaptation does somewhat disrupt the original closed ending of *An Enemy of the People*. In both the original and the adaptation, it turns out that Doctor Stockmann's wife's father has bought up a huge number of shares in the baths using what would be Stockmann's wife's inheritance. In other words, Doctor Stockmann's future personal financial security is inextricably bound up with the economic success of the baths. In the original, the play ends with Doctor Stockmann disgusted with the society and world in which he lives and determined to continue alone in his political mission even at the cost of isolation and destitution. In Borchmeyer's adaptation, the play ends slightly less clearly: Doctor Stockmann and their wife sit onstage, having both been fired from their jobs, evicted, and abandoned by family and friends. Their baby cries persistently in the background. There is no clear next step. As Alisa Zhulina writes, the Schaubühne version casts "a shadow of doubt over Thomas Stockmann's ability to resist [financial security]."[45] Even with this somewhat uncertain ending, however, the play is still unequivocally about Doctor Stockmann's journey. By the end of the play, almost every other character has turned against them. The doctor is the one aggressively attacked and pelted with white-paint-filled balloons at the end of the town hall, earning sympathy as the unfortunate target of the onstage majority – even if the offstage majority in the audience was on their side.

The idea of "the majority" is actually a recurrent one in the show. The play depicts a classic conflict between an individual and society: a lone activist against a monolithic crowd. In the traditional Ibsen text, the doctor decries, "The most dangerous enemy of truth and freedom amongst us is the compact majority – yes, the damned compact Liberal majority!"[46] and "It is the majority in our community that denies me my freedom and seeks to prevent my speaking the truth … the majority *never* has right on its side."[47] Doctor Stockmann is figured as the minority who is right, against a majority that is wrong. This framing of majority vs. minority was maintained in Borchmeyer's adapted translation: Doctor Stockmann claims that "Truth's worst enemy is this fucking liberal majority"[48] and "I'm pretty certain, everyone in the theatre agrees…We, the minority. We are right."[49] This categorization breaks down somewhat, however. As soon as we, the audience, all become the minority – as soon as we are all on the side of Doctor Stockmann – we are technically the majority. This contradiction is obvious in Doctor Stockmann's line that "everyone in the theatre agrees." Quite evidently, the majority *is* in agreement with Stockmann.

THE PERFORMANCE OF
THE (REAL) SOCIAL-POLITICAL SELF

It is important to return once more to Collini's definition of politics as power relations in a given space.[50] Exactly what power is offered to audiences in *An Enemy of the People*, if any, is important to consider when thinking through the effect and impact of the audience participation. It would be incorrect, after all, to state that everyone in the theatre *is* unequivocally on Doctor Stockmann's side. It is impossible to know the real opinions of the audience. It may be the case that there were audience members opposed to the doctor who didn't speak up; it may be that there were also audience members who simply opposed the audience participation, didn't understand its parameters, or otherwise did not want to take up the invitation to speak and instead asserted their power to abstain. It is also difficult to know if there were audience members who were simply "playing a part" and didn't really believe that Doctor Stockmann was in the right but decided, for one reason or another, to pretend to agree with them. Evidence of some, admittedly limited, audience dissent comes from one actor who described in a talkback that, "Sometimes you meet people afterwards who go 'I was going to say' but, because the tone is that you should be agreeing with Doctor Stockmann [they didn't]." The actor continued, "in this environment it's very hard. I've had friends go 'I did kind of want to say, maybe, but I didn't want to,'" a response the actor sums up as "very truthful to politics."[51] If, optimistically, democracy purports that each voice has equal weighting, the actor's remark is a more realist view: some voices are less welcome in certain spaces and contexts.

This idea of hesitating to participate also came up in another talkback, wherein an actor described "a lot of people going 'Should I say something or should I not? I don't know the rules of the game.'"[52] Theatre critic Cushman similarly describes a kind of reluctance to speak up the night he attended, writing that, "The night I went, most of us were too shy to contribute, and the vital questions were asked by people I took to be plants, who would be necessary anyway to keep the show on track and to give the actors their cues. Which is why I think this kind of theatre, though it can undoubtedly be exciting, is fundamentally dishonest; the performers have rehearsed, the spectators haven't, so it isn't an equal contest."[53] These two remarks clearly speak to a sense of power relations. In referring to the town hall as a kind of game, as the actor describes, or contest, as Cushman does, they offer ways of reading the town hall as a different kind of binary struggle between two sides – this time not between Doctor Stockmann and Peter Stockmann but between the performer and audience. These two sides, of audience and performer, are not weighted equally in their knowledge of the "rules of the game," not least because of the thorough rehearsal of the performers and their repeated experience in the political forum being staged.

To turn to broad concepts of participation, Markus Miessen's *The Nightmare of Participation* suggests that "conventional models of participation are based on inclusion and assume that it goes hand in hand with the social democratic protocol of everyone's voice having an equal weight … in the simple act of proposing a structure or situation in which this bottom-up inclusion is promoted, the political actor or agency that proposes it will most likely be understood as a 'good doer.'"[54] For *An Enemy of the People* to directly engage the audience, the production seems to be encouraging a multiplicity of voices and staging a kind of civic engagement that relies on such a bottom-up form of inclusion where each voice has, ostensibly, the same weight. And yet, as Miessen goes on, such participation requires participants to acquiesce to the structures that currently exist which may already be affecting the relative weight of certain voices.[55] This presents an issue if the structures themselves are what one wishes to take issue with. The town hall being staged, in other words, is not neutral territory – the actors have an advantage through their repeated experience and rehearsal. The exercise also favours those audience members who are most comfortable voicing their opinions in a middle-class Toronto theatre. In their analysis of performance and civic engagement Ananda Breed and Tim Prentki offer that civic engagement "is predicated on the assumption that the citizen or young person is looking to engage with state institutions, either at national or local levels; to become more actively involved in the workings of those institutions, rather than reforming or overthrowing them which might be outcomes arising from community engagement."[56] To return to an earlier excerpt from the script, the invitation to audiences to participate is crafted within a narrow, pressurized situation full of apparent institutional structure. Peter says, "All of you. You gotta make a decision now."[57] There is thus an implied time limit. Decide now. Only a limited range of options or opinions are offered: are you with Doctor Stockmann or against Doctor Stockmann? There is thus only a simple binary from which audience members can choose, and in order to do so they must engage with pre-existing structures. These factors reinforce that the participation being invited is far from neutral or egalitarian.

It is also not just that the structures of performance and differing understandings of this scene – from fictional character perspectives for the actors, and for some unclear, possibly fictional or possibly real perspective for the audience – create unequal participatory footing but also that the strictures of acceptability, consensus, and majority create for the audience the impression or feeling that one's voice is actually not equally weighted. In the case of *An Enemy of the People*, this means participating in a forum that does not necessarily make clear its own scaffolding: it is offering audience members a chance to behave outside of the normal expectations of theatre etiquette insofar as audience members are not asked to remain quiet and immobile, but what exactly the new rules of participation are remains obscured. If a dissenting audience member is immediately presumed to be a fictional plant (as critics J. Kelly Nestruck and Robert Cushman suggested) they can be quickly discounted. A dissenting voice, then, loses power. Instead, the pressure exists to follow the majority, save the protagonist, and speak against the antagonist. These socially inflected power relations are powerful: this kind of pure democracy, wherein everyone has a voice in the theatre and everyone can speak up, is always already imbricated in pre-existing structures that shape its progression and ultimately results in a limited forum of participation, compounded by the script and production structures.

Following Claire Bishop's definition of participation as that "in which people constitute the central artistic medium and material, in the manner of theatre and performance,"[58] it is clear that participation does not necessarily constitute power. As Jenn Stephenson describes in an article about the "audience-citizen," "Power is held by politicians and by artists; they are makers and givers – they are the initiators of policies and ideas that shape experience, whereas citizens and audiences are receivers. Where audiences diverge from democratic citizens is in the transferability of that power. Audiences do not stand as representatives. There is no mechanism for audiences to assume the mantle of power."[59] Because the rules of the game and the structures of participation are already dictated by *An Enemy of the People*, the audience is still under the control of the play even as they are encouraged to offer their real-world experiences and perspectives. This is epistemologically troubling, since the basis of the issue ostensibly up for debate is within the fictional world (that of the baths) and thus out of the ultimate control of the real-world audience. These two ontologies, fictive and real, are thus neither juxtaposed nor layered but obfuscated out of the control of the audience.

By inviting the real world into the performance vis-à-vis the audience, but not permitting them co-creative roles, audience members are essentially providing raw material for a sense of the real-ish. Participation in this case is a means of generating a feeling of realness – unpredictability, reference to real-world events, etc. – without an actual engagement with it. There is, I would offer, a potential danger in inviting audience participation with no real shift in power: making the contribution of "real" opinions at best ineffectual and at worst risky and revelatory for those audience members participating. As Liz Tomlin writes in her analysis of political dramaturgies, "the dramaturgy of real people closes down the potential for two-way dialogic engagement between spectator and performer due to the absence of character that eliminates the critical field on which such engagement might be possible. By so doing, such practice can evade the agonistic debate that is required to accommodate the complexities of the political situation in question."[60] While Tomlin is referring to a lack of character for performers onstage, the same lack of character for the audience may result in a similarly limited sense of discussion. Lack of a site of common analytical reflection – the actors playing fully in character, the audience unsure of their setting, are we in Norway, or are we in Canada? Are we characters or are we ourselves? – limits the ability of the audience to engage in real discussion. Political scientist Margaret Kohn agrees, writing that one of the reasons theatre can potentially foster critical dialogue is because "people meet together and have a shared text in common. According to this perspective, the subject–object relationship in the theater is a precursor to the intersubjectivity that emerges after the performance."[61] A shared text means that an audience has fictional characters and fictional situations that they may hold up against the reality of their real world, to critically reflect on the complexity of the situation and the parallels they might find in the larger macrocosm of the real world outside the theatrical microcosm. The conflating of the "cosms," as it were, of *An Enemy of the People* potentially leaves spectators unmoored.

Lest this line of argumentation be taken as a repudiation of *An Enemy of the People*, I want to turn to Liz Tomlin's analysis of political dramaturgy and spectatorship in an age of precarity. She argues that theatre that is more explicitly political, more explicitly slanted, ideological, or one-sided may be precisely what is needed as "an invitation to step onto firmer ground in which subjecthood and future actions take on concrete form."[62] The audience's adoption of Doctor Stockmann's side follows Tomlin's assertion: that people are keen to find an ideological grounding and a material experience of what position they might (should) take in a real debate about environmental contamination. The effect at work is not that there is no opportunity to invoke dissensus or agonism in *An Enemy of the People* but that finding a clear position to adopt that puts them in step with their fellow audience members is simply a much preferable experience for spectators. An invitation to take an ideological position aligned with most mainstream liberal views feels solid in ways that precarious, multiple, poststructuralist spectatorship cannot. Perhaps this is what *An Enemy of the People* wants to demonstrate – how easily the majority will flock to the side that is perceived as "right." This is then less about political effect than demonstrating the potency of affect: "the conviction of being right is an emotional, identarian commitment as much as, if not much more than, a rational one."[63] To speak against Doctor Stockmann simply *feels* wrong: this is suggested by not just the lack of voices taking on that position but also the belief that those who did were fictional plants. Those who had real-world opinions that did not support Doctor Stockmann kept those views largely to themselves and shared them only afterwards, outside the theatre, preserving them for the real, real world. This is, in itself, a powerful provocation for thinking about political engagement and performance; what roles are audience members willing and unwilling to adopt in fictional vs. real worlds?

This question becomes pressingly important when considering the proliferation of identities constructed and performed in contemporary societies as a result of social media and online life. This topic is worth a short diversion. The parallels between theatre and social media are frequently invoked to describe how online modes of communication frequently involve a degree of performance. Profiles and posts on Facebook, Twitter, and Instagram are frequently curated so as to perform certain identities.[64] Erving Goffman's *The Presentation of the Self In Everyday Life* has, Bernie Hogan writes, become an important frame of reference for scholars analyzing online performance. Goffman's metaphor offers the idea that life is a kind of stage and that people engage in performance or what he describes as the "activity of an individual which occurs during a period marked by his continuous presence before a particular set of observers and which has some influence on the observers."[65] This definition offers a familiar theatrical marker in its description of a co-present audience for whom someone performs. Nicolette Vittadini and Francesca Pasquali also utilize theatrical language in their writing about audience research in social networks. They cite danah boyd when they describe how "networked publics [referring to both the space constructed through networked technologies and the imagined collective that emerges as a result] are embedded in communicative infrastructures where identities, activities, and relations are literally staged"[66] or, as Jenny Sundén suggests, "typed into being."[67] Social media, then, affords individuals a space to perform their own identities. Nicholas Abercrombie and Brian Longhurst confirm that "one of the effects of the intrusion of the media into everyday life is the way that formerly innocent events become turned into performances with the further result that the people involved in those events come to see themselves as performers."[68] This is not to say that such a performance invalidates the identities as untruthful or unreal; in *Theatre & Social Media* Patrick Lonergan outlines the case of Sam Gardiner, a fifteen-year-old who masqueraded (convincingly) as a professional, adult football commentator. Lonergan writes, "The construction of his online persona was an act of creativity, but it was also an act of self-expression, a revelation of something authentic about the real person."[69] Indeed, Gardiner was a very capable football commentator and was subsequently employed to do just that, despite his deceit online.

Regardless, *An Enemy of the People* in some ways replicates the conscious performance of identity that is brought into being in online worlds. Audience members participating in the town hall are managing and performing identities for a very real audience. But the actual realness of the identities being performed is debateable: audience members may really feel the way they suggest in their vocalized pronouncements. Or, they may just be playing a role. Again, the political dimension of this performance is important to consider and offers a further parallel to what scholars have termed "online activism" or, pejoratively "performative activism." In so-called slacktivism, social media users quickly and nearly effortlessly share a post, use a hashtag, or click a button that doesn't actually contribute to a cause, mobilize, or otherwise imply actual participation in a movement.[70] It may not even indicate if a person truly cares or supports a social cause: an Instagram user expressing solidarity with the Black Lives Matter protest may really be an ally. Or, they may just be performing for an imagined audience.[71] The notion of performance of certain roles, alongside questions of what constitutes real or truthful participation, has resonance with *An Enemy of the People* and the ways in which participating audience members may elect to or feel pressured to perform particular roles. The result of the proliferation of curated and dramaturged selves online and in public may be an increasingly hard to access authentic, private self. But in studying *Enemy* we may better understand what compels people to perform particular public identities – in this case a desire to follow the majority, fight for the perceived minority, and further the perceived protagonist's narrative journey – and how that kind of performance, while it may offer a semblance of the real, can still be very much unreal. Has *An Enemy of the People* managed to raise the environmental consciousness of its spectators? Or has it just appeared to? And, maybe more importantly, did it intend to?

REAL POLITIC

There is a final tension between the fictive and real to address: that of effect. The question of political theatre having real effect is a frequent area of interest for scholars who wonder how a theatre audience might become active, politically engaged participants in and, ideally, by virtue of said participation, beyond the show. Ultimately, states Joe Kelleher, "the arbitrary and incalculable nature of theatre's effects ... [mean that] there is no saying for sure what will appear, or how, or as what, or to whom. From this perspective, theatre's instrumentality (in political terms) is defeated."[72] He goes on, however, to say that "This is not to say, by any means, that theatre does not have effects, and it is in the encounter of theatre's singular appearances and the unforeseen destiny of such appearances in the experience of those who take the theatre seriously (including the latecomers) that theatre's political potential may reside."[73] To sum, while the direct effects of any given political message or piece of theatre may be unknowable, there are still effects and those effects are centred in the experiences of the audience: "Theatre remains unpredictable in its effects, given that its effects reside largely not in the theatrical spectacle itself but in the spectators and what they are capable of making of it."[74]

Accordingly, this question of effect was also raised by audience members of *An Enemy of the People*. One audience member asked the actors in a talkback about the result of letting the audience speak during the town hall: "when you give them the opportunity to give feedback and talk back – you could take this as your opportunity to rally and speak up and engage, or you might say the politicians in the show allow the people to speak because it sort of deflates their cathartic position ... it deflates them, [the audience] get to say their piece, they feel good about themselves, and then they don't have to do anything."[75] This audience member persuasively brings up the idea of a cathartic release to suggest that the town hall might make the audience feel they have done their bit: they can feel good about themselves for having participated *in* the theatre, diffusing any potential after-effects of participation in civics *outside* the theatre.

Dylan Robinson, writing in the context of Indigenous-settler relationships and reconciliation in the lands now known as the United States and Canada, articulates the dangers of "felt truth" in his concept of sensory veracity. His ideas as related to performance are highly useful for considering potential political effect. He describes how "the intensity of affect when experiencing socially and politically oriented performance allows for a conflation of affect with efficacy" such that attendees feel they have accomplished some positive outcome by simply attending a performance.[76] He goes on to describe the dangers of situations in which "it is much easier … to allow the feelings of being transformed to satisfy, rather than to unsettle and engage with the enormous amount of work that must still be done" in order for what is felt to be brought into material existence.[77] Audience participation in *An Enemy of the People* as a highly embodied, engaged, and affective experience, may offer the kind of outcome that Robinson warns about: audience members feel validated in their fight for Doctor Stockmann but this quickly becomes the entirety of their engagement with environmental issues. As Robinson goes on, "this conflation of affect with efficacy is confirmed, and perhaps redoubled, when a consensus of response in fellow audience members is perceived."[78] In the case of *An Enemy of the People*, the operation of the majority in support of the doctor may offer this kind of perceived consensus. Robinson's arguments affirm that feelings, though powerful, can be dangerously illusory when it comes to political import. This is not to say that *An Enemy of the People* has a clear or even implied desired outcome: this is not applied theatre. Rather, I bring up the idea of political effect because it was brought up by audience members: a repeated assumption that the participation was supposed to be doing something productive politically, possibly acting as a kind of rehearsal for democracy that the audience might partake in and then re-enact (for real) outside the theatre.

Alisa Zhulina cites Thomas Ostermeier's (director of the Schaubühne production of *An Enemy of the People*) talk at the Brooklyn Academy of Arts to similarly argue that "Theatre is not political action. Political action happens in the streets." She ends her paper by suggesting that "this is how the theatre of capital performs the task of the immanent critique of political economy. Now the real work begins."[79] Like the audience member quoted earlier, she thus draws a clear line between the real politics outside the theatre and the unreal play inside it. I am prompted to return to my earlier questions surrounding the blurring of the real and fictional worlds. Ostermeier's assertions about the potential effect of political theatre establish clear boundaries between real and fictional. But audience participation, as I have described, is far less delineated: are audience members meant to be their real selves or take on fictional characters? Are they meant to address real world issues or stay within the fictional plotline? And what structures, rules, or guidelines shape this participation in seen and unseen ways?

In *An Enemy of the People* the boundaries between the real and fictive are malleable rather than strict. The audience is real. Real-world events, like upcoming Canadian elections, are brought into the theatre and audiences comment upon them as aspects of reality. Real affects are also generated. And yet, simultaneously, the structures of fiction remain and the storyline plays through. Audience participation, I argue, can serve to generate a sense of the real-ish and this is, in effect, the effect of such participation: an experience that feels real-ish provokes consideration of hypothetical worlds that likewise straddle the real/unreal binary. Wood, for instance, suggests that *An Enemy of the People* is interested in asking "what would happen in real life? The play's abstract set design illustrates its cynical answer: Messages scrawled in chalk across a wall-to-wall blackboard – 'This is a test. The eyes of the world are watching'; in French, 'I participate, you participate, she participates, he participates, you (plural) participate, we participate, they profit.'"[80] Who participates, and who profits, indeed. In *An Enemy of the People*, the real-not-real status of the audience in the town hall scene ultimately pessimistically serves to reflect core issues of civic engagement and democracy; the unequal weighting of voices, the always, already inescapable pre-existing structures of ideology, and the tenuous nature of participation and performance of self as simultaneously real and not real, effective and ineffective.

4

"You Will Long Remember"

The Nostalgic Real in Site-Specific Historical Re-enactment

When I asked the audience members of Rising Tide Theatre's Trinity Pageant which part of their theatrical experience was most real, the church scene was repeatedly cited. In it, spectators slowly file into St Paul's, a nineteenth-century church in Trinity, Newfoundland, Canada while a choir comprised of actors in nineteenth-century period costume sings hymns. As the spectators take their seats in the church pews, an actor dressed as a minister begins a memorial service in which he describes the "recent" tragedy that has taken several lives from the surrounding community: the Trinity Bay Disaster of 1892. The real-world audience is visually demarcated from the characters in the fictional narrative because of their lack of nineteenth-century costumes. References made in the scene to the "current" event of the sealing disaster, in which several men died while hunting seals due to a swift and unexpected change in the weather, likewise separate the audience from the play world by more than one hundred years. And yet, the audience is seated in the same space that a real memorial service likely would have happened in 1892. The minister also recounts the names of real historical victims, reinforcing the apparent realness of the scene. Moreover, because of the setting of the church, potent real-world conventions, especially related to liturgy and singing, compel the audience to actively participate. In fact, falling into the familiar ritual, audience members respond to the minister's call of "Peace be with you" with the proper service reply. Both choir and audience then sing a closing hymn that is still used in the church today. As a result, the present-day audience and the historical service unite in time as the audience members effectively play the role of a church congregation, hailed into a fictional role as they sit in place and are directly addressed by the actor-minister. The spectators are simultaneously real-world audience and play-world congregation. The church is both the "new" church the minister refers to in the nineteenth-century play world and an old, now-historic site that audience members surreptitiously sneak photos of during the performance. As the scene unfolds, the fiction of the play world becomes mixed up with the real world. Is this just a fictional scene? Or is it a real memorial service? As two audience members described it:

AUD 3b: And I looked at him and I said "This is not a real church."
AUD 3a: This is not a real service, but we just said the real response.[1]

The perceived realness of this moment is complex: although the audience member states, "This is not a real church," St Paul's is, in fact, a real church and still an active site of worship for the town of Trinity. Yet, it is also not real in the sense that the scene and service are theatrical. Another audience member articulated the scene as *feeling* real, regardless of whether it was "really real" or not: "It felt very real in the church for sure."[2] What these audience members highlight are the ways in which realness may be perceived and felt in complex and complicating ways. This sense of what I refer to as real-ish-ness – experiences of the apparently real produced, perceived, and/or felt by the audience within the given time and space of a performance – in turn raises the further question of whether such complexity and indeterminacy when it comes to what is real is problematic or not, especially when applied to historical events.

The scene in the church is just a small part of the two-hour promenade performance of the Trinity Pageant, the content of which is ostensibly rooted in local history and real past events. The pageant has been the anchor event of Rising Tide Theatre company's annual summer season since 1993 and is very popular: the show's audiences range from fifty to 150 every performance, rivalling the entire town's population of 169 (according to the 2016 census).[3] The longest running of any of the company's shows, the pageant involves the entire company of actors who have been hired for the summer season, all of whom have ties to the local area through family, education, or work, as a general hiring policy of the company. During the performance, audiences follow the large cast of actors around the small outport town of Trin-

Figure 4.1 The audience in St Paul's church interior, Trinity, NL, 27 August 2016

ity in northeast Newfoundland. They travel to several primarily outdoor performance locations including the church graveyard, two different beaches, and several green spaces next to restored historical buildings and watch various scenes of historical re-enactment. The scenes loosely follow a chronological order that details the first European explorers' discovery of Newfoundland, the growth of the cod fishing industry, and the day-to-day life of the people inhabiting Newfoundland in the eighteenth and nineteenth centuries. The production is very much ensemble-based, with each scene introducing one or two primary characters and large portions of the cast filling it out as "background" or running ahead to the next stop to set up.

The overall tone of the Trinity Pageant is one of pride. The actors showcase the historical struggle, hardship, and resultant "grit" of the Newfoundland people – a group who face starvation from dictatorial fishery owners and the loss of loved ones to the elements but who ultimately persevere and create their own Newfoundlander culture and nation. Over the course of ten scenes, audience members meet and interact with a variety of characters who reflect this sentiment: early eighteenth-century settlers who were the first to inhabit the island year-round and who, we are led to believe, were a feisty and flirtatious group; a series of pirates; a local religious Quaker; a mourning widow; the district's court magistrate; down-at-heel fishermen; and finally, local nineteenth-century politicians.

While surface considerations of the pageant may lead audiences to determine that the show is innocuous, folksy, and feel-good, the phrasing used to advertise it is more sombre:

> You will meet an array of colourful characters as our past unfolds in story and song. You will long remember Dustabella Durdle's first winter here, Peter Easton and his band of pirates, the Minister consoling his parishioners at St Paul's Church ... And you will surely sing the Ode to Newfoundland as you bid farewell to a great and grand recreation of our cherished past.[4]

This deceptively simple description of a "walkabout" in the town of Trinity largely encapsulates the ways in which Rising Tide's pageant blends historical past with present and future. It highlights that audiences "will remember" the region's history. This phrase, which uses the future tense – "will" – while summoning the past into the present as an act of remembering, indicates more specifically how the pageant manages to create a kind of affective web across time. The temporal blending that the Trinity Pageant employs, as in the blend of history and present day in the church scene, is thus at work even before spectators attend the performance.

The pageant's ties to notions of realness come, initially, from its objective to animate the history and culture of Newfoundland but ultimately are the result of a kind of tripartite operation: the pageant relies on ostensibly real content as it re-enacts moments from the town's history; it locates its performances in real present-day, site-specific locations like St Paul's Church; and it contributes to the town's economic future vis-à-vis the audience members' ticket fees and tourism spending. In fact, the economically depleted town depends on commodified events such as Rising Tide's version of Newfoundland history. The pageant thus uses history as a means of blending past, present, and future into a weave of performative time that is both affectively and effectively real for audiences. As Artistic Director

Donna Butt suggested, "we [as audience members] are a part of the story," caught in this cross temporality and motivated to preserve the unique Newfoundland culture we've just witnessed.[5]

This chapter focuses on the use of site-specific practice and historical re-enactment as two strategies of theatre of the real. While the previous two chapters looked at the construction of felt realness as relates to politicized issues, this chapter is focused on examining historical records, both official and unofficial, and their theatricalization in emplaced locations. Using data collected from observation and attendance at four performances of the Trinity Pageant and interviews with twenty-three audience members, I examine the apparent realness of historical past and how it has the potential to haunt both present and future realities and thus create a potent affective time that feels real for audiences. Importantly, I consider how performed, or real-ish, history may be used as a marker and maker of real national and cultural identity, regardless of its facticity. This has consequences for community, belonging, and identity-formation writ large, as well as understanding of the limits of historical "truth."

THE "REAL" NEWFOUNDLAND: PERFORMING HISTORY AS IDENTITY-CREATION

Attendees of Rising Tide's performances laud the shows as providing authentic, genuine, or real Newfoundland experiences, especially as evidenced in more than one hundred and fifty five-star TripAdvisor reviews.[6] Audience members whom I spoke with also enthusiastically reported on the pageant's authenticity. While the audience members I interviewed were neither asked nor required to disclose whether they themselves were Newfoundlanders, many stated or implied that they were originally from Newfoundland but now lived "away," often returning to the province for the summer holiday. Full of recognizable regionalisms, fishing families, and a blend of humour and tragedy that audience members described as "quintessential Newfoundland," the Trinity Pageant is particularly "Newfoundlandish." Below are a number of audience descriptions:

> AUD 1b: And the kind of, the humour was kind of – you know growing up in Newfoundland you'd probably recognize it a bit more than, than if you're from away.

AUD 1d: I liked the accents and the colloquialisms. A lot of Newfoundland-isms to it, you know. Some people would have to think before they realized what they, what they were saying, you know? I really enjoyed that part as well.[7]

AUD 3a: Well it's a re-enactment of history and being from the province it just brings to life what you've read in history books and it's uh, like they've added Newfoundland sayings it's not just proper English and whatever but the proper history and culture comes through in the language.[8]

The above audience responses suggest that Newfoundland has a unique culture and that the Trinity Pageant is an authentic expression of that culture. One audience member actually stated that, "One sense I had was that this is a different country," suggesting that the propagation or reinforcement of Newfoundland's culture as special, in the context of Canadian culture as a whole, is certainly in operation.[9] A particularly interesting moment that supported the perception of this show as specific to a unique cultural identity occurred following a performance in unpleasant weather. Huddled outdoors under the overhanging cover of the theatre's balcony on a cold and rainy afternoon, audience members asserted a Newfoundland nationality by drawing a connection between the stories of the past presented in the pageant and their own analysis of who would volunteer to be interviewed post-show for my research: "We're all Newfoundlanders, eh? That's interesting. Who comes to help you, right?"[10] They drew a connection between the hardy Newfoundlanders portrayed in the pageant who weathered harsh life in a new colonial settlement and those volunteering to be interviewed by a researcher from Toronto. In doing so, they identified what it means for them to "be a Newfoundlander." The historical pageant thus acts as a means of gesturing both backwards (to the creation of a culture) and forwards (towards a kind of solidifying of true Newfoundland identity). Such culture-creation invokes important questions of acceptance, belonging, and exclusion: how is history a means of identity-creation and more specifically how might real-ish history serve to create (sometimes exclusionary) affective communities?

Newfoundland remained independent from the colonial nation-state of Canada until 1949, and this distinct history has helped to shape its identity as culturally unique. Ideals like friendliness, quirkiness, and being down-to-earth are projected in representations of Newfoundland, most recently popularized in the musical *Come From Away* and its depiction of a community's response to hundreds of passengers being re-routed to a Newfoundland airport following the 9/11 attacks. James Overton, a political science scholar who writes on Newfoundland economy and culture, offers a particular image of Newfoundland he calls the "Real Newfoundland."[11] According to him, this culture is something that can be harnessed for profit – packaged and thematized for use in the tourism economy as a sort of romanticized and sanitized presentation of primarily rural and historic Newfoundland. The image of the "Real Newfoundland" focuses on the small, isolated fishing communities known (in another example of regionalism) as outports, in which closely-knit populations live.[12] Sanitized descriptions of outports depict communities of "'quaint little houses' and 'good wives knitting' in a 'cove of bliss'"[13] or offer romanticized ideals about a way of life that is tied closely to the sea and demands a "communalistic, egalitarian ethic."[14] This image drove the majority of the government's tourism efforts in the late-twentieth century.[15] In these campaigns, the province's rural, outport culture was lauded as an authentic and genuine tourist experience. This cultural image is similarly enacted by the Trinity Pageant, with its emphasis on a particularly local and historical Newfoundland. The "Real Newfoundland" performed in the pageant is not, however, entirely "real": it uses history selectively and adds fictional accounts. As such, it is only real in the sense that it seems to subscribe to this accepted and conventional representation of romanticized, nostalgic, or mythologized Newfoundland. In other words, the "Real Newfoundland" feels more real than it is.

The "Real Newfoundland" at work in tourism efforts and for economic profit may not be entirely real, but it may nevertheless be operationalized for real effects, particularly in relation to its nation-building capacity. I use here the term nation-building with reference to Newfoundland because, although it is a province within the nation-state of Canada, with Newfoundland's longstanding resistance to amalgamation, the preservation of Newfoundland's unique "nationality" (alternatively, national identity or cultural identity) prevails. As Overton writes, "the significance of mythologies which deal with cultural origins and distinctiveness" are primarily of value in nation-making.[16] He adds, "it is the vision of the province enshrined in the 'Real Newfoundland', which is largely the mythical core of the emerging national culture. As an image it is a symbol for all that is distinctive and essential about the Newfoundland character and way of life."[17] Thus, the belief in a unique, valuable, individual, and historic culture, at least as far as the tourism industry is concerned, is a prevailing notion in Newfoundland. This "Real Newfoundland" persists as the original and essential culture, even if it seems at once paradoxical in Overton's conflation of the "real" and the mythic in his descriptions.

Perhaps the government of Newfoundland and Labrador best demonstrates claims to this idea in their 1975 statement, "Nobody has been living in North America longer than Newfoundlanders, so they are rich in folklore, song and inherited crafts. Fortunately, Newfoundland has been able to preserve this rare culture in the face of space-age technology, sophistication and industrial progress."[18] This is a highly problematic description not least because of its disregard for the Indigenous Beothuk and Mi'kmaq peoples who populated the region well before and during the European settlement. Such gaps of representation in the otherwise totalizing notion of the "rare culture" of Newfoundland already begin to destabilize any positivist notions of what a "Real Newfoundland" might look like. The simultaneous selective facticity and creative editing of who belongs within that "original" or "Real Newfoundland" culture suggests both the utility and danger of an apparent, though not necessarily factually correct, realness. The "Real Newfoundland" is both a means of solidifying national myth for tourist output and a means of nation-making beyond the tourist industry, with clear repercussions stemming from its inclusion and/or exclusion of certain bodies.

To illustrate this point, it is helpful to consider more specifically the ways in which history is used in the Trinity Pageant. The performance relies upon the unique local culture of the "Real Newfoundland" in its exclusive use of Trinity's outport history. Trinity was one of the first summer fishing camps in the late sixteenth century and later became a thriving fishing outport that Janet Pitt describes as "a major fortified fishing and trading centre" through to the 1850s, when the dominant, wealthy merchant class eventually withdrew.[19] Pitt writes, however, that "because of its considerable past, the preservation of many of its historic buildings and records, and the restoration of some merchant premises, Trinity retains much of the look and flavor of a 19th-century town."[20] Trinity's municipal government received funds to restore several historic buildings in town in the late 1980s as an attempt to preserve some of its cultural past for tourists but, as Artistic Director Donna Butt suggests, that act privileged a certain history: that of the merchant class who had largely built and used those buildings.

By contrast, her aim in the Trinity Pageant is to tell the "real" story of Trinity by "interpreting the working people" rather than the wealthier merchant class.[21] She also has a vested interest in telling the stories of women and includes scenes depicting the struggles and challenges of the first female settlers whose lives were largely unrecorded in conventional historic sources. However, even if it is "more real" than some stories in its focus on the working class and women, certain dramaturgical choices in the pageant exacerbate this still selective view of history. In short, the Trinity Pageant presents only a limited scope of the region's human experience in order to maintain its "Real Newfoundland" character. For example, the absence of any actors or characters of Indigenous background in the pageant suggests that this version also fails to tell the whole story. The Trinity Pageant does not erase Indigenous presence as wholly as the 1975 tourism slogan does, but the only mention of Indigenous people in the pageant occurs in a short exchange in which two Caucasian fishermen consider that their fishing vessel is missing. The content of the Trinity Pageant is clearly not a corrective antidote to exclusionary history, even as Butt may hope it to be. Of course, given the sheer volume and diversity of historical perspectives, delivering the story of Newfoundland is an ultimately unattainable objective. But, that the "real" history that is performed in the Pageant is no more real than other representations of history must not be overlooked.

Sarah Ahmed's analysis of the relationship between emotion and nation-building provides a useful means for describing the exclusionary operation of culture as identity-building. She uses a Derridean philosophy of language to suggest that the repetition of words detaches them from their contexts of production and thus allows them to accumulate cultural meaning and value, particularly in terms of generating bodily affects. The effect is that the "repetition of signs designates which bodies belong to the imagined community of the nation and which bodies are abject to it."[22] If we consider cultural narratives, such as the "Real Newfoundland" and its rural, fishing outport contingents as a kind of language, then we might examine the particular emotions generated by the repetition and vaunting of the cultural images at work in the Trinity Pageant. The creation of a kind of "affective economy," to use Ahmed's term, has the power to "do things" and "align individuals with communities – or bodily space with social space – through the very intensity of their attachments," including an explicit memorialization or production of nostalgia.[23] If one's body responds with nostalgia to a specific event, then one's body becomes a part of the nation. In the case of the Trinity Pageant, the nostalgic response is a pledging of love to idealized Newfoundland. The pageant in fact begins with a performance of the Newfoundland anthem. When the audience is invited to join in and sing "Ode to Newfoundland" – an anthem penned in 1902 by Sir Cavendish Boyle, well before Newfoundland joined Canada – many members do so with nostalgic vigour:

We love thee, we love thee
We love thee windswept land.
As loved our fathers, so we love,
Where once they stood, we stand;
Their prayer we raise to Heaven above,
God guard thee, Newfoundland.

The performative nature of the language contained within the anthem strengthens the generation of an affective pledge: following J.L. Austin, singers are actively praying for Newfoundland.[24] I did not, in my first two experiences of the pageant, have the requisite knowledge to join in the song. However, by my third attendance, a part of me felt compelled to join the group. I opened my program to the printed lyrics and followed along. I wished to join in the repetition of the cultural sign of Newfoundland as special and unique – as something other than just another part of Canada. Not all bodies will have, or are able to have, such a nostalgic impulse. Indigenous populations ignored by the 1975 governmental slogan, for instance, undoubtedly have a non-nostalgic response to the anthem as a product of settler colonies whose cultural and physical violence caused irreparable harm. Such a non-nostalgic response is relegated, however, to outside the accepted nation. In fact, the emotional power residing here predominantly in the impulse for nostalgia (following Overton's descriptions of the "Real Newfoundland") operates with a kind of political power that solidifies the colonial nation-state and clearly defines its borders, and contingently, who is included and who is excluded.

In their reflection on the connections between site, applied performance, and community Sally Mackey and Nicolas Whybrow write that "nostalgia is an interesting term to consider with regard to place. It literally splits ... into the pain suffered (*algos*) as a consequence of being unable to fulfill the dream of return (*nostos*) to a location perceived to be 'home.'"[25] As the "Real Newfoundland" identity is ultimately mythic and unreal, the nostalgic urge of many of its inhabitants prompts them to reach for something unattainable: They are not truly capable of returning home when their historical perspective is not realistic. However, affect is still an active means of making that "home" even if it cannot really exist. In fact, following Ahmed, that the nation for which one feels nostalgia is ultimately unreal may actually act to extract even further investment from its members.[26] Thus, even if that affect is predicated on what Overton calls a "mythical core" – itself garnered from nostalgia and predicated on fiction – the affect remains real and directive.

In the case of the Trinity Pageant, affect is activated vis-à-vis the "Real Newfoundland" cultural sign. For instance, a scene dramatizing the election of 1832 is loosely based on historical records that recount John Bingley Garland's failure to complete his elected term as the first speaker of the House of Assembly because he and his family returned to their home in England. In the pageant performance, Garland and his wife are portrayed as wholly distasteful, with a lascivious Mr Garland flirting with his wife's maid and Mrs Garland describing how much she dislikes Newfoundland. Shortly following their exit, another character assesses with pride that "true Newfoundlanders" stay in Newfoundland because it's "home." In performances that I attended, audience members laughed at the Garlands' snobbery and the actors' hyperbolic performances. More important than historical accuracy, at least for the audience experience, is that the scene encourages the creation of community within the audience; they team up against the dislikeable Mr and Mrs Garland, who are not "true" Newfoundlanders. As Overton goes on to say, "It is important to stress that the mythologizing process does not simply create an illusion. Myths and ideology are real, they are a material force ... they guide action."[27] Accordingly, the enactment of the pageant, though dependent on a particular version of history that is exclusionary, incomplete, and thus not comprehensively real, is nevertheless an active force for generating a real cultural identity. Those Newfoundlanders who best emulate accepted cultural Newfoundland-isms feel most real and are treated as such, reinforcing a cultural identity.

Mimetic theory helps further illustrate the possibility of identity-building through performance. According to Hans-Thies Lehmann's definition of mimesis in *Postdramatic Theatre*, the representational reality of theatrical performance can be understood as a variable that is dependent on another reality.[28] In such a scenario, he writes, "reality always precedes the double of theatre as the original."[29] Lehmann goes on to point out the limitations of this thinking. If we deem the real as the precedent and the imitation as its successor, then we have omitted from the equation the idea that

> All that we recognize and feel in life is thoroughly shaped and structured by art: shaped and structured by ways of seeing, feeling, thinking, "ways of meaning" (Benjamin's "Art des Meinens") articulated only in and by art – so much so that we would have to admit that the real of our experiential worlds is to a large extent created by art in the first place.[30]

This notion of art as a means of constructing reality, or "making real," has clear implications for culture as a form of nationalization. If we concede that the mimetic act is an imitation of something real, then since "cultural production depicts the nation's attributes onstage; this makes 'the nation' those depictions' ultimate referee and guarantor of meaning. Granting the nation referent status through performance effectively establishes the off-stage 'nation' as fact."[31] This occurs even if that nation is predicated on a mythos (such as the "Real Newfoundland"), as it becomes a kind of real ideal or "fact" by virtue of being referenced. The maintenance of Newfoundland's distinctive identity, then, could potentially be achieved deictically through performance: the representation of something onstage solidifying its referent as real. In this way, the real history at work in the Trinity Pageant is not so much real by definition but by operation. The performance of historical stories, regardless of their actual facticity, points back to those stories as belonging to "real" history and thus endorses them as real. However, while the idea of a representation pointing back to a reality implies a temporal order in which the referent precedes the reference, in the Trinity Pageant the establishment of the "Real Newfoundland" happens during or following the performative pointing back. The relationship, then, is not just from the real to the fictive, as in a typical stage representation, but *through* the fictive to the real, in which a real is established through a kind of reverse engineering in the act of mimesis.

What does it mean, though, to gesturally point back or make reference to something that has no original model beyond its own iterative re-performance? With regard to the historical inventions and fictional liberties of the pageant, the pointing back can only be to itself, to past performances of the pageant, rather than to some distant history. This citationality echoes Derridean notions of an endlessly circuitous "real" that acts as a free-floating signifier without foundation. For the twenty-something-year-old pageant, the performances' references to events that happen solely in previous performances still cultivate a kind of real material: the pageant as a historical artifact in and of itself. In this way, the repetitive temporal gestures of the pageant enliven a real historical past, even if it is not the one we may have initially assumed. Instead of reinforcing the real history of Trinity, the pageant makes real the work of the pageant itself: a fiction making real a fiction.

Referring to the past as distinct from the future and present, however, still misrepresents the actual fluidity of the performance, in which past is punctuated with present and future references. For instance, historical characters interact with present-day audience members: Sir Richard Whitbourne, author of the 1620 text *A Discourse and Discovery of the New Founde Lande* kisses the hand of a lucky (or unlucky) audience member in one of the first scenes in the show. References to court cases from the nineteenth century are coupled with references to Muskrat Falls, a planned future hydroelectric project still in the process of construction. Rather than a strict one-to-one representational-referent relationship, the mimesis enacted in the pageant is a both/and relationship that moves flexibly between real and unreal and past/present/future. Present action in performance, then, can mimetically point to a future potentiality or a remembered past. Rebecca Schneider, in her pivotal study of liveness, temporality, and archive vis-à-vis American Civil War re-enactments, troubles notions of linear time by suggesting how visceral and affective engagements with history can create moments in which "times touch" and the past meets the present.[32] Aptly, Overton provides evidence for such a flexible operation of multiple temporal worlds in the "Real Newfoundland" tourism plan, which suggests how history might be utilized for economic benefit: its slogan of turning "the past into the future,"[33] is a phrase notably similar to the historical war re-enactors that Schneider describes who fight to "keep the past alive."[34] The unique, historic Newfoundland performed in the pageant and tourism material – that is mythic, real, or some combination of the two – both solidifies historic source as fact and generates resources and income for future industries. Pointing back to Newfoundland history, then, is both a temporal gesture forwards and backwards, to present and future possibilities.

REAL(-ISH) HISTORY FOR REAL AFFECT

The real-ish history in the Trinity Pageant also functions to elicit highly affective responses in audience members, which I argue in turn helps reinforce impressions of realness. Spectators described moments of "real" emotion, especially after watching a scene depicting the struggle and rejection of Newfoundland settlers working under the truck system of the fishing industry. Under the truck system, "fishing merchants would provide goods and materials to fishermen at the beginning of the season against the fisherman's catch … At the end of the season, the fisherman would bring his total catch to the merchant's shed for weighing and credit against his account".[35] This meant that fishers could easily go into debt and even be cut off from the merchant's supplies. Without a connection to supplies from England, many fishers and their families slowly starved over the winter. In a scene in the Trinity Pageant, we, as audience members, watched a merchant turn down desperate settlers, knowing they were being condemned to a winter without supplies. As one audience member described, "I felt as though you got to know the players and I was hurting inside when they were hurting. It became so real, so quickly."[36] Another audience member articulated a complicated reaction to the scene:

> That one scene over [there] in the [yard] with all the people who starved in that, like the acting was very good but because it was a true story in some ways I felt like I want to applaud the acting but in some ways I don't want to because it was such a horrible thing that happened in history. So I felt really torn then because I thought they did a very good job of, of depicting the um, the horror of, of that time so yeah. It was a really great way to learn history because um you know it was very interactive.[37]

Amidst the real history being enacted, clear departures from realism also occurred. For example, this brief, emotional scene also included a highly theatrical musical performance, during which I could spot actors trying to inconspicuously get set for the next scene. These theatrical moments complicated the audience's affective reaction. As the above audience member notes, they could simultaneously feel admiration for the real actors and feel hurt for the apparently real historical events.

My consideration of the real affect that this representation generates may be examined using insights from studies on "simming," defined by Scott Magelssen as "deliberate, embodied practice" within "live, three-dimensional, immersive environments" where "spectator-participants engage in the intentionally simulated production of some aspect of real or imagined society."[38] Simming might also be used to describe living history museums and immersive theatre experiences that similarly immerse spectators in created environments that are meant to feel real even though both audience members and those participating in simulations are aware of their inherent fakeness. In the Trinity Pageant audience members are immersed in the town's actual historic sites and encouraged to participate as church congregants and even, in one particularly memorable scene, as pirates newly landed in Trinity Bay. They are well aware of the theatricality of their participation but are nevertheless immersed in an experience that engages them in an active, embodied way. Writing on living history museums, tourism experiences, and applied simulations for military and healthcare workers, Scott Magelssen points to the immense performative power such experiences can have: "a simming can ... change participants' perception of that original, so that the representation itself begins to constitute the reality of what it points to ... soldiers increasingly refer to combat as feeling like the a video game they've played to practice [for real life]."[39] Such a statement suggests shifting perceptions of both real affect and real source: What both feels and is real may be shifted through simulation experiences.

It must be reiterated that the ostensibly real history – or "original" history, to use Magelssen's term – at work in the Trinity Pageant is, at best, only somewhat real or real-ish; that is to say, while many of the scenes are based on historical events that are recorded in local and official archives and records, the majority of the characters themselves are invented.[40] Furthermore, many moments are magnified, altered, or otherwise caricatured for entertainment purposes, as the show fluctuates between comedy and tragedy. A useful illustration of this real-ish quality comes from a scene dramatizing a court case of animal abuse. Local historian Kevin Toope offers a historic tour of Trinity separate from the Trinity Pageant.[41] During it, he details a sober excerpt from Trinity's court records that states, "December 27th, 1841. Charles Phillips fined one? [sic] pound or eighteen days for cruelly and maliciously driving James Dwyer's pig into a cauldron of boiling seal fat." The Trinity Pageant makes use of this same historical source, but the scene that enacts this brief court record, unlike Toope's tour, is raucous, fun, and silly in equal parts. The actor playing Dwyer appears to have been inappropriately enamoured with his now dead pig, and the actor playing Phillips provides a farcical re-enactment of the incident that incited a great deal of audience laughter during the performances I attended. Often, at the end of the scene, audience members would stop to chat and joke with one of the unfortunate actors who ended up condemned to the stocks. There is even a moment where the judge's chair falls into the water. Of course, historically, court would not have been held outdoors, much less so close to the water, especially with the town courthouse being only yards away. But, the physical humour and embodied, at times participatory, quality of the experience "embroiders" the historical record such that it becomes, as one audience member stated, more than a just text, "Bringing life to the history, making it real."[42] Another audience member continued, "You can read a book, you can watch a movie, [but] to wander around like that, the movement and everything else …,"[43] implying again the "added value" of the embodied experience.

Though Magelssen speaks of the potential for simming to enact a changed perception of the original or real, in the case of the Trinity Pageant, it is again less about changing the perception of the original than actually constituting a new original. What the pageant is able to do is to make real, or constitute in reality, an affective bodily response that comes to assign realness to the experience itself. In fact, is not just that the original history referred to in the Trinity Pageant comes to gain real status despite its above-described unrealness but that the performed history may come to feel more real than the recorded history because it has been "embroidered" and supplemented. For audience members, this was manifest in the pageant feeling real not because of historical fact but because of an impression of things that "probably" happened. As one audience member noted, "And like the stories you know like felt very real because you know like, well I found it a lot easier to block out the fact that we're watching actors just because you know it seemed like such a realistic thing that probably happened here, you know."[44] In other words, the pageant's performed scenarios felt real and thus prompted audience members to believe in the probability of the scenes having historically occurred. To use Clifford Geertz's anthropological term "thick description," which he uses to refer to descriptions that include analysis, context, or other more subjective voices, feelings, or interpretations, the pageant presented "thickened" experiences in which people behaved as real people; they were not simply "thin" historical accounts on paper.[45] The court case, for instance, was not just a few lines recorded in local archives but a fully fledged court scene. The question is thus less one of what is or is not real but instead a question of what might feel real, and thus become real, through the power of the theatrical process. In the pageant the audience-participant-sims are having a real experience – really walking, running, laughing, getting dampened by the rain – in amidst the fiction. The experience is "thick" and thus really felt, even if it is far from real.

AUTHENTICITY IN, THROUGH, AND IN SPITE OF HISTORICITY

Necessarily, the question of authenticity must also be raised, given the close association between historical re-enactment, living history museums, and questions of an "authentic experience" in the Trinity Pageant. Alan Gordon, when writing about living history museums in Canada, suggests that authenticity is one of the dominant values of the entire living history movement, adding that audience demand for authenticity is what has driven its current popularity.[46] Magelssen concurs that visitors to historic sites are encouraged to believe they are entering an "accurate, authentic representation of the past."[47] The Trinity Pageant has a relationship to authenticity insofar as it is clearly and self-consciously a play, but it does attempt to enact historical record and authentically represent a different time. This different time, however, is not necessarily a specific historical period: we, as audience members, are aware of the theatricality of the production and own our place in the present day, an awareness reinforced by the multitude of times represented in the production from the sixteenth century to present day. Instead, then, the "real" past meets our present moment of watching in a kind of blended temporality. This creates a different sense of the "real" than the authenticity Magelssen and Gordon describe. The Trinity Pageant is not seeking exact historical accuracy but a "realness" born of the perception of an authentic culture, sometimes at the cost of historical fact, exclusionary practice, and misrepresentation.[48] The clear impetus is not on re-creating an accurate historical past or authentic experience of a past time but on creating for present-day audiences an experience that affectively feels real

One particularly evocative scene from the Trinity Pageant, which illustrates a complex relationship between authenticity and realness, takes place in an active port where local fishers keep their boats (see figure 4.2). In this scene, actors portray an eighteenth-century minister, named Balfour, and a contingent of labourers who are working to clean and dry codfish on flakes. Though the actors are essentially miming the process of drying and cleaning the fish flakes using primarily rubber foam props, the method they are enacting is "authentic," by hand, and is thus a part of the Newfoundland cod-fishing identity and tradition: a kind of everyday experience that has all but disappeared along with the Newfoundland cod-fishing industry. Gordon states that one of the reasons for the increased popularity in living history museums and the feelings of authenticity they produce in audiences is modernity's challenge to the authenticity of the everyday experience.

In the face of rapid change and progress, the everyday has become heavily mediated through technology. Consequently, it has lost some of its authenticity.[49] Fittingly, during one performance of the Trinity Pageant's authentic fish flake scene, a few Trinity locals positioned near the scene were actually cleaning fish.[50] These modern-day fishers were approximating the traditional methods but were using plastic gloves and ready-made tables rather than the rough-hewn spruce flakes the actors were using to dry the fish. In this instance, the distance between real and authentic is unclear. The performers with their fake fish use authentic methods, while the fishers with their real fish supplement the historic practice with modern, inauthentic tools. During a later performance, I overheard Artistic Director Donna Butt explain to a curious audience member that the actors previously used more real fish as props but that these real specimens were growing increasingly difficult to acquire. As traditional methods lapse further and further into the storied past, the fake stand-ins are now more readily accessible than the real fish. A characteristic feature of simulated heritage and commemorative performance in general is such a complex and tenuous relationship to the real. It is not immediately clear by which standards we ought to measure the realness of the cleaning and drying of the cod flakes; which is a more authentic representation of the real Newfoundland?

Figure 4.2 The pageant scene at Harvey's Cove set in 1760 in foreground, community fishermen in 2016 in background, Trinity, NL, 20 August 2016

Butt is interested in developing a particular kind of realness: "[The pageant is] real in a number of senses. I think it's a true story ... I'm not convinced that there is objective history. People are not objective. You write the facts but the facts are influenced by who you are."[51] Though a scene might be able to be traced back to a singular source within court records, for example, the authenticity for Butt comes from the human dimension: stories of people trying to live together peacefully within the same community. The authenticity at work in the pageant, then, is not grounded in the ability to trace a character or event to a real moment in historical record. Instead, seeking authenticity means presenting what feels real or authentic to a contemporary audience. An audience member corroborated this view, saying that for them, "Historical facts aren't good enough. And, those tales about peoples' joys and pains are very much a part of the history telling."[52] Another interviewee responded to the first's remark: "the thing that really captured my imagination was, you know, the sense of community."[53] Through these remarks both audience members reinforced the reliance on relationality, highlighting the importance of the community and the "human" side of the stories. The pageant attempts to re-write or at least re-feel the past, to use Schneider's thinking, through a more emotional, personal, representation.

The performance seems to have a meta-level awareness and acceptance, or even celebration, of its own questionable accuracy. For example, two characters argue about a minor historical fact respecting the arrival of Vikings on the coast of Newfoundland. One asserts that the presence of Vikings in Trinity "has not been proved," and the other replies, "yeah but we know it happened."[54] This short repartee, exchanged as audiences walk from one scene to another, establishes that these characters are part of an "in-group," whose knowledge arguably outranks historical record. Even if the arrival of Vikings hasn't been officially proven, their presence is unofficially confirmed through a kind of folk-wisdom: the characters are essentially educating the audience about acceptable forms of knowing. In this way, writes Overton, "The spectacle, the mythical structure, has some correspondence with actual circumstances and does make many connections with popular views, and sentiments."[55] In so doing, the spectacle – in this case, the pageant – further strengthens its claims to authenticity or realness. The pageant's performance fits within the region's folk-wisdom, in other words, which itself has adopted its own kind of accepted, community-based cultural reality. These aspects of the stories – their humanness and the ways in which they are relatable to a community – are more important than a factual source. In the case of the Trinity Pageant, the community comprises Newfoundlanders and their traditions as well as audience members, the latter of whom learn to accept the stories as authentic parts of Newfoundland's past.

The prioritizing of community and folk-wisdom over reliable historical sources has significant implications for what constitutes authenticity: It suggests a relationality and a performativity that is not "a universal value attributed once and for all to a text or any other cultural artifact, but it happens or takes place in the specific time and space of a performance" as David Bousquet writes in his study of authenticity in dub-poetry performance.[56] Janelle Reinelt similarly writes that "performance events which have their most potent incarnation in a particular venue, for a particular community of spectators

... are quite changed when moved to other, more available sites."[57] In saying this, Reinelt points to the powerful effect a "localized" theatre event might have on audiences and the ways in which authenticity or realness is cultivated. For the Trinity Pageant, the community of spectators joins forces with a larger Newfoundland community. We, as an audience, become witnesses to a unique, particular history – a past that exists only in this place, where the events are brought to life on the very ground where they ostensibly historically happened. The effect is that, as Bousquet suggests:

> For each new performance, the audience's adhesion to the process of performance is renegotiated, and so the sense of identity and community (just like authenticity) is not rooted in an abstract essence, which would stay the same at all times and in all places, but is produced in the contingency of a unique performance and celebrates its very transience and specificity.[58]

The pageant's presentation feels real because the company grounds their history in individual, localized stories from a particular historical past. The audience accepts its authenticity because the stories cohere with their accepted knowledge of what Newfoundlanders are like. Historical past re-enacted in the present feels authentic because of its ties to both temporal past (as presumed fact) and temporal present (relationally accepted by the audience).

It is important to highlight the potential danger of this form of real-ish-ness: If the local knowledge – complete with its local prejudices or exclusion of certain bodies and/or stories – stands in for the authentic, then it can potentially become self-perpetuating in a kind of tautological mechanism. The implications for history and epistemology are clear, as scholar Natalie Alvarez articulates in her question about the effect of immersive performance encounters: "When performance is instrumentalized and made coextensive with knowing or a means to know, in what respects does it advance the imperial imperatives of archival thinking that seeks to house knowledge?"[59] While Alvarez's examples are perhaps more obviously high stakes (military training settings, staged illegal border crossings, simulated insurgency), the invocation of archive is especially relevant. In the acts of moving together throughout the town of Trinity, witnessing the various actors perform in roles, and perceiving the enlivening of historical text, the audience becomes a community that acts as arbiter of real history and real archive: it accepts the version of real that is on display in the pageant as authentically Newfoundland-ish because it feels real and is relationally supported by the community of viewers. This raises a question: how do members of an audience who do not represent the accepted Newfoundland local culture complicate the authenticity status of the show? Does the pageant's authenticity depend on its closed, self-confirming mythology? And, if so, what is the future of the pageant in a theatrical ecology and society increasingly aware of its exclusionary practices and desirous of a more diverse audience?

In short, authenticity or realness can be a cultivated quality, confirmed and created by a community. In the same way that the "Real Newfoundland" described above can paradoxically be a storied myth, authentic history, both generally and in the Trinity Pageant, is ultimately left open to potential "punctures" – to disputes that complicate or challenge the real through the display, subtle or explicit, of contradictory material. The real past presented in the pageant is not so much real as "not not-real": It cannot be written off as fabricated since parts of it are real – or, might be real as audiences describe in their awareness of things having "probably" happened.[60] It has a historic quality that is tied to specific facts without being beholden to them. Its ties are instead to an emotional or affective experience for the spectators. It is invested in simulations, and the identity-building operation it may serve for nation or community constitutes a marker of authentic experience. The exclusionary possibilities of such a use of real-ish-ness, or performed authenticity, are important especially because of the difficult historiographical task the pageant has set for itself in its attempts to enliven history.

Anthropologists Richard Handler and Eric Gable identify two opposite impulses for producing living history experiences. Realist/objectivist models promote re-enactment as "mimetic" or "progressive realism," with accuracy as an achievable aim. In this sense, history can be resuscitated for educational purposes, and the past can "come alive."[61] On the other hand, "constructionist" historians are skeptical about ever achieving historical accuracy, understanding that our perception of history is in constant flux. They advocate a model of presentation in which historical interpreters present the lives and history of their subjects with an added layer of awareness that history is subjective. Constructionists recognize that there are gaps in our received histories and that our understanding of the past is based upon certain documents whose survival depended on those who held positions of power.[62] There is thus potential for a framework that can be a political act against patriarchal and colonial structures.

While Donna Butt's choices for the Trinity Pageant certainly place the performance in the constructionist camp, by attempting to fill in holes in the historical record the pageant also reveals or widens existing gaps of representation. In light of this, it is important for us to consider what exactly the Trinity Pageant preserves since how we perceive the past in the present can have very potent effects on the future. Writing on American Civil War re-enactors, Schneider describes the fraught relationship she negotiates with re-enactors who feel that the South should have won and who see the re-enactment as a potential re-envisioning, or at least re-feeling, of what could have been.[63] The ideological conservatism implicit in a preservation of the past, as seen in both the Trinity Pageant and Civil War re-enactments, is a necessary object of interrogation, particularly when the past enacted is not so much factually real as affectively real-ish. Returning to Rising Tide, Butt created the pageant with the aim of bringing to life the stories of those people whose lives remain unrecorded in official history, including the working classes and women. In doing so, the company succeeds in offering a broader history of Trinity's official past than most historical documents preserve. Nevertheless, the pageant is still limited and narrow. If, as an audience member attested, the pageant "causes you to think and think through things, history, and also where we're going," it is important to consider just what is being preserved – and with what outcomes for the present and future.[64]

PERFORMING IN REAL SPACES: OUTPORT CULTURE, SITE SPECIFICITY, AND SOCIAL RELATIONS

In addition to the affective real cultivated by the historical-temporal nature of the pageant, the use of particular, site-specific places also works to cultivate a sense of realness. As I briefly mentioned in my description of the church scene, space and place are two of the most important aspects of the Trinity Pageant: "The place, where it is, is really important to what it is ... I wanted to put it in the place where the stories came from." Describing her perception of what audience members desire in the pageant experience, Butt continues "I think they're looking for an experience of Newfoundland, I think they're definitely looking for an experience of a place ... I think people come to Newfoundland with the sense that it is a separate place. And they expect their experience to somehow reflect this land they've come to ... I think everyone wants to belong to something, whether it's family or work or geographical location."[65] Butt is not alone in her interpretation of what audiences crave. Theatre artist Dustin Scott Harvey, for example, highlights that contemporary audiences desire a sense of belonging: "theatre now needs to place emphasis on being present at this moment, at this place, at this time, with this group of people. It needs to establish a sense of belonging."[66]

For the Trinity Pageant, it is crucial that the play is set in, and staged in, an outport town. Butt describes how the Trinity Pageant's dependence on local people and culture, and the emphasis on the real and performed place as a singular, conflated site – this particular outport town – is required for the pageant to have a "natural" or "home-grown" feel.[67] Interestingly, in relation to the question of "Real Newfoundland," Overton points out that this mythic place is not the city of St John's; instead, it is found in remote parts of the province: "To find 'the Real Newfoundland' visitors are urged to 'go down the side roads' and 'poke into the bays'; to 'turn to the ocean and 'test' the breeze; smell the salt, the wave torn kelp, the spray washed air, the saturated, aged sand'. 'The real Newfoundland' is the outports," of which Trinity is a prime example.[68] Indeed, the Trinity Pageant takes audience members to the "landwash" (beach) twice, where they can smell, taste, and feel the "Real Newfoundland." As Susan Bennett argues, writing about tourism and theatre, "local cultural practices have come to be valued as distinctive mobile 'baits' to lure tourists to a particular place."[69] Accordingly, commenters on Rising Tide Theatre's TripAdvisor page reference the ways in which a sense of space, place, and local culture add to audience perceptions of learning about true Newfoundland: "We followed the 2 pm Pageant around the village and learned more about the history and human component of the island and its people than anything else we did in Newfoundland. Even in the cool, misty weather of the day of the last performance of the season it was enjoyable."[70]

Building on anthropologist Robert Redfield's model of a "folk society," folklorist Peter Narváez suggests that Newfoundland outport culture has a distinct sense of time and space. It is "an oral-aural community that, among other characteristics, is spatially 'small' and 'isolated.'"[71] He summarizes that such a culture is predicated on continuous time and discontinuous space: the past, the present, and the future are viewed holistically such that time is continuous, while the "spatially slow-moving, high distortion tendencies of spoken language foster a contractionist worldview which is geographically limited."[72] Both these aspects of culture are in operation in the Trinity Pageant: the present-day presentation of "real" past creates a sense of continuous time wherein much of the culture remains constant, while the use of the town's specific sites make settings localized and distinct as discontinuous space. Narváez juxtaposes settings like these with the fast-paced, globalized, and connected culture of the present day, in which he considers time to be discontinuous ("now" and "immediate") and space to be increasingly continuous.[73]

This is important to my analysis of inclusionary and exclusionary forces at work in the performance of the pageant. While Narváez seems to position outport culture as a stronghold that resists the globalized, fast-paced world of modernity, geographer Doreen Massey problematizes any such characterization in her work on social relations and space. She does not necessarily view the preserved local as an antidote to the contemporary "time–space compression" – a compression in which globalization and fragmentation have left many feeling a loss of security and stability: "The occasional longing for such coherence is none the less a sign of the geographic fragmentation, the spatial disruption, of our times. And occasionally, too, it has been part of what has given rise to defensive and reactionary responses – certain forms of nationalism, sentimentalized recovering of sanitized 'heritages', and outright antagonism to newcomers and 'outsiders.'"[74] Certainly, the Trinity Pageant may be considered a "sanitized heritage" that is related to the production of "nationalism" or at least the production of a unique cultural identity. The cultural concept of the "Real Newfoundland" reinforced by the pageant may not be openly hostile towards outsiders – or at least, not to tourists – but even with the historical violence of the site as colonial settlement and erasure of Indigenous peoples notwithstanding, there are still localized feelings of exclusion (including Butt, who has lived in Trinity for more than twenty years). Regarding this feeling of being an outsider, Butt says, "If you didn't grow up here, you're always to some degree someone from outside. That, that will never go away."[75]

The highly localized space of performance is not merely a reaction to contemporary concerns over fragmentation and globalization (an effort to preserve the way things really were) but also an active and present-day means of establishing a new "real." It is worth quoting Massey at length to consider the danger of viewing an emphasis on local place as simply reactionary to contemporary concerns over globalization and fragmentation:

> Many of those who write about time–space compression emphasize the insecurity and unsettling impact of its effects, the feelings of vulnerability which it can produce. Some therefore go on from this to argue that, in the middle of all this flux, people desperately need a bit of peace and quiet – and that a strong sense of place, or locality, can form one kind of refuge from the hubbub. So the search after the "real" meanings of places, the unearthing of heritages and so forth, is interpreted as being, in part, a response to desire for fixity and for security of identity in the middle of all the movement and change ... In that guise, however, place and the spatially local are then rejected by many progressive people as almost necessarily reactionary. They are interpreted as an evasion; as a retreat from the (actually unavoidable) dynamic and change of "real life," which is what we must seize if we are to change things for the better. On this reading, place and locality are foci for a form of romanticized escapism from the real business of the world.[76]

What is important about this passage is that, as I have earlier argued, even if such romanticized heritage sites like the Trinity Pageant appear to be an escape from the "real business of the world" they are not: the pageant is a clear boon to the present-day tourism economy and reinforces Newfoundland culture. It is less a retreat from "real life" and more an *establishment of* the real. The place constituted has very real effect and affect, and so cannot really be considered a removal from the real world.

Chris Morash and Shaun Richards, writing on Irish theatre, articulate similar relationships between place, nation, and stage representation and the ways in which they mutually construct each other. They suggest that Irish audiences bring to the theatre a notion of space that is rooted firmly in a concept of nationhood. More specifically, they argue that the space of the nation is embedded in a mythology of, and nostalgia for, the rural west of Ireland. The "dominant space on the Irish stage" during the first half of the twentieth century, they write, was "the metonymic representation of the nation – the cottage kitchen."[77] The audience's preconceived notions of Irishness and what constitutes Irish theatre in turn directly inform their reception of stage realism. Drawing on Yi-Fu Tuan, Morash and Richards consider a distinction between *space* and *place*. Tuan defines "space" as a location with no social connections or meanings for humans. Conversely, he defines "place" as a location that has been created by human experiences.[78] Morash and Richards use these distinctions to frame one of their key assertions: that theatre operates as a "machine for making place from space."[79] Such a statement, of course, leads to questions of what, how, and to what end theatre creates place.

Turning back to the Trinity Pageant, for Overton, "A particular version of Newfoundland was 'invented' for tourists. But it was not invented just for tourists. The same totems, icons, and images highlighted for tourists came to be seen as the essential symbols of Newfoundland national identity ... From the late nineteenth century a host of local writers emerged to sing the praises of Newfoundland's fisher-folk and scenery. Ideas about landscape became central to notions of nationhood."[80] Overton is asserting that performances of the "Real Newfoundland" in turn create the "Real Newfoundland" – for tourists but also for locals. What happens, however, when lived experience of *space* does not measure up to perceived notions of *place*, as defined by Morash and Richards via Tuan? When the reality, say, of rural Newfoundland does not cohere with its romanticized ideal as "Real Newfoundland"? Furthermore, when issues of gender, Indigeneity, and colonialism remain markedly absent, what metonymizes the place? What is problematically excluded? As Massey goes on in *Space, Place, and Gender*, "We need, therefore, to think through what might be an adequately progressive sense of place ... the question is how to hold on to that notion of geographical difference, of uniqueness, even of rootedness if people want that, without it being reactionary."[81]

LOCATED IN REAL SPACE/LOCATING THE AUDIENCE: SPATIALITY AND RELATIONALITY

One of the ways in which the Trinity Pageant might partially eschew a static sense of place is through a layering of multiple temporalities, most significantly in emphasizing not only historical place as content but also present-day site as frame. I want to now turn to consider how site-specificity impacts the creation of a sense of real-ish-ness, with all its repercussions for establishment of culture, nation, and the real. The use of real, present-day, site-specific places allows for the explicit coinciding of two times – past and present. Mike Pearson and Michael Shanks describe site-specific performances as involving "a location at which other occupations – their material traces and histories – are still apparent."[82] As an example, the Trinity Pageant concludes with a re-enactment of the election of politician John Bingley Garland to the District of Trinity in 1832. This reproduction occurs on land adjacent to John Bingley Garland's actual property, now the historical Lester-Garland house. This reconstructed home, a construction project funded by the historical society of Trinity and the Newfoundland government, incorporates the original ruin. This means that the other occupations of the site of performance are already multiple, and audiences can see this multiplicity: Both the history (historical ruin) and the present-day preservation of that history (the reconstructed house) are visible. In the case of the Lester-Garland house, even the possibility of future is invoked in the cast's invitation to later visit the house as a ticketed tourist site. Amongst this blended past/present/future place, it must be pointed out that non-colonial presence is markedly absent, much as in the script of the Pageant itself.

Place also dominates in the marketing materials for the Trinity Pageant: Continual references are made to the landscape of Newfoundland on the company's website, in spoken interviews with artistic staff for promotion, and in photos and video footage from the pageant itself. In fact, some images on the theatre company's website showcase no theatrical activity or stage whatsoever, instead simply displaying photos of the local area. The landscape and seascape are consistently foregrounded in the staging of theatrical moments too: The audience often faces the scenic bay, and the majority of the action takes place in front of some sort of picturesque, natural landscape. Further, many scenes exploit the natural landscape: The scenery or set is not "made to look like" the town and land surrounding Trinity; it *is* Trinity. The production thus disrupts conventional indexicality or iconicity in rejecting a representation. The set is, essentially, real.

As a direct reaction against what Dan Rebellato calls "McTheatre" – that is, theatre with a "near total disregard for geographical or cultural specificity" – Morash and Richards distinguish between "place-specific work" and truly "site-specific work."[83] In the former, the performance site draws on the resonances of the place, but the form of the play is not dependent on being staged there. In the latter, "the form and meaning of the production are inextricably bound to the site of performance, usually (but not always) such that it could not be staged elsewhere."[84] The Trinity Pageant certainly qualifies as "site-specific work." In its use of historic buildings, centuries-old beaches, and the town's scenic backdrop, it is dependent on and entrenched within the real space of present-day Trinity, a dependency in turn reflected in the omnipresence of signifiers of place in marketing and staging.

Audience members accordingly routinely highlighted the unique nature of the pageant's location as one in which story setting is eclipsed by real set. They noted in interviews that this was a dynamic method of enacting history. After being asked what was unique or special about the pageant, the following audience members contemplated the importance of space to the pageant –how its "located-ness" was clearly tied to this particular place:

> AUD 1a: I feel like what's so special about this one is, you know, like, instead of sitting down at a theatre they obviously have you walk –
> AUD 1b: Travelling around town.
> AUD 1a: You know you're actually seeing, you're in the middle of all the, the place.
> AUD 1b: You can imagine what it was at that time.
> AUD 1a: They're telling stories about this place and you're actually seeing the place at the same time, so it's cool.
> AUD 1g: Everything [was] set at a place. That was really significant.
> AUD 1a: And the history of, of each place, area ... and each setting fit, fit so beautifully with whatever the message was, which was really valuable. And having not been to Trinity until an hour before it all happened, it added to the interest of all – added to the credibility and reality of it all.[85]

The realness of the pageant is thus arguably magnified by situating it within the place that it ostensibly "actually" happened. Another audience member in a different interview concurred that "to have it in surroundings where it actually happened, and walking from one place to another place where, where you know, well that's where they would have been doing the, the different activities and that was you know, that was a real – that was where it took place. Where it was over there. You know that added the set – it was authentic."[86] The opening words of this audience member's analysis are particularly interesting: "to have *it* in surroundings where *it* actually happened." By referring to both the performed pageant and the real history as "it," the interviewee appears to conflate them. In this way, the site-specificity of the pageant makes audience members feel they are "in the middle of it" – surrounded by "realness."

The embodied activity required by the pageant, as an ambulatory, active, physical experience, also creates a palpable realness for audiences. This is not simply because of its being local to Newfoundland but also because of its more particular site-specificity to places in and around Trinity. As the company performs the past in present-day locations, it attempts a dynamism that is more flexible than fixed realism. The audience literally retraces the steps of characters in the stories, both activating a present-day consideration of one's own body and movement through space, and pointing back to a historic event. For instance, for scenes in which the actors dry cod flakes, the company takes the audience to beaches where fishers have worked their trade for centuries. They then guide the audience from the beach to the church, following a path that locals have taken since the church's establishment centuries earlier. In so doing, Rising Tide is successful in creating "authentic culture" by engaging audience members in present-day, real-time activities that simultaneously point back to the ostensibly true history of Newfoundland.

The operation of space, then, as suggested by the audience remarks about the church scene described at the beginning of this chapter, results in a particular affective real for audience members. Rather than a static reading of place as site of fixed and sanitized nostalgia (church as a historic site) that is separate to, or a retreat from, "real life,"[87] to use Massey's phrasing, when place is able to operate in multiple ways (or in multiple times) it allows for an affective experience that resonates with audiences as particularly real. As audience members remarked after the pageant, the line between reality and theatricality became truly blurred during the church scene:

AUD 3b: Well when the minister said – what did he say?
AUD 3e: You know, something like peace be with you –

AUD 3b: Yeah what they say at the end of the church service. It was so real the two of us piped up and said the response automatically!
AUD 3c: I did too, I did too![88]

Many audience members read the church as a both/and mimetic operation; it was a real church, and it was a fictive church:

AUD 4a: It felt very real in the church for sure.
...
AUD 4a: Probably, maybe because we were in the interior at that point. In that very real, you know – you could really compare it to –
AUD 4c: the worship space.[89]

For these audience members the church scene felt particularly real because, as they articulated it, their experience in it was comparable to what might unfold in a real worship space: there was a marriage of place and practice. This is an interesting comment, since it suggests that the church they were in for the performance was not a real worship space (which it is). They have thus complicated how the term "real" is applied in site-specific performance, particularly as regards the difference between *being* and *feeling* real. Arguably, the church *feels* more real for the audience members because it both is and is not real in the performance. A church that stays firmly only within the realm of the real (as a historic site or place of worship) does not *feel* as real as a church that is simultaneously also placed within a fictive frame. In other words, their comments suggest that things feel most real when we are referring to them from a place of presumed un-realness, as in a performance.

Of course, much like the "Real Newfoundland" tourism strategy, which presents a place that is more mythical than real, many of the scenes do not occur precisely where their historical antecedents did. Moreover, in the case of the fictionalized moments, there is no "real place" for them to be staged. Audience members were not duped into any kind of misreading of reality, however, as their comments suggest an awareness of the storied nature of the performance. For many, it was not the historical fact that was important but rather the overall impression of realness: "Historical facts aren't good enough."[90] As such, in a nuanced paradox that distinguishes history from reality, the site-specificity of the performance had the effect of "bringing life to the history, making it real," as one audience member put it.[91] It is not, therefore, facticity that is the important operator. Instead, if something feels real, it has the power to pull the past into the present, to "bring it to life." Regardless of the stability of the one-to-one relationship between site of performance and site of real history, it is obvious from the audience members' comments that the pageant's site-specificity generates "real affect" by allowing for a both/and perception of past and present.

Gay McAuley writes that theatre "is always local and must be local," noting that this results in a "double quality of being both local and located."[92] Her observation resonates with the duality we encounter in the Trinity Pageant, which is local in both its material content and its literal location. We can add, however, a third layer in the case of the pageant, which is not just local and located, but is also locating: It deliberately positions the audience in a particular place, both physically and perceptually, actively locating them in time and space. As an audience member remarked, "We walked through the life of it."[93] The sense of real place in the pageant is tripartite: it is "local" due to its reliance on specific outport culture, "located" in terms of its particular use of site-specific places, and "locating" as an action of relational space-making. Rather than remaining static and located, the Trinity Pageant actively establishes and maintains place. Through performance, it locates Newfoundland in a constantly shifting constellation of institutional and personal pasts and presents, and interpersonal interaction. As audience members, for example, we move swiftly from a scene in which a fictional character directly addresses the audience and jokes about recent American tourists releasing lobsters into the forest instead of eating them, to a scene dramatizing the successful government election of the historical figure, Mr Garland, beside the site of his rebuilt historical home. In both instances, we are invited to build social relations amongst ourselves: laughing at the hapless Americans and the snobbish Mr and Mrs Garland.

The necessary activity of the audience within the pageant, invoked by the unique sense the performance offers of real, local Newfoundland culture and of real, site-specific space, is significant precisely because it invites relationships to form amongst and between the audience members, and the local community. For instance, it is certainly no accident that the pageant begins with the performance of the provincial anthem "Ode to Newfoundland." As noted earlier, although it is performed by three young actresses, many audience members join in. They have been invited to do so in Artistic Director Donna Butt's introductory remarks: "We would love to hear your voices blended with ours."[94] This immediate, active offering of allegiance to the province prepares the audience to be more involved as the pageant unfolds and even more broadly participatory in Newfoundland culture through the influx of their tourist dollars. In the ambulatory procession of the remainder of the two-hour performance, the audience is essentially onstage themselves: They are participants in this activity of making culture and thus, to follow Hurley, also making a nation.[95] Site-specific performance, Susan Bennett and Mary Polito argue, "converts landscape into taskscape."[96] They cite Mike Pearson's argument that "in the present, [site] is experienced as muscular engagement but it also involves retentions from the past, as experience and memory; and projections for the future, as hopes, aspirations. To perceive it, is always to carry out acts of memory and remembrance, engaging constantly with an environment within which the past is embedded."[97] The situating of the pageant in present-day sites allows audience members to be engaged in the present while feeling nostalgic about an ostensibly real past; they become bound up in the "web" created by the meeting of past and present in real space and actively contribute to the preservation and creation of a culture.

Audiences are, as noted, also invited to join in with a hymn in the church scene. They are provided with the lyrics on a program insert. On all four occasions that I attended, audiences willingly sang together. One audience member described how she "sang the hymn. It was a really heartfelt moment."[98] In this remark, the audience member explicitly ties her physical involvement (singing) to an emotional response (it was "heartfelt"). This kind of embodied action also serves to emphasize the present-ness of the pageant: Bodily processes such as the audience members' participation in the singing of the hymn, and the consequent emotional response to such a moment, cannot but occur in real time. The audience, in other words, is really singing, and that action occurs in real time.

In a sort of community-building exercise, this embodied interaction also necessitated a relation not only between audience and actor but also between audience members as they sang together and, occasionally, shared lyric sheets. As one audience member put it, "It got more real as we went on. You got to know the people, feel more comfortable. At the beginning, there was a little bit of distance, we were separate. But then we kind of become part of the life. So yeah, by the end it was very, very real."[99] This audience member is clearly not referring to literal distance. Instead, she appears to be speaking about the imagined space of social relations and, most importantly, how the development of social relations contributed to the show's realness. The embodied action was not simply an individual activity – it was also a relational one, and it contributed to the pageant's realness. The act of singing together brought the audience figuratively closer through the communal nature of the act. A locating of the real, then, might be found in specific, literal, geographic space, as in the church scene of the pageant which elides fictional set and real space but also in the emergent connections and social relations that a performance in that space informs.

It is worth noting the specificity of the hymn sung by audience and actors. Written in 1827, "We Love the Place, O God" was composed by St Paul's church's then rector, Reverend William Bullock, to celebrate the consecrating of the church of that year. (That structure would be replaced in 1892, which is the church that is still standing today.) Massey writes, "what gives a place its specificity is not some long internalized history but the fact that it is constructed out of a particular constellation of social relations, meeting and weaving together at a particular locus."[100] The particular locus of the church is what prompts the singing of this hymn, fittingly titled to emphasize the importance of "the Place." However, it is not the building itself but the "constellation" of relations beyond the church that is invoked. We can imagine the social relations that led to the writing and first singing of the hymn in 1827, but we can also imagine the community of audience members of the Trinity Pageant who have come together to sing the hymn under much different circumstances since the pageant's premiere in 1992. Cliff McLucas who worked with Mike Pearson in Brith Gof developed an understanding of site-specific theatre as being composed of "The Place (the Host), The Performance (The Ghost) and The Public (The Witness)."[101] Andy Houston picks up on this metaphor to highlight the importance of the audience in site-specific theatre: "a site is always shadowed by the possibility of other versions or perspectives on these details, and the work of the artists is to try to keep the possibility of these other versions viable for interpretation by the audience. Here the 'ghosts' are the various approaches to animating the host created by the artists and interpreted by the audience. McLucas calls the audience 'witnesses' because ultimately they play a crucial collaborative role in piecing together the 'ghost stories' however they may be conveyed."[102] Audiences here are invited to imagine these various "ghost stories" all while collaboratively coming together for communal hymn-singing: the experience was, resultantly, reported to be highly affecting by audience members.

The use of the verb "locating" to describe the method of site-specific performance in the Trinity Pageant is thus more apt than calling the show simply local or located. The term "locating" maintains a multifaceted flexibility necessary for encompassing the very active process of relationship-building that is enacted by virtue of the real place. As Kirsty Sedgman notes in her study of Welsh audiences, "At its broadest, the role of located art is therefore to bring into view the many different layers of experience, history, politics, architecture and memory of which a place is formed. To put it differently, it is not about *location* but *locating*, making room for audiences to situate themselves in space (and time) rather than setting them down into an existing version of place."[103] The pageant is local, as previously described in sections on authenticity and outport culture. It is also located insofar as it is tied to a particular geographic space that allows for dimensions of both past and present to meet. But most importantly it is also actively locating its audience in a web of relational space that is made and unmade during each performance. Space, as an active operation, thus helps contribute to the feeling of realness through not only its site-specific ties to geographic space and cultural place but also through its relationship building between audience members (that is, through its construction of an affective web of time).

Choosing to perform in real spaces is, for Butt, a means of encouraging audience members to consider where they have come from, where they currently are, and what their connection to Newfoundland is. As Butt recalls, in designing the Trinity Pageant she wanted to "Write a script that would leave you with a profound sense of where you were." This same impulse is reflected in her choice to perform pageant-style: "You do it outside, it becomes tied to here, this place."[104] This phrasing highlights not only the necessity of location but also how the present-day act of performance engages that location and "ties" it to a very specific time and space. For McAuley, writing on site-specific performance, "spectators experience these places in new ways and are obliged to engage in new ways with the political issues that seem to be an inevitable consequence of being in place."[105] Real place and location are integral to the pageant's engagement with present-day visitors; they help to build an affective attachment that in turn encourages audiences to consider the current economic, social, and political issues of that place. A scene with late sixteenth-century Sir Richard Whitbourne is followed by a reference to a recent hydro-electric project in the province. By virtue of the space in which the show is located, audiences are asked to temporarily embody the community and consider its concerns. They are asked to become, at least momentarily, identified in relation to present-day Trinity as community members.

However, Butt also highlighted the power of specific sites to instigate a reflection on the past: "It's important people know who they are and where they came from. What's running through their veins … You belong to this place … [and] need to live in a place you belong and belong to."[106] McAuley also argues that "Places raise questions about memory and about group and individual identity: who we are is intimately bound up with where we are, and where we come from."[107] These questions of identity and belonging, however, imply a very selective and particular past: "Who belongs," after all, is a limited category since the majority of places visited during the pageant are colonial buildings from the Western Europeans who arrived in the seventeenth and eighteenth centuries. The site-specificity of the performance also limits the experience to those with particular abilities, who can stand and walk for the two-hour performance and hear without amplification in the natural settings, among other possible accessibility issues. Consequently, just as the historical accuracy at work in the pageant is selective, so too is the notion of belonging and social communing: The politics of identity and inclusion/exclusion inform and qualify the extent to which the Trinity Pageant is "real." Of course, if as I have argued, audience members are able to momentarily become a part of the Trinity community, then possibly these categories of belonging/not belonging to the outport are productively expanded by the pageant, as more and more audience members "from away" come to participate in the culture-making process of attending the pageant.

THE CHIASMUS OF AFFECT: THINKING ABOUT SPACE TEMPORALLY, THINKING ABOUT TIME SPATIALLY

Schneider suggests that it is necessary to move beyond Western temporal linearity in her analysis of theatrical re-enactment and consider instead a cross-temporal liminality. She proposes that this can be achieved by introducing spatial metaphors to concepts of time to imagine "crossing disparate and multiple historical moments to explore the ways that past, present, and future occur and recur *out of sequence* in a complex crosshatch."[108] Schneider posits that an approach to history that involves any kind of remains "engages temporality at (and as) a chiasm, where times cross and, in crossing, in some way touch."[109] In the case of the Trinity Pageant, the "remains" include a variety of tangible and intangible pasts, from historic buildings, to court documents, to folk stories. The way in which temporalities blend in the Trinity Pageant can be felt in the church scene where a service is held for a present-day congregation in the historic building. Past meets present again in the cod-fishing scene, where twenty-first-century fishing methods formed the backdrop for a historical scene during one performance. This cross-temporality can be pushed further to consider that the pageant does not just present time out of sequence but as a simultaneous multiplicity. In this way, time and (re)presentations within the pageant become an assemblage that echoes, as Schneider goes on, "the Deleuzean notion of assemblage [...] to gesture not only to mobility but also to the always already *crossingness*, or *betweenness*, or *relationality* of the sets of associations that make up something resembling identity."[110] The pageant offers moments of historical re-enactment, contemporary community-building, factual references, entirely fictitious scenes, and many instances that fall somewhere between those poles all as it performs and re-performs Newfoundland's cultural identity.

This chapter has argued that Newfoundland's cultural identity is tied to a sense of place that is performed (and performative) in the Trinity Pageant, and it is important to note how such ideas of place are tied to a complicated temporality: "clearly places do not have single, unique 'identities'; they are full of internal conflicts" that span past, present, and future.[111] Butt asserted something similar when I asked her about the spatial location of the pageant:

So the history of what was on this site is kind of important because it was, this is where, this is one of the places where the fishing industry was, happened. Right, so it was one time a place where that industry, which was a part of ... what kept things going here happened and now this is, now you have on it, you know, I guess another kind of work ... So it's a different kind of work that's going on here that hopefully contributes in some significant way both to the place in terms of what it represents, both in terms of providing work and so on and so forth and helping in some way to, to enable things to carry on and also sort of to continue with the cultural and sharing the culture and the history of what those kinds of things. So it's all intertwined, really.[112]

She points to space in terms of past, present, and future, invoking temporal dimensions to describe the sites (and work) of the pageant.

This impact of experiencing multiple times vis-à-vis space is one of Rising Tide's goals and informs the company's mode of presentation. Butt explained that her initial aim with the company was "To present Newfoundland work in a setting where it would have sprung from. So that you were doing it in a place where the landscape and the seascape ... [were those] in which these things had happened." She explained a consequence of the method they used to achieve this: "the past and the present really intrude on each other, you know? They really do. Because here the past and the present meet all the time ... it does so in what you're seeing physically and it also does so in the stories that are being told."[113] For Morash and Richards, site-specific performance can collapse the present, day-to-day function of a space with another time and space – that of the play world.[114] In the case of the Trinity Pageant, the present converges with multiple play worlds *and* real worlds, at times ranging across centuries, all active in a single place. This is more closely aligned with Massey's idea of a "plurality of trajectories" such that places are a "simultaneity of stories-so-far."[115] A scene on the beach might invoke the past of European settlers, the present-day fishers, and also a future question about the viability of the cod industry.

This notion of pulling the past into the present was not just observable on a general conceptual level; it was also evident in the personal phenomenological experience of the audience members. One audience member remarked upon the church as being "So real. Just the smell of it brought back so many memories."[116] In noting this, the audience member suggests that her own past had been pulled into the present by the sensation this real place provoked; the production tied real sensation, with real space, with real personal memory. To take Ahmed's notion of the "stickiness" of affect, Schneider describes how "histories of events and historical effects of identity fixing, *stick* to any mobility, *dragging* ... the temporal past into the sticky substance of any present."[117] Place thus operates to facilitate this sticky "dragging" or pulling of personal and historical pasts into the present. The effect is the generation of an affectively real experience for audience members.

One way to generate a potently affective experience for an audience is thus for a production company to surround an audience with a syncopated presentation of past/present/future, and to link multiple times through a particular space. Jen Harvie describes how site-specific performance can be a "potent mnemonic trigger" by which audiences become engaged in "negotiating, formulating, and changing their relationships to their pasts – and also to their presents and futures."[118] As one audience member put it, describing the effect of watching the pageant's historical re-enactments where they "really happened," "It was real enough to me: I cried."[119] As this quote demonstrates, temporal blending can be thickly affecting in instances in which the past is not just behind us but also feels present. It achieves what Schneider calls a "viscous, affective surround."[120] Fittingly, following the show, audience members had a variety of affective responses. To return to a quote cited earlier in this chapter, one audience member stated that

> That one scene over in the ... with all the people who starved in that, like the acting was very good but because it was a true story in some ways I felt like I want to applaud the acting but in some ways I don't want to because it was such a horrible thing that happened in history. So I felt really torn then because I thought they did a very good job of, of depicting the um, the horror of, of that time so yeah.[121]

This audience member's remarks point to the effect of conflating past with present: The past feels so present for her that she is not sure if she should applaud the skill of the actors. Her affective response is complicated because the representation has stirred "real" feelings.

Many of the pageant's audience members whom I interviewed for my research described the multiplicity of times the performance (re)presented to them within the deceptively limited present of the performance. As an example: "The pageant allowed you to focus on what you're actually seeing, observing with your eyes going okay the buildings and reading the history you know that's one thing but actually having a little scene played out you go 'This is how it could have been.'"[122] This comment combines a focus on the present sensation of "what you're actually seeing," namely the buildings, a historic sense of the past, and a resultant imagining of what could have been that is speculative. Another audience member spoke emotionally about the need to share stories widely in Canada and her own personal, affecting recollections:

> Yeah, it has made me think a lot about things. And I certainly will be talking to my friends at home ... You know like I mean so what? But I thought it's important to recognize um you know like the sealing [referring to the sealing disaster described in the church scene], I didn't – you know we'd been to the interpretation centre but I didn't think of, God, you know they were here, it was here too. It wasn't just in one place. And that story needs – I think it's important to tell it, to keep it as part of the history of Canada. Yeah.[123]

Such comments illustrate not only the affective power of temporal blending but also its necessary multiplicity and varying character, much like my earlier stated ideas of multiple places cultivated through the performance. Schneider writes, "Time, engaged *in* time, is always a matter of crossing, or passing, or touching, and perhaps always (at least) double,"[124] which suggests that we cannot, for instance, simply refer to the past, present, and future when considering performance. Instead, we must invoke several of each, considered in terms of spatial relationships; several potential futures are presented in front of us (some actually gesturing back to the past) and the audience is (at least symbolically) imbued with the power to enact one or more of them. In the case of the audience member quoted directly above, she is empowered to, in the future, talk about the show with "friends at home." In this way, the real setting creates a temporal chiasm in which a present-day performance of a past act might spark future action. When we think about time spatially, it becomes an expansive and open way of considering the affective potential of the theatrical's apparent "real."

Notably, Butt begins each performance by outlining the decline of the community in which the pageant is being performed: She explains that there are "as many people here in winter as here on this block right now [referring to the assembled audience of the pageant]."[125] She then asks the audience to drop a coin in the historic Trinity church donation box for future roof repairs, but despite the bleak picture painted, adds, "you don't need to be walking around today thinking of us freezing in the winter."[126] The concept of theatrical utopia can help us better understand both the affective impact of and the temporal blend at work in this simple opening: as Magelssen writes, "In the case of what Jill Dolan calls the utopian performative, simmings need to reference the known world but be conspicuously unlike the world enough to offer a hopeful vision of what we might strive for – what Dolan describes as fleeting moments of 'intense, sincere, generous romanticism' that inspire and move those gathered toward 'feelings of possibility, hope, and political agency.'"[127] The Trinity Pageant's presentation of history, including Butt's opening remarks, are such a call to sentimentalism. They implore and empower the audience to support the community. The company's actions should not be characterized as insidious, and neither are they profit-mongering, except insofar as the dominant political and economic order impacts all such moments of cultural exchange. The past-ness of the church building and its need for roof repairs, coupled with the affective invocation of the town's population in winter, encourages a present-moment action – that is, the dropping of a coin into the donation box – which generates future effect (a preserved building). Another audience member stated that the pageant "causes you to think and think through things, history, and also where we're going."[128] This remark points to a variety of possible pasts and futures that are dependent on choices made in the present; will this past be forgotten in the future? It can be argued, then, that Newfoundland's historic past, full of tragedy, challenge, and resilience, enacted in present-day sites, compels tourists to act in the future (post-performance) to preserve its heritage.

The first page in the 2016 season brochure further reinforces the role of temporality in the pageant: "Come to our 'time' and celebrate our heritage and culture set against the magnificent backdrops of Trinity Bight, where the past and present meet as surely as the waves embrace the shore and the moon shines on the harbour ... You'll cherish the memories all winter long." The apparently affective power of time that the brochure invites readers to consider is perhaps unsurprising. Time is, after all, often highly affective in language: The enjoyment of something makes it go by "too fast" while tedious tasks make time "move slowly." Even before audiences see the show, the company invokes, through the brochure, a particular time – one that is removed from the vagaries of "real time." They cunningly claim it as their own; it is "Our 'time.'" This unique time is beholden not to the linearity of past and present, as the two will "surely meet." In declaring that time is not linear, the company reinforces the existence of a special performance time. The language in the brochure invokes a dizzying, non-sequential explanation of temporal events: a potential future filled with past memories that will be made in the reader's future attendance at a performance about the past.

It is worth considering why Newfoundland culture, and the Trinity Pageant in particular, are expressed temporally and what that temporal expression accomplishes. Newfoundland culture is presented as out of time: its outport culture separates it from modernity/modern time, and its tourist culture offers visitors a time away from time (a "vacation time"). It is also, however, portrayed as running out of time and requiring preservation. The pageant manages to create (re-enact) a particular Newfoundland time – one that inspires audiences to contribute to the preservation of the region's future. As Barbara Kirshenblatt-Gimblett argues, "When a way of life disappears, with the ... economy that once sustained it ... tourism is ready to step in. The formula for revitalizing the economy of a depressed region is the resurrection theatre of the heritage industry. While tourist attractions may seem like oases of time out, they are implicated in a larger political economy of transnational flows of money, people and symbolic capital."[129] Fittingly, the clash between times is portrayed as one in which time has been lost: modernity has stolen time, or sped up time, and Newfoundland's unique culture is able to pause time. It is cast as both a special time and a time in need of preservation. Though it may feel like an "oasis" or a "time out," this Newfoundland time requires financial support (it is not absolved from "real life," to borrow again from Massey as quoted earlier in this chapter).[130] It is still a part of a larger economy in which audience economic contribution is vital.

Considering notions of preservation more broadly, Overton writes that, in the use of the "Real Newfoundland" as a tourism strategy, "an idealized rural life is set against the problems of the present and the uncertainty and instability of the future in a nostalgic celebration of the (lost) values of community, simplicity and stability."[131] The preservation of such a place – or, if we follow the claims of the Rising Tide brochure, the preservation of such a time – requires action. It must be remembered or lost. Overton goes on to note that "It is even popular in some tourist literature to introduce the idea of the imminent demise of 'the Real Newfoundland' making it even more urgent for tourists to 'taste' a way of life which is in jeopardy."[132] On a scale much broader than the maintenance of the church roof, tourists are compelled to spend their tourist dollars tasting, and thereby preserving, the "Real Newfoundland." The website of Rising Tide fittingly contains links to accommodation, activities, hiking trails, restaurants, and shopping destinations. It is clearly implying that the pageant audience may feel inspired to pay more, to inject tourist dollars into the town in order to avoid repeating the misery of the town following the loss of their previous economic driver. Rising Tide's pageant, in presenting a particularly Newfoundland performance of historic identity, makes use of flexible time modalities to cultivate a kind of future imperative that in turn incites appropriate audience action to preserve. In other words, the past of Newfoundland's particular place becomes, in the present performance, something that will require (i.e., in the future) preservation.

The "Real Newfoundland" is, paradoxically, a highly constructed myth that merely *feels* real. It is a concept that Rising Tide's Trinity Pageant makes full use of – from its apparently real historic content, to its site-specific locations, to its attempts to garner a real result in terms of the growth and maintenance of a strong and healthy tourist economy for Newfoundland. To return to the temporally complex phrase from the season's brochure, "you will long remember" used in the title of this chapter, it seems to point both backwards and forwards in time by suggesting a future action of recalling the past. The wording encapsulates what Schneider calls "a more porous approach to time and to art – time as full of holes or gaps and art as capable of falling or crossing in and out of the spaces between live iterations."[133] If the conceptualizing of time and space are integral to the generation of an affectively real experience – one that feels real irrespective of how real it really is – then study of the flexible and multiple ways in which time–space acts to shift audience perception on issues as wide reaching as historical origin, national identity, and cultural norms is necessary. For Rising Tide, there is a simultaneous looking back, present locating, and an exercise in distinct culture-making practice for the future, with real effects for Newfoundland. The production of cultural identity ensconced within the pageant suggests the necessity of recognizing exactly whose culture or history is preserved and/or made and the boundaries and biases of cultural identity in terms of what narratives, bodies, and even facts are accepted or rejected. Studying the pageant thus prompts questions of applicability to other culture- and nation-building practices and the apparent real-ish-ness that is generated in such practices.

5

Constructing Immersive Experiences for "Real" Engagement

KJ: *And what do you mean by immersive?*
AUD 1a: Like, you get to choose. You choose your experience, but you don't know what you're going to experience. Um, I don't know. Like, it made me cry.[1]

The audience member in the above interview excerpt is describing their experience of *TomorrowLove™*, a production by self-defined immersive theatre company Outside the March located in Toronto, Canada. Directed by Mitchell Cushman, the show uses a cast of eight actors, four identifying as female and four identifying as male, to perform fifteen two-person vignettes written by Rosamund Small about relationships and the future. The show begins with a dance choreographed by Robert Binet, in which the actors constantly change pairs.

When a brave (or possibly just curious) audience member pushes a large red button, the actors freeze in the couples they currently find themselves in. Each pair takes a quarter of the audience and leaves to a different room to perform a scene. After the scene, audience members then choose which of the two actors they wish to follow to a different room, for a different scene performed by the actor with a new scene partner. This pattern repeats itself throughout the show; audience members watch three or four scenes, choosing an actor to follow each time. This multitrack route option was described by many audience members as a kind of choose your own adventure,[2] or, as the aforementioned audience member described, "you get to choose. You choose your experience but you don't know what you're going to experience." The show is structured in such a way that an audience member will see three or four vignettes in one performance. The roles

Figure 5.1 Actors Cyrus Lane and Katherine Cullen dance in the chapel at *TomorrowLove™*, December 2016

in each vignette may be played by different actors on different nights, depending on the pairs selected during the opening dance. For instance, the night I attended, I watched a scene between two of the male actors, but the scene can also be played by two female actors or any other combination of genders. The performers you see in each vignette depends on chance: What pairs the actors are in when the button is pushed dictates the sequence of vignettes each performer will perform.

The scenes themselves are connected only by the amorphous theme of futuristic relationships; the actors take on different characters from scene to scene, and the stories the audience observes do not directly relate to each other. The scenes are brief but generally emotionally intense, ranging from the presentation of a new invention that lets people speak to deceased loved ones, to a story involving space travel as a means of closing a large age gap between two lovers. Two actors learned each of the thirty possible parts, and the writing was designed so that the roles are not dependent on a person of any particular gender or race performing them. The production offers numerous possibilities for different routes, different sequences of scenes, and different experiences: 472, according to one critic.[3] This scenario seems to highlight many of the production components the audience member quoted above described as immersive: chance, risk, and participation.

And yet, the immersive nature of this show may not be immediately apparent – at least, not insofar as the term is usually applied. Gareth White defines immersive theatre as "a trend for performances which use installations and expansive environments, which have mobile audiences, and which invite audience participation."[4] Discussions of immersive theatre cannot ignore Punchdrunk, a theatre company established in London, UK, in 1999, whose large-scale immersive projects such as *The Drowned Man*, *Sleep No More*, and *The Burnt City* have made it "the game-changing company who've done more to catapult this kind of work into the heart of our culture than any other."[5] Punchdrunk's expansive, multi-story, multi-sensory experiences in which masked audience members follow actors around large-scale environments serve as a prime example of immersive theatre as defined by White. Josephine Machon problematizes White's succinct definition, however, highlighting how the term "immersive" has become convoluted; she argues that it is now used "as a promotional adjective to market games," with the result being that "immersion" is synonymous with "good."[6] White's analysis does not fully contradict this. Indeed, he announces that "so prevalent has the use of this term become in the UK that theatre journalists have begun to propose that this trend has had its day."[7] He cites Charlotte Higgins who decried immersive theatre in 2009 as "tired and hackneyed" after attending an immersive theatre performance in which she reports thinking, "Oh, not blindfolded *again*."[8] Eleven years later artists and scholars are still debating the utility of the word, with Ramos, Dunne-Howrie, Maravala, and Simon declaring the need for a post-immersive manifesto, given the term's repeated use in not only theatre but also extending into games, marketing, and even shopping malls.[9] I raise this point to signal that the term "immersive" has come to be applied in a manner that obscures what it might actually define. In other words, the category is so large that it seems that either not every immersive theatre performance employs the original tactics of the genre or performances are doing so merely superficially.

In light of how problematic the term has become, it is central to my investigation of the relationship between immersive theatre and realness to have participating audience members clarify themselves what they meant by immersive. This is similar to Kirsty Sedgman's impulse in her article "Ladies and Gentlemen Follow Me, Please Put on Your Beards: Risk, Rules, and Audience Reception in National Theatre Wales" to focus on reception rather than intention when it comes to terms like immersion.[10] As Matthew Reason similarly argues, "What is needed are not competing over-statements of idealised or imagined possibilities ... [but] a serious focus on reception processes, and an analysis of the manners in which actual audiences engage with different kinds of audience–performer relationships to produce different kinds of experience."[11] I felt this was particularly crucial with regard to *TomorrowLove™* since the company defines the show as immersive even though it lacks a themed installation design (such as audiences might observe in Broadway's *The Great Comet*), or a free-wandering component (such as audiences experience in Punchdrunk productions).

Rather than having a singular definition, immersive practice involves a constellation of qualities, all of which imply different relationships to perceived realness and offer varying perceptions of what constitutes audience participation. *TomorrowLove™* appears to check only some of the requisite boxes of conventional immersive theatre. There is a large, staged environment to explore, but the set itself, as I will show below, is relatively sparse. As well, although the audience is mobile, it is difficult to articulate how the required walking from scene to scene is really any different from a pageant-style performance (such as the Trinity Pageant discussed in the previous chapter). Because of the pattern of following actors, audience members are never travelling alone. Instead, they are led alongside other audience members down pre-determined routes throughout the show's multi-story, multi-room set. The audiences of *TomorrowLove™* thus walk from room to room, but then promptly sit down to watch a fairly traditional theatrical scene (only one of the four scenes I personally witnessed broke the fourth wall). With regard to participation, audiences are compelled to make decisions about which of the actors to follow at the culmination of each scene. They are also occasionally – in interstitial moments between scenes – asked to complete a short activity. These range from passing a model spaceship from one person to another, to writing on windows about why they love someone. The audience members do not, however, appear to have any significant impact on the show itself: Nothing is actually altered as a result of the actions of the audience members, aside from the promising moment during the opening when an audience member pushes a button to determine when the dancing stops. This chapter thus considers why both company members and audience members whom I interviewed deemed *TomorrowLove™* to be immersive and how its perceived immersiveness resulted in a perceived realness. Core to this consideration is a thorough examination of what constitutes productive engagement in immersive theatre; what allows audiences to feel that they have had real involvement? What real impact do audiences have in immersive theatre? How does immersive theatre create a potentially more real, or real-ish, experience for audience members and to what end?

To answer these questions, I narrow my focus in this chapter primarily to the nature of the engagement required of audience members in *TomorrowLove™* and how that connects to perceived realness. In the case of this production, the necessary audience participation is not solely a result of their experience of the site itself, nor their navigation through it, nor even their interaction with materials of the environment. Instead, I turn to Adam Alston who "recognises productive participation as a feature of immersive theatre aesthetics that stems from demands that are often made of audiences – demands to make more, do more, feel more, and to feel more intensely."[12] I place particular emphasis on this last sentiment: feeling more intensely. Indeed, the audience member's remarks with which I opened this chapter are not about the theatre space or the story content; rather, they are about her individual emotional experience: "Like, it made me cry."[13]

While I primarily utilize data collected from attending four performances and interviewing thirty-seven audience members from *TomorrowLove™*, I also consider other immersive theatre productions. In particular, I draw on my experiences attending Mitchell Cushman and Julie Tepperman's 2015 large-scale immersive musical *Brantwood*, the largest immersive, site-specific musical theatre production in Canadian history thus far, centred on telling the story of a school's imagined 110-year history. I also compare *TomorrowLove™* with works by immersive theatre company Punchdrunk, again using my own experience attending their performances, as well as online and social media responses from audiences. Putting this well-established UK company in conversation with Toronto's Outside the March company is a useful means for considering the specific immersive dramaturgical strategies at work and their resultant effects.

IMMERSIVE SPACES AS INTIMATE, EXPANSIVE, AND DEMANDING

One of the most recognizable markers of immersive theatre is its use of space, often placing audiences in novel large-scale environments or rearticulating an audience member's relationship to a known site. This consequently creates a unique relationship between audience and site that requires both mobility and interactivity. An immersive production may for instance reanimate real-world spaces. Take the spectrum of plays produced by Outside the March: Performance spaces have included a kindergarten classroom, the streets of downtown Toronto, and a dilapidated movie theatre used primarily for screenings of pornographic videos, the latter of which was transformed into a site of refuge post-apocalypse in their production of *Mr. Burns, A Post-electric Play* by Anne Washburn. The original function and use of these spaces was visible to theatregoers and used to further the story being portrayed in the fiction. Immersive theatre productions may also construct entirely new environments, such as those spaces created by the epitomic immersive theatre company Punchdrunk, which feel closer to an expansive movie set than a theatre space. Punchdrunk, for instance, utilized a 4,000-square-foot former mail sorting facility for *The Drowned Man*, transforming it into a highly detailed and fully conceived trailer park, movie theatre, motel, and desert, among other settings. The original use of the space was obscured and its past as a mail sorting facility purposefully hidden.

The result of this emphasis on space, whether highlighting the previous function of the space or obscuring it entirely, is that audiences are often required to remain ambulatory throughout performances. *Brantwood*, as an example, made use of a large elementary school slated for demolition. Audience members were dressed in school graduation robes and driven by school bus to the site. Free to explore the building's interior and exterior, they were invited to roam the expansive space at will before the show began. From scenes imagining the school's future as an apartment complex, to scenes depicting pre-war student romances, audience members were asked to step into role as alumni returning for a visit and wander the school grounds at large for three hours, experiencing eleven different storylines, each set in a particular decade from 1920 to 2020.

The use of such exploratory spaces also invites a specific kind of interactive relationship with the audience. In fact, Jonathan Mandell suggests that immersive shows double as hands-on museums or art installations.[14] For example, audience members in *The Drowned Man* were free to follow characters loosely enacting Büchner's 1837 play *Woyzeck*. They were also at liberty to wander independently and investigate anything that crossed their paths, from bundles of letters to bottles of tequila, using any or all of their five senses. *Brantwood* also involved highly detailed sets, such as a school cafeteria stocked with edible veggie dogs and juice boxes. The result for the spectators was a spacious world, ripe for exploration. In these cases, the space – as both vast and full – demanded a mobile, interactive audience.

The effect of these expansive exploratory spaces also creates a sense of the epic. Game designer Jane McGonigal defines an epic environment as "a space that, by virtue of its extreme scale, provokes a profound sense of awe and wonder."[15] In shows such as Punchdrunk's *The Drowned Man*, the vast scale and minute detail of the many different spaces do fill audience members with awe: From a trailer park replete with birch trees, to sand dunes made from real sand, to a fully stocked bar, movie theatre, and locker rooms, *The Drowned Man*'s scale and scope is remarkable. While not all immersive shows utilize an "extreme scale," the scope of the site of most immersive shows is usually magnified conceptually, if not literally. In other words, an immersive show might allow audiences to move around the stage, backstage, lobby, and theatre auditorium, rather than require them to remain seated in one place. The actual physical site of the theatre may not be any larger, but the different audience relationship to the site – one that fosters exploration – makes it feel more expansive. In her exploration of epic environments, McGonigal goes on to describe how a synthetic (as opposed to a natural) environment can inspire two responses: humility in the face of such an impressive scale and empowerment through an awareness of what humans can achieve.[16] I wish to add the idea that this "impressive scale" may not need to relate to the physical construction undertaken by the company itself. It may instead take the form of the complex logistics and the number and coordination of the performances within a space, as in *Brantwood*. In this show, audience members were free to enter the production's "control room." Here, they saw the vast number of technical operators running the lights, sound, and other show elements.

This making visible the impressiveness of such an undertaking has a complicated effect on spectators of immersive theatre. In this genre, the communal act of spectating typically collides with an enfranchisement more commonly found in first-person video games, where one is free to explore on one's own. In a kind of paradoxical effect, audience members are both made to feel humbled by the epic nature of the sets and productions, and simultaneously empowered as a leading figure in a participatory narrative in which an entire world full of minute details has been crafted for one's personal consumption. There is both the obvious work of many people having worked together to create the environment and the sense of communal achievement but simultaneously the invocation of a highly individuated, almost narcissistic experience of personal choice within the environment. As Allison Oddey and Christine White argue in their book *Modes of Spectating*, immersive theatre is ideal for "the new mode of spectating," in which the audience member is like a first-person gamer.[17] They use the first-person perspective to articulate this new mode of spectating: one in which I "focus only on what 'I' want to see; on my perception of the world as 'I' see it."[18] In my interview with Mitchell Cushman, the co-creator and director of *Brantwood* and director of *TomorrowLove™*, he similarly described how immersive theatre is often driven by a first-person perspective and personalization of experience:

The first immersive experience that our company did to help us form our identity and the first thing I ever worked on like this was a piece called *Mr. Marmalade*, which we did in a kindergarten classroom. And the audience and the actors inhabited the classroom, and there was no part of the classroom that was designated as the stage or playing area. The actors just ran around the room and the audience of about thirty people followed them. And by definition, directing it, there was no way to think about sightlines because the audience created their own sightlines. They were their own cameras and I couldn't control where they would go, so it was a very different way of working ... right now, I'm working in a proscenium theatre and I'm thinking about sightlines and stage picture and all these things that you're really putting in the hands of the actors and the audience when you're working in this more immersive way. To me the payoff of that is that every audience member, fundamentally, is having their own experience that they're involved with creating, and that they'll take something away that no one else will. They will see some version of the show that is just theirs, and I think to me that makes things more real because it makes them more personally valuable. I really feel like live theatre truly has the power to do things that other mediums like films can't, because it's happening live in the moment and each audience member can take away something different and I think there's certain kinds of theatre that don't harness that as much as immersive theatre does.[19]

Part of why Cushman values the genre is because it empowers audiences to craft highly unique experiences. His description of the simultaneous privilege and responsibility that audiences are imbued with in immersive theatre dovetails nicely with the idea of the audience as first-person gamer: Based on my own actions, I will see some version of the show that is "just mine." Thus, the large scale of most immersive experiences invokes both a sense of the epic and yet, at the same time, can offer an experience that is highly personalized and individuated.

In fact, while immersive theatre is frequently epic in scale and grandeur, it is often simultaneously intensely intimate. In his book project on authenticity in contemporary theatre, Daniel Schulze defines intimate theatre as theatre in which the viewer is placed at "the centre of attention." Intimate theatre, he says, focuses "on individual, unique experience and personal narratives as opposed to a commodified, uniform product."[20] This definition seems equally applicable to immersive theatre, especially following Cushman's suggestion above that a single audience member in an immersive theatre experience crafts a unique experience for themselves. The intimacy is often also achieved through one-to-one performances, which Punchdrunk frequently uses and which were also present in *Brantwood*. Machon defines one-to-one performances as "performances made for one recipient at a time that explore the direct connection between performer, performance and individual audience member and usually encourage that individual's solitary and sentient interaction with(in) the space."[21] Accordingly, one of the most memorable moments for me as an audience member of *Brantwood* occurred in a one-to-one experience with an actor: He was an older man who placed his hands on my shoulders, asked my name, and asked if I would help him. I was then shut in a small room in the back of the school library with this stranger, helping him to change into a mascot costume while catching glimpses of a concealed gun and a young man tied up to a chair in an adjacent room. The man threatened me, demanding that I not tell anyone about what I had seen, before abruptly pushing me back out into the library. In that moment, I was experiencing an epic intimacy: The set, containing a complete library and offices, was thoroughly detailed and expansive, but I still felt the intimate thrill of being alone, at the centre of attention with an actor. The intimacy of the one-to-one experience builds upon the impression of the environment as epic such that it feels like the show is an expansive undertaking crafted solely for my own personal consumption.

Machon actually explicitly conflates the epic and the intimate in her analysis of one-to-one performances. In these, she argues, one can experience "the epic in an intimate immersive encounter."[22] Different from McGonigal, Machon defines the epic as "the authenticity of human connection often lacking in workaday lives."[23] She thus makes a distinct connection between relational affect, here characterized as authentic "human connection," and the epic. It is not immediately obvious, however, that the intense implication, threat, and collusion required of me as an audience member in *Brantwood* as I helped a performer change costume were authentic moments of "human connection." I would argue, in fact, that the experience felt distinctly unreal: In my real life, I would not likely be asked to follow a strange man into a room, and I would be even less likely to acquiesce. And yet, the intense intimacy of this moment may reflect what Machon describes as an authentic human connection precisely because such a high stakes situation with a stranger is unlikely in my day-to-day life. This is not to say that the experience was more real than real life. Nevertheless, such intensely heightened pretending brought me into real human contact with another person. If I encountered such a situation in the real world, I would be implicated in something for which I would need to immediately alert authorities. By encountering it in the world of make-believe, I can arguably engage more deeply in the experience, become implicated, and experience a real adrenaline rush.

I also experienced this intense intimacy in Punchdrunk's *The Drowned Man*. A man dressed as a doctor took me by the hand, locked me in a small room that reeked of rubbing alcohol, and proceeded to whisper urgently and kiss my cheek while I listened to other audience members rattle the doorknob, trying to enter. The theatrical frame of the experience meant that I could act like a bold protagonist: I engaged in calculated risks that I would not carry out in the real world. Because of the safety frame of the theatre, I was able to take chances and embark on risky adventures. Again, this intense experience with a stranger was beyond the realm of my real "workaday" life, but it still felt real in terms of the risk I encountered in engaging with a real stranger. As Felix Barrett, artistic director of Punchdrunk, describes, "A lot of what we are excited about is heightening real life – how can you feel as though you're the hero of your own movie,"[24] echoing the impressions of singularity, individuality, and heroism I experienced as an audience member engaged in this "heightening of real life."

It cannot be ignored how well these descriptions of immersive experiences as single-person journeys follow notions of neoliberal principles through their necessary individualism and risk-for-reward structuring. Alston has thoroughly examined this argument. He maintains that situating immersive theatre within an economy of neoliberal principles affects the form of the artwork itself. Alston articulates the ways in which immersive theatre can be co-opted by a neoliberal agenda that privileges those artists and audiences who are the most fulfilling of the neoliberal tenets of individualism, entrepreneurialism, and self-interest.[25] For instance, the National Theatre's introductory webpage to Punchdrunk's *The Drowned Man* states: "Your curiosity is key. The more you explore, the richer your experience will be. Delve in, be bold, and immerse yourself."[26] Such a command clearly prioritizes autonomous exploration, and it also places the onus of ensuring a positive experience on the consumer rather than on the artwork. In fact, the show encourages independence even before audience members arrive: An e-mail that members receive before they attend encourages parties to separate during the show. The show then effectively forces parties to break up during an elevator ride at the outset of the performance: Only a few audience members are let out at each floor. It also compels audiences to make choices and consider the stakes attached to each decision (e.g., if you explore this room, will you see a key scene, find a hidden clue, or end up far from the action?).

Part of what fosters the neoliberal behaviours that Alston describes is the fact that one-to-one experiences are a significant part of Punchdrunk's work. These intimate experiences are offered to only a few audience members and occur as direct encounters between one performer and one audience member, like my interaction with the doctor related earlier. Many online bloggers describe their desire to have one: "I was dressed in lace, and one of my fellow Execs gave my dress a once over and remarked, 'If you want to be molested by Claude, I'd say tonight's the night.'"[27] That same blogger went on to say, "Which, as you'll see in my next post, is precisely what I set about doing."[28] As these quotes show, guests would even strategize to ensure they received one-to-one experiences. As a first-time visitor, I experienced a one-to-one performance in what felt like an opportunity equally available to all audience members present, but "The opportunity to exploit this selection process [… exists, as] those with enough experience [...] of Punchdrunk's work are more likely to be ahead of the game when it comes to exploiting participatory opportunity."[29] I believe that the drive to have a one-to-one experience was part of what made people aggressive during *The Drowned Man*. This, coupled with the fact that spectators are requested to wear anonymizing white masks may have liberated their latent aggression and resulted in jostling and racing to achieve the best sightline or get closest to the actors. The audience's desire to "win" a one-to-one experience or the best sightline to watch a scene prompted audience members to be in it for themselves. Keren Zaiontz writes about what she calls presumptive intimacy in immersive theatre, which "fosters an explicit lack of generosity that ensures that the spectator maintains her place at the centre of her own singular journey."[30] This seems fitting when considering the experience cultivated by immersive theatre in which the audience member is the star of a journey that fosters epic intimacy through a highly detailed alternative world: an experience of individuated consumption that cannot help but reflect neoliberal principles.

In contrast to the highly detailed set, one-to-one performances, and free-wandering audience components of Punchdrunk and *Brantwood*, however, *TomorrowLove™*'s set is bare, it offers no one-to-one experiences, and audience members are not permitted to explore the space independently. To begin with a consideration of the set itself, *TomorrowLove™* uses the site of the "Aorta," an empty former funeral home north of the city centre in Toronto that was renamed for the show. The space felt much like a sprawling maze, with several small rooms, staircases, and narrow hallways branching off from a large central chapel. The rooms were not heavily altered from their original state, aside from being painted white. They were also left essentially empty, with only slightly theatrical lighting effects creating washes of pink and blue. Each scene made use of only one prop that was in some way representative of the story. For example, a small, handheld rocket ship was the designated prop for a story about a full-grown adult who travels in space in order to minimize the age difference between himself and the twelve-year-old child to whom he has pledged his love. There were no additional set decorations or props save for differently coloured tape lines that served as directions or pathways for the different stories (see example in the lower centre of figure 5.2). Cushman decided against creating a highly detailed set with many props and set pieces – one that would be ripe for exploration by the audience members. Instead, he pursued a "blank" or "bare" aesthetic.[31] He articulated his thoughts about this set aesthetic for *TomorrowLove™* as follows:

> Hopefully at a base level, when you're actually in the room with the material, it is achieving a real kind of intimacy because it's so bare. We knew we didn't want to do anything with the sets. We wanted to keep the audience to twenty to twenty-five people at a time so that you are – yeah, I just feel like, both for the actors and the audience there's sort of nowhere to hide. So, the reason I got interested in doing this kind of work in the first place was having some really affecting experiences as an audience member in some really intimate found spaces that I felt like were just so different from how I – from the barriers I put despite myself in a more traditional theatre space.[32]

Figure 5.2 Performers Paul Dunn and Katherine Cullen amidst the "barebones" aesthetic of the set and space in *TomorrowLove™*, December 2016

One reviewer, J. Kelly Nestruck, negatively critiqued Cushman's aesthetic choice in *TomorrowLove™*:

> Cushman has done impressive immersive work before with *Vitals*, his previous collaboration with [playwright Rosamund] Small, and the extraordinary *Brantwood*, a musical-theatre flash mob that took over an entire school in Oakville. *TomorrowLove™* seems a step back, in a way – staged in chilly rooms painted white and filled with folding chairs. The site is as non-specific as the writing. If the novelty of trudging up and down stairs between scenes has worn off for you, you might wonder why you're not immersed in a comfortable theatre seat somewhere for an hour and a half.[33]

Precisely because Cushman's stark departure from the usual tenets of immersive theatre may seem strange, it is important to consider its effect. *TomorrowLove™*'s "non-specific" set reinforces the show's central conceit by drawing attention to relationships with others and to

Constructing Immersive Experiences for "Real" Engagement   161

Figure 5.3 Performers Anand Rajaram and Oyin Oladejo perform in front of audience members in *TomorrowLove™*, December 2016

relationality in general. With its bare aesthetic, there was less to attend to within the space; consequently, audience attention was trained on other audience members and the actors. This is not to say that all the apparatuses of theatre (e.g., lighting, set, and sound) are distinct components that vie independently for our attention (rather than as parts of a conceptual whole); instead, it points to the convention in immersive theatre of having sets that are detailed to explicitly allow for audience members to focus on and explore the materiality of the space. For instance, when a relative attended Punchdrunk's *The Drowned Man*, she spent a significant amount of time reading letters that she pulled from a mailbox on the set. She favoured this over following a performer around the space.[34] In *TomorrowLove™*, by contrast, with the absence of detailed set pieces to attend to and experience, audience attention was directed at the only other thing filling the space: the other human bodies contained within.

As described by two audience members, the lack of detail actually fostered a sense of intimacy:

AUD 3g: You feel like you're on a journey because you're moving through things and it's very intimate because you're right there with them instead of – as they were saying about props – you're really watching their face because, it feels to me like it's about the acting and not the set, the grandeur, not the room. It's really about what's happening. And that's what a relationship is. It's really about what's happening and you're just waiting for those key lines. Because you're right there.

AUD 3c: [...] It was very naked.[35]

The particular word choice "naked," is interesting. It connotes intimacy, vulnerability, and realness, all of which the show's narrative, with its exploration of relationships, investigates. The audience member's comment, "That's what a relationship is. It's really about what's happening and you're just waiting for those key lines," is likewise significant since it points to the actors' performances as the show's most important element. These descriptions highlight the kind of implicit relationship encouraged between the audience members and the actors – a relationship in which the audience members are poised, waiting to receive important communication from the actors. The ways in which the audience–performer relationships develop are also significant because they occur with a proximity that replicates human interactions in the real world. In other words, audiences and performers are not divided like they would be in a conventional theatre piece, where the audience sits in front of the stage and the actors remain on the stage. This proximity distinguishes their relationship from that which would (or, rather, would not) be developed in other theatres. Not only is the actor in a different position, literally closer to the audience and thus inviting a different relationship, but the audience too is, according to Cushman, in a physical and psychological space in which the "barriers" of the "traditional theatre space" have been lifted. Rather than "the set, the grandeur ... the room" being the focal point, the audience member is focused on the face of the actor. The focus is *here*, in the scene playing out in front of the audience; there is no need to seek it elsewhere.

This also distinguishes *TomorrowLove*™ from other immersive theatre experiences in other ways. In *Brantwood* and *The Drowned Man*, there is always the potential that a better, more exciting piece of action is happening elsewhere – one that spectators must seek out, which resulted for me in a constant sort of hurrying through the space. In

TomorrowLove™, the audience cannot leave the space of the scene partway. As a result, audience members can concentrate fully on the two actors. While this is far less emancipatory, it is a departure from the neoliberal-inflected, "every-person-for-themself" chasing that other immersive theatre productions encourage. The smaller scale and proximity of the piece, coupled with its relative barrenness, communicates that the experience the spectators are seeking is right in front of them: There is no need to compete for the intimate one-to-one experience because this is as intimate, personal, and intense as it will get – fitting for a piece that examines relationships. Rather than encouraging the kind of entrepreneurial spirit that *Brantwood* or Punchdrunk productions foster, the staging choices for *TomorrowLove™* meant that the other human beings in the room were hyper-visible. This visibility in turn discouraged competitive individualism.

There were also no one-to-one performances in *TomorrowLove™*: no instances in which an audience member is selected and separated from the other audience members to have a special experience without other spectators. Instead, the moments identified by audience members as being most intimate during interviews with me often *involved* other audience members. For example, in one interactive moment between two scenes, the audience was asked to work together to pass a prop around a small room. One audience member commented on these collaborations as follows:

> AUD 5b: It's moments that you share with people that are more intimate in a way. Especially in smaller groups. During this one, I had to get in a very tight, claustrophobic room and have a very like selective, singular moment with one of the characters and it was way more unique than usual.[36]

I initially took this response to mean that the audience member had had a one-to-one performance (based on their description of a "singular moment"). However, when I asked for more details, they offered this clarification:

> AUD 5b: We were in the room and [the performer] was playing with his spaceship and the lights were going off like I'd say, I'd say it's kind of a supernova like style up at the ceiling and we all just got to pass along this spaceship while we waited for the next scene change.[37]

The audience member actually highlights the teamwork required in sharing this one prop. While this is not a one-to-one performance, it is nevertheless intimate. I also often observed different audience members showing care for one another by notifying each other of low ceilings or holding curtains open for one another. In the final scene of the performance, wherein everyone returns to the central chapel, actors took turns reading cards on which audience members had written what they love about someone else. In this action, diverse members were united in their listening to others' love notes.

This consistent collaboration among the audience also resulted in a more explicit awareness of each other. When I asked a group of audience members how real they felt the production was, one of them responded:

> I found what really made things really real, um, was there was the performances which obviously had emotional uh realness and connection, but then those moments in between where you're walking with the audience members and you can look and you see the relationships between the people that you're travelling with and that sort of had – there was this lovely duality and really creating, that made it, it made it more real. You know we're talking about people, and we're talking about relationships, and you see people who are obviously partners rubbing each other's' backs as they're walking to the next story and it was like – yeah that was, that really lovely duality to that.[38]

This audience member highlights actions of care-giving between the audience members who, unlike in Punchdrunk with the use of anonymizing masks, were clearly visible along with their interconnections and relationships, even "rubbing each other's backs." As such, the intimacy in *TomorrowLove™* was not cultivated by individual, one-to-one experiences wherein other audience members were absent from the moment. Instead, intimacy was cultivated through relationship-building *between* audience members. What is more, the absolute visibility of the other audience members put that intimacy on display.

In most Punchdrunk shows, as well as in *Brantwood*, the invitation to explore is implicit: Spectators are freely released into a highly detailed world, which they are encouraged to survey. By contrast, the navigation in *TomorrowLove™* is explicit. While audiences for *Brantwood* and *The Drowned Man* were free to wander the space and investigate on their own, *TomorrowLove™*'s audience members were required to follow an actor through the space. Of course, following an actor is possible in both *Brantwood* and *The Drowned Man* but not explicitly required. Thus, though it was an individual decision-making process of which actor to follow, *TomorrowLove™* fostered relationship-building insofar as audience members *had* to embark on a deliberate journey with others, following a single actor but also accompanying other audience members.

Because of this necessity of moving in a group, individual audience members were compelled to consider their own presence in relation to others. Most obviously, in selecting an actor to follow, the audience was engaging in the beginning of a relationship. It is worth sharing here two separate interview sessions, in which participants collectively articulated relationship-building between the actor they chose to follow throughout the space and themselves:

> AUD 3b: I felt a deeper connection to the actors as well. We actually ended up following the same actor the entire way. After a couple of scenes with him I was like, "I can't, I can't leave this guy!" I want to follow his story.
> AUD 3a: You get attached!
> AUD 3d: Yeah, me too.
> AUD 3e: And even, they're not all same characters. They're different characters in different rooms, but you still feel like-
> AUD 3d: You get attached. You're like, yeah that's my guy. And follow him around.[39]

The next night a group of audience members again brought up the idea of creating a relationship with the actor they decided to follow:

> AUD 5a: And it's like you're following, you're going on this journey with someone. You're not just watching at a distance.
> AUD 5b: Yeah I didn't want to break away from the person.
> AUD 5a: Yeah I followed, we followed the same person. So we watched like an evolution of like different, just like the different –
> AUD 5b: I couldn't break up with him (laughing).[40]

The language of relationships is clearly in operation in these conversations, as audience members describe a sense of loyalty and commitment to the actor. This echoes Rose Biggin's similar finding in an examination of fan mail sent to Punchdrunk, in which the notion of building a relationship with a particular performer, usually in a one-to-one experience, was prevalent in her data.[41] What is notable in *TomorrowLove™* is that there were no individuated experiences or one-or-ones to craft the kinds of intensely intimate encounters that Biggin's fans report. Further, the actors in *TomorrowLove™* changed characters from scene to scene – the actor did not maintain a continuous fictional identity – and despite this, individual audience members still felt loyal to a single actor. They couldn't "break up with him." Instead of the heroic journey of the individual explorer (that is, the audience member in their explorer persona), the audience members describe the process of a journey with someone. For one audience member, this act of journeying together sparked a reflection on her own relationships with others outside of the theatrical space: "Well, going back to choosing who to follow, there was an emotional component to that too, because um the first scene I saw was one girl was getting rejected while the other one was doing the rejecting and at the end when you choose who to follow I ended up choosing the girl who got rejected and I ended up staying with her the entire time. It's kind of – maybe that tells me a little bit about me, you know?"[42] Again *TomorrowLove™* manages to encourage interrelations between and among audience members and actors. In fact, one audience member explicitly described the journey as its own kind of relationship building:

AUD 3g: I felt that moving also felt like a relationship. Because a relationship is chaotic … And it just feels like life, like when you're trying to relate and you're just moving and you're saying yeah but you like – and then you jump. I felt that. Like I felt that, that craziness. There's no sanity in love, like there's no –
KJ: *It physicalizes it?*
AUD 3g: Yeah.[43]

It is clear that the physical effect of moving through the space in *TomorrowLove™* is different from the wandering that is possible in *Brantwood* or *The Drowned Man*: In *TomorrowLove™* I cannot wander aimlessly as a spectator; instead, I have to choose to follow a specific actor down a specific path. I have no way of knowing where the actor might take me or what scene or activity might follow. This meant that there was still an insecure element in the wandering – as there might be in *Brantwood* or *The Drowned Man*. But it nevertheless fostered a specific kind of relationship-building that wasn't possible in those other shows. By following someone, I was implicitly trusting that they would take me on the "right" journey. I was also a part of a team of journeyers, led as a group and often involved as a group, even in activities as simple as holding a curtain open for each other or offering a hand to an elderly group member as we descended stairs.

Audience members from *TomorrowLove™* frequently described the act of decision making as integral to the feeling of being on a journey:

> AUD 3b: Traditional theatre really needs that deep, rich story to be able to take you on the journey, while I felt here we were physically going on that journey. It [*TomorrowLove™*] just created that wonderfully.
> [...]
> AUD 3d: So if you would stay in some significant place through the whole show it would be like um the place is not real. And in this it always evolves and changes so you feel like you are going somewhere to see something. You're not just watching different stories in some place.
> KJ: *You're making a choice.*[44]

It was this journeying that created a sense of realness for some audience members: They felt they were "going somewhere to see something." I shared this sense of purpose in my experience as an audience member: During one performance, I made my way upstairs, downstairs, through large, cold, industrial rooms and tiny cozy spaces, sometimes moving straight into a scene and other times being asked to complete some kind of activity before proceeding. No matter the place or the action, I maintained a sense of purpose throughout the journey because I was making decisions about which actor to follow, even though I never knew what might happen next and had to willingly accept the unknown. The site became, essentially, maze-like: not knowing what came next or where a trail might lead but with an ultimate goal in mind. In her writing about interactive audience-centred experience, Esther Belvis Pons describes how "Mazes offer intricate experiences that play with mirroring effects and create disorienting situations; the strange and the familiar are counterparts in the perennially interrupted desire to reach the exit. Mazes evoke restlessness, risk, and mystery through their whimsical, interconnected pathways. They are intrinsically immersive as, once inside, we are fully committed to their possibilities."[45] Audience members similarly pointed to the feeling of insecurity created by the space's several rooms, staircases, and narrow hallways:

> KJ: *And does the particular staging of the show add to or take away from the sense of the real? ... Why?*
> AUD 3g: Mystery. I didn't know where I was being taken. Is it going to end now, or is it going to build? Is it going to get more intimate or is it going to turn into a [large] cast now? Or is it – I just had no idea what was going on. [laughs] It was exciting.[46]

Notably, the audience member quoted above laughs and describes how the insecurity of the maze-aesthetic was "exciting." Rather than the insecurity of the unknown producing fear or danger, the disorientation was pleasurable for the audience member. Audiences may not have had any idea what was going to happen next, but the suspense was not unbearable because they were in it together, with other audience members. The space, then, contributed to a sense of realness by requiring real navigation and invoking real unknowns: The audience members were really ignorant about what they might encounter next as they made their way physically through the site. This insecurity and lack of knowing could, in turn, lead to the creation of further relationships. As Bill Mitchell, one of the artistic directors of immersive theatre company Wildworks puts it, in the act of moving through an immersive space, the audience member transforms into percipient, becoming: "more alert, looking for clues. They are insecure, unsure of what might happen next. Their senses are heightened. They are more aware of each other and become a temporary community experiencing something new together."[47] In *TomorrowLove™*, the maze-like aesthetic and the requirement to choose and follow (and trust) an actor facilitated the creation of small communities or teams. This is not to say that the same kind of community building is not possible in other immersive theatre: Immersive shows often encourage or result in group travel when several spectators follow the same performer out of interest. What distinguishes *TomorrowLove™* from, for example, Punchdrunk is the explicit orchestration of group movement: audience members *must* move in groups.

This eschewing of unguided individual exploration in favour of following a specific person in *TomorrowLove™* changes the notion of the journey for audience members by encouraging a constant negotiation of one's own experience in response to others: I cannot pause on the stairs to examine something as I would hold up my group, or I might alert my fellow audience members to the low-hanging ceiling they are about to encounter. We move as a part of a collective of mutual concern. As audience members highlighted, this experience resulted in a heightened awareness of one's perceived "place" in both the real world of the set and the fictional play world:

> AUD 3d: And you don't just watch something, you became a part of this experience. When you walk around with the actors. And when you're in the room and they're fighting, you don't actually do that when real people fight in their relationships. And I think this is important because you are actually a part of that fight when you're there.
> KJ: *You feel sort of implicated I guess.*
> AUD 3d: Yeah.[48]

The lack of individual navigation offers the potential for a relationship-building experience precisely because it demands the relinquishing of control. You are not solely responsible for giving yourself the best experience; you are not alone in seeking, searching, risking, and exploring, as in usual first-person immersive tactics. Instead, you follow a collective that both increases the perceived safety of the moment and invites a relationality.

The ways in which *TomorrowLove™* enacts relationality through group-navigation also highlights how the show requires a constant negotiation between the real and not real. The production encourages relationships that may be either temporary or lasting, from the fictive or the real world. These relationships are either forged within the confines of the play world (as audience members follow their favourite actor) or brought into the space from the real world (as spectators come with partners, friends, children, and dates). The space feels resultantly real-ish, a quality of being that was explained by audience members as a "different reality":

> AUD 2e: Well, I feel like real is immersed. Which is one way maybe of talking about it. And I kind of get lost in this building, it's very – I don't know if I could find my way to rooms I was in. And that was a way of – even as I was going the scenes were interrupted I

still felt like I was in a space that was created apart from the world and I was kind of sunk into it. So that's not real, but it's immersed in a different reality.

KJ: *It feels real?*

AUD 2e: It feels real and in a way it – sometimes you want the reality that you're going to in the theatre to not be the one you experience every day. You obviously want it to be a space that is kind of foreign to you and this felt like a very foreign space, not only because it's in a different time in some cases but also, it's very, you don't spend time in a funeral home very often.[49]

This establishment of an entire world – a "reality," as the audience member describes it above – compels the audience to explore it. While this may seem to suggest at best a virtual reality or hyperreal world, this mode of experiencing is actually most similar to an audience member's other main experience of being a first-person-player: the real world. As Carl Lavery argues in his ecological understanding of audience participation, we are already always immersed in real life.[50] The human condition is one of sensory immersion, so the key to immersive theatre and its thrilling immersion is a change in immersive medium. Schulze articulates this connection between immersive production and real life by stating that "the appeal to individual perception, narration and interpretation, which often closely links the life of the spectator to the spectacle on stage, is one fairly prominent strategy of metareference that is able to effect authenticity."[51] In other words, navigating an immersive "other" reality feels in many ways similar to navigating one's current reality. When these two worlds or realities collide, they become less defined, more porous, and more unstable; they allow an invasion of each into the other and a sense of real-ish-ness: something that feels real even if it is not entirely so.

An example of this friction between the real and not-real can be found in the fact that the site of *TomorrowLove™* was a former funeral home. Producer Michelle Yagi described in an interview one particular instance in which a patron requested a refund because the funeral home was, for them, a site with many personal memories attached to it involving the death of a loved one. As such, they did not feel comfortable attending a theatrical performance there.[52] Cushman similarly pointed to the pervasiveness of the space's former life as a funeral home in his interview:

I mean, the most complicated part of the project was finding the space to do it in. We knew we were looking for somewhere that would have a number of different spaces that could function kind of independent from one another. We knew that sound bleed was going to be really important to control, as was audience flow. And we didn't set out looking for a funeral home, but when we found this space, it was just so perfect in terms of – it had that – I don't think we ever could have dreamed of a space that would have that kind of, that central chapel in terms of what that offered in the beginning and end of the experience. We tried to, I mean, yeah, my goal was not necessarily – I mean, we didn't keep it a secret that it was a funeral home, but we did consciously sort of rename and try to change the aesthetic of the space as much as possible. I kind of felt that the ideal was that people showed up and there was an uncanny thing that they felt like they had been in a place like this before and also that they hadn't. And that was something, to think about a place that has disassociation and an atmosphere and aura that you can't quite place that felt relevant and connected to the idea that we were trying to depict: the future.[53]

By contrast, *Brantwood* utilized a real school that was being demolished, which was precisely the location in which the story was set. The show's use of a real former school allowed for a potent bleeding through – of the real world into the story world – which invoked memories or nostalgia. After all, the site of a generic former school potentially carries baggage for all those who are familiar with the spatial "genre" of public-school buildings. In Punchdrunk's productions, the real identity of the spaces they use is not apparent. For example, there is nothing in the expansive 1950s set of the *The Drowned Man* that would point to or reveal the building's former use as a mail-sorting facility. *TomorrowLove™*, is unique in its creation of an "other world" because the real site conflicts with its fictional site, and the real site has not been entirely concealed. The former funeral home bears no relevance to the stories being told, except in so far as the mood induced permeates the story world. As one audience member articulated:

AUD 2g: The last scene we saw was about an app that would let you communicate with your loved ones after death, and I thought that was really interesting, given the space we were in. We were in

the basement which almost felt like, this is going to sound really creepy, I think it might be an embalming room.
AUD 2a: I thought it was an embalming room.
AUD 2g: So I thought that was cool and I almost wished that they played with the fact that this was a funeral home more. And maybe played on what might have happened throughout time in each of these rooms. So that's another story.[54]

In some ways, then, *TomorrowLove™* did not entirely ignore the building's former status in making use of its atmospheric impact, but the show is nevertheless neither site-specific nor even site-responsive. And yet, the real history of the building manages to bleed through into the performance. This company uses this irruption of a particular real – the previous function of the building – primarily for its capacity to induce affect. The atmosphere and mood evoked by the embalming room creates a particular kind of affect that is effective on a visceral or bodily level, rather than on any kind of intellectual or narrative level. This unsettling experiencing of the real within the fictive generates a strong emotional response in turn. To put it differently, the immersivity of the experience establishes an "other world," with its own time and space. This "other world," however, is still subject to moments in which the real world appears to invade it. This is in part because both are experienced in the same "first-person player" perspective. Spaces of immersive performance can thus end up straddling worlds and enacting an unsettling relationship between the fictive and the real.

Using Foucault's concept of heterotopia can help illustrate how the real/unreal nature of the performance space might impact audience behaviour. Analyzing Punchdrunk shows, Schulze describes them as "spaces that are closer to utopia or dystopia than to the real world but have nonetheless gained a partial existence in it ... a space in between fact and fiction."[55] These sites of performance, in other words, are fictional places whose existence is based in the real world or, following Foucault's analysis, are the partial realization of fiction in the real world.[56] Schulze utilizes Foucault's definition of heterotopias as "countersites, a kind of effectively enacted utopia in which the real sites, all the other real sites that can be found within the culture, are simultaneously represented, contested, and inverted"[57] to argue that immersive performance spaces can change visitors' behaviour because these are worlds in which different rules apply than in the real world.[58] Immersive theatre, he writes, "allows for strong emotional responses and for different behaviour than in normal life."[59] In Punchdrunk's *The Drowned Man* I may be inclined to describe my experience of the space as espousing a very neoliberal set of rules in which the "best person wins," exaggerating (or making more visible to me) the existing power and social structures in the present-day zeitgeist and thus impacting my behaviour. *TomorrowLove™* conversely created a series of rules that centred on relations to others. I was more aware of the other audience members as I moved throughout the building, and I was conscious of the role I played in selecting what actors to follow, therefore moderating my behaviour appropriately so as to not negatively impact other spectators' experiences. The unique configuration of *TomorrowLove™* thus encouraged a particular kind of heterotopia to engage in, which in turn prompted a more affective, relational response from audience members.

One of the more pressing outcomes of immersive theatre having garnered a "partial existence" in the real world (to follow Schulze) is the potential for it to invoke real emotion. Take, for instance, the one-to-one performances in Punchdrunk in which the spectator's white, anonymizing mask is removed. This is in direct violation of the rules of engagement that spectators of Punchdrunk shows are told, including one that specifically prohibits removing one's mask. Of this moment, White writes that "[The performers] report that they are often resisted, and when they do succeed in removing [the mask] they might be met with tears, confessions, and sometimes anger. In these moments, they have achieved an intimacy, which is sometimes disturbing to both parties, and which brings into question that this work is as purely escapist as they believe it is."[60] What White highlights is a real emotional response to a highly constructed world and set of rules. As Schulze goes on to describe, "the fun of exploration can quickly turn from amusing game to a situation of very real emotional turmoil."[61] This is the possible effect of interplay between unreal and real: When I have my mask on, I am not real and am playing a part, but when my mask is removed, I become real – or at least, more real than I was previously.

I posit that the highly controlled and highly intimate encounters possible in immersive theatre can in fact be characterized as extra real rather than real or, as Lois Keidan from the Live Arts Development Agency articulates it, "more real than real life."[62] After all, in the real world I would not regularly have encounters in which I am locked in a room with a stranger, as I have already argued above. In the unreal context of the immersive play world, the real actually becomes extra-real and resultantly extra-affective. In the real world I do not wear a mask. However, because I began with a mask in the fictional world and it has now been taken away, I feel its absence more. Of course, in *TomorrowLove™* there are no masks, but the space itself manages to invite a similar kind of affective experience. The former funeral home bleeds through the fictional story world in a visceral way – one that is felt without necessarily being analyzed. While the space has been designed to facilitate the audience's understanding of it in relation to the story world as a futuristic, minimalistic place, it nevertheless generates its own independent effect because of its history as a real funeral home. Being in a funeral home can be unnerving regardless of one's experience with death. Experiencing those unnerving feelings without the knowledge of the real history of the site works to heighten its uncanniness. Frictions with the real-world space thus craft an extra-real or extra-affective experience for *TomorrowLove™*.

TomorrowLove™ both replicates and subverts many of the markers of immersive theatre by virtue of its unique use of space. The set is not intricately detailed like those of *Brantwood* and *The Drowned Man*. Its relative simplicity means that audience members will potentially focus on other audience members and the actors rather than on the set. Additionally, they will aim their attention at building relationship(s) with their fellow audience members and the actors. The realness of the space and its historical usage as a funeral home also manages to permeate into the alternate reality of the story world, thereby creating potent affective responses. Furthermore, the space is large, inviting audiences to explore. Their journey through this space, however, is not so much an individual's heroic journey. Instead, it is one that invites observation and reinforces the virtues of instigating or reinforcing relationships with "the people you're travelling with,"[63] as one audience member put it. In this way, *TomorrowLove™* extends beyond the individualistic timbre of Punchdrunk and encourages an awareness of relationality.

REAL BODIES, REAL SENSATIONS, REAL TIMES

As suggested by my earlier descriptions of *Brantwood* and *The Drowned Man*, immersive performance often includes everything from touching and being touched, to smelling, moving, seeing, and sometimes even tasting. In considering the operation of time in immersive theatre, as well as the genre's creation and use of realness, it is necessary to examine how spectator bodies are used differently in immersive theatre than they are in proscenium or other conventional theatres and to consider how this different bodily engagement creates a different temporal impression. In light of the multi-sensory experience immersive theatre offers, the usual terms "audience" or "spectator" may seem insufficient since the immersive theatre experience often demands the engagement of the whole body. Machon, for instance, states that while conventional performance typically prioritizes visual spectacle or auditory quality, the priority placed on the olfactory, aural, and tactile is one of the clear distinctions of immersive theatre.[64] Elinor Fuchs similarly posits the necessary acknowledgement of the full-body quality of immersive theatre: "In the conventional theatre I am 'audience' or 'spectator', all ears or all eyes, and otherwise cut off from the full response of my body. But *Tamara* [an immersive theatre show] wants my body."[65] Finally, Alston offers a tentative definition of immersive theatre as a genre which "may be distinguished by the sensory acts that it demands of audiences, such as touching and being touched, tasting, smelling and moving": live acts of sensory experience that occur in real time.[66]

In *Brantwood*, I was able to explore two floors of a real school, slated for demolition, ranging from classrooms to the cafeteria, from asphalt areas outside to a closet under the stairs. I was free to follow characters or wander independently and use any or all of my five senses to investigate anything that crossed my path, from library books to cafeteria hot dogs. In light of all this, as Fuchs suggests, perhaps the term "consumer" is more appropriate than "audience" or "spectator" when it comes to immersive theatre – or Fuchs aptly calls it "shopping theatre."[67] Audiences affect the performance when they, like consumers, touch, take, feel, smell, taste, see, hear, and move around the immersive environment, sometimes literally consuming the materials of the set. In this way, immersive theatre both acts on the body vis-à-vis the senses and is acted upon by the bodies of the audience members as they consume and experience it through all their senses. This allows audiences to craft their own, unique experiences that feel real precisely because they are engaging with audiences' real sensory organs. The connection to consumerism is particularly apt: economists B. Joseph Pine II and James Gilmore in *The Experience Economy: Work Is Theater & Every Business a Stage* argue that ideal commodification is no longer tied to physical takeaway objects but rather to full sensory experiences, actually making immersive experiences even more attractive than material goods to modern audiences.[68] In fact, Pine and Gilmore's experience economy actually replaces tangible objects altogether, substituting the term "commodity" with "experience."[69] From voluntourism to "brand experience" stores, realness-as-experience seems to be the newest prized commodity, and its popularity within the theatre world is no different.

The effect of this real bodily engagement implies a certain kind of relationship with notions of liveness. Liveness, it is well known, has been a point of contention in performance studies but remains one of the core, identifiable qualities of performance as an art form. Peggy Phelan in her seminal text *Unmarked: The Politics of Performance* writes that "Performance's only life is in the present. Performance cannot be saved, recorded, documented, or otherwise participate in the circulation of representations *of* representations: once it does so, it becomes something other than performance."[70] By utilizing an intensely sensory experience, immersive theatre seems unequivocally ephemeral. After all, audience members in immersive theatre can be observed moving, touching, eating, and smelling – all basic bodily functions that can only occur in real time. Each distinct sensory moment is so fleeting and unique that even if one were to exactly retrace their steps, they would experience the same thing in a slightly different manner. Fuchs actually argues for an implicit connection between liveness and sensuality, based on Elaine Scarry's explication of the word "presence," highlighting its etymological roots in prae-sens: "that which stands before the senses."[71] Machon similarly notes that, "What is clear is that the sensual worlds created exploit the power of live performance. Immersive practice harnesses the lasting ephemerality of performance as an artistic medium of expression."[72] The perceptual liveness, then, of immersive theatre, is partially achieved through utilizing real sensory experiences that occur in real time and are ephemeral: if I eat this veggie dog in *Brantwood* I am really eating, in real time – and irrevocably consuming this prop such that no one else can eat it. For Phelan, this is where performance's power lies: in its refusal to be repeatable. She goes so far as to invoke economic terminology to point to performance's separation from the economy "Performance clogs the smooth machinery of reproductive representation ... Performance resists the balanced circulations of finance. It saves nothing; it only spends."[73] The perceptual liveness, then, of immersive theatre, which it achieves through utilizing real sensory experiences that occur in real time, heightens its realness because of its unrepeatability.

All the above notwithstanding, audiences often desire to attend immersive theatre performances more than once. Punchdrunk's *Sleep No More* and *The Drowned Man* both have active online communities in which bloggers describe upwards of seventeen trips to *The Drowned Man*.[74] Tara Isabella Burton profiles a "superfan" called Jim Stark who now creates his own immersive one-to-one performances after having attended *Sleep No More* eighty-eight times[75] and Rose Biggin in her book on Punchdrunk's audiences suggests that there are audience members who have seen Punchdrunk's *Sleep No More* more than one hundred times.[76] In other words, even though one of immersive theatre's defining features is its ephemerality, audience-consumers buy (or even create, as in Jim Stark's case) "reproductions" of their original experience by attending the ostensibly same event multiple times. In fact, the means by which immersive theatre is able to create an ephemeral experience may paradoxically be the same means by which it becomes a reproducible experience for the audience.

Turning to *TomorrowLove™*, the show arguably makes less use of sensory engagement than other immersive theatre might. With its lack of a highly detailed set, there was nothing for audiences to eat or smell and very little for us to actually touch. However, if we distill the impact of the sensorial in *Brantwood* or *The Drowned Man*, the effect seems to be the creation of a highly unique experience for each audience member that is so unrepeatable that, paradoxically, it encourages attendees to repeat the experience. Accordingly, when asked about what made the performances of *TomorrowLove™* particularly unique, interesting, or important, many audiences highlighted the show's similar repeatability/unrepeatability paradox by remarking on the way in which it compelled audiences to want to see it more than once:

> AUD 1g: I think the multiple story lines, like the different things that could be happening that played out in many different ways makes it a very unique play and if I had endless money I would have purchased tickets to visit it again.
>
> KJ: *Yeah, there's definitely a craving for more, or at least that's what I felt.*
>
> AUD 1a: Uh, I think the app story that I just watched, about the app for death or whatever it was, you didn't pick it up initially –

[reacting to another audience member's inaudible reaction] I know right?

AUD 1C: I'm like, what part was that, I didn't see that![77]

Just like in Punchdrunk shows or *Brantwood*, the fact that the show could potentially be different upon repeat visits cultivated an attractive individuation of the experience. Of course, this paradox resonates with the anomaly of an actor performing the same part differently at each performance of a more conventional show and thus having a different embodied experience each night, despite performing the same role over and over. The difference is that this experience is typically limited to the actor, not the audience.

TomorrowLove™ capitalized on this potential for audiences to have several different experiences of the same show by running a contest: Audience members who completed their "bingo card," which signified their having seen all fifteen possible scenes, were entered into a draw to win theatre tickets for a different production. Each time an audience member attended *TomorrowLove™*, they would see only three or four of the fifteen possible vignettes, depending on which actors they followed at what point in the show. In order to complete the bingo card audience members would need to attend the show multiple times, attempting to follow different actors in different orders. This ability to repeat the experience differently, or, rather, to revel in its unrepeatability, thus drew audiences back to the show in order to experience scenes they had not yet encountered. Unlike conventional, non-immersive productions where repeat visits result in one's viewing essentially the same show, audiences cannot risk boredom through repetition in *TomorrowLove™*. In other words, the show made use of the singular experience of "real" time to invite audiences to return multiple times.

While other immersive theatre experiences, such as Punchdrunk shows or *Brantwood* also vary widely on account of different audience members' varying activations of the senses, or how they choose to move around the space, *TomorrowLove™*'s unrepeatability was more explicit. This was in part a result of its use of game and chance in a highly overt way: As described above, the show begins with a carefully choreographed dance in which the actors continually switch partners until a button is pushed. Then, in the pairs they find themselves in, they officially begin the show by leaving the dancing area with a portion of the audience. Depending on who audiences follow, the scenes they watch will be completely different from ones they have previously experienced as well as from ones that others are contemporaneously experiencing. Moreover, since it seems impossible that the button would be pushed at the exact same moment each night, *Tomorrow-Love™* appears to present itself as a game of chance. Of course, the dance is choreographed in such a way that the actors will never be forced into performing a scene they are not prepared for. The gamification of this apparent element of chance, nevertheless, reinforces the apparent uniqueness, and liveness, of the event. One audience member helpfully explained the result of this production choice, speaking about how it personalized the experience: "The personalization. You could come see this twelve, fifteen, twenty times and it's going to be a different show every single time. It's a more personal interaction than I think traditional theatre."[78] The personalization in this instance comes not from a one-to-one performance or intense sensory experience mediated by one's own personal body but from the mathematical gestures of the performance: The possible permutations suggest that the experience an audience member is about to receive is one in 472 (as noted earlier). It is like playing the lottery or otherwise considering the odds insofar as the individual experience you "win" is the result of 1 of 472 possible outcomes. While in a Punchdrunk show one might be able to return even more than 472 times and have a unique experience each time by differently navigating the space, engaging sensorially, following actors, etc., the effect of the gamification in *Tomorrow-Love™* is such that the "edges" of possibility are made clear and the notion of collecting every permutation (or at least all fifteen vignettes) becomes achievable rather than infinite.

Just as the use of space in *TomorrowLove™* promotes relationship building, its different invocation of temporal liveness also highlights relationality over individuality: My experience is partially dependent on when another audience member pushes a button. Especially because this game of chance occurs at the outset of the show, the implication that my experience will be affected by those around me is very clearly underscored. To refer back to the experience created by the space of *TomorrowLove™*, audience members often highlighted the presence of other audience members because of the group-style journeying the show required. My individual experience depends on several uncontrollable factors: it is not just my individual choices respecting where to sit and who to follow that determine the course of events for me but that what happens to me also depends on choices made by the other audience members. Will I be the only person to follow this actor, or will all of us follow her? Will my fellow audience members gamely participate when we have to pass a spaceship between us, or will they resist? Will I see other audience members crying, laughing, or helping each other up and down staircases as we move around the building? My experience is very much based on chance, including not only the button-pushing game of chance at the opening but also the chance that my fellow audience members will behave in different ways each time I attend. Moreover, I might also find myself in a different mood, with a different horizon of expectations, each time I attend. The audience thus becomes an element of the scenographic experience, affecting my experience while I affect theirs.

Immersive theatre's invocation of a sense of liveness, whether through sensory invocation or perceptual chance, imbues the experience with a commodifiable value: It entices audiences to return again and again. Intriguingly, then, immersive theatre commodifies the very aspects of live performance that seem to resist commodification: Philip Auslander's writing on interactive theatre states that "Because they are designed to offer a different experience at each visit, they can be merchandised as events that must be purchased over and over again: the ostensible evanescence and non-repeatability of the live experience ironically become selling points to promote a product that must be fundamentally the same in each of its instantiations."[79] Although Phelan argues that "Performance's independence from mass reproduction, technologically, economically, and linguistically is its greatest strength,"[80] immersive theatre seems to have lighted upon an almost infinitely reproducible model that has audiences repeatedly returning not in spite of the potential re-productions but because of them.

As the preceding paragraphs have established, an immersive theatre experience has the potential to be simultaneously unique and replicable. We can likewise destabilize conceptions of liveness beyond Fuchs's aforementioned insights by suggesting that the term "live" as it relates to immersive is not ontologically intrinsic to the work of art but is rather largely cultivated; in other words, it is a kind of aestheticized realness. Martin Barker, for instance, suggests that the valorization of the spontaneity of live theatre is more affective than actual.[81] This is simply to say that audiences want to experience theatrical events *"as if* they had elements of uniqueness"[82] – even if the actual variations between performances are miniscule. As Rose Biggin writes in her analysis of audience response to Punchdrunk, "It may not matter if the experience created is truly bespoke: what is at stake is that it is *felt* to be personal."[83] It is the *feeling* of personalization that is heralded as a vital aspect of immersive theatre experience.

To return to the perceived game of chance at the outset of *Tomorrow-Love*™, as an audience member I know that the dance is not entirely random; I realize that it must actually be carefully timed and choreographed. I also know that the one-to-one experience I had in *Brantwood* was not unique: a colleague experienced an identical series of events. My one-to-one experience in *The Drowned Man* felt unique because the actor picked me out from a group of masked audience members and then responded to my unique presence and conversation. However, the uniqueness of this one-to-one experience is illusory. In actuality, it is repeated not only every night the show plays but multiple times during the same night. This is because the show operates on a system of performance loops in which characters have a series of scenes they perform repeatedly and in the same order. During a return visit to the show, I actually experienced one small one-to-one performance, in which a greengrocer fed me a single pea, twice in the same night. This of course decreased my perception of it being special since it underscored that my "unique experience" was actually one that has been repeated hundreds of times and to hundreds of people over the course of the run. The feeling of unique privilege and liveness I experienced was not accurate; instead, it was a carefully cultivated aestheticization in which the appearance of uniqueness was reinforced by being alone, being picked, and through my limited improvised interaction with the actor.

This points to liveness as an affective quality, with the potential to be extrinsically crafted and constructed within the minds of the audience. On this subject, Auslander writes, "The emerging definition of liveness may be built primarily around the audience's affective experience. To the extent that websites and other virtual entities respond to us in real time, they *feel* live to us, and this may be the kind of liveness we now value."[84] Following this, it may be argued that immersive theatre often utilizes liveness not necessarily denotatively but rather affectively. Aesthetic tactics make shows *feel* live and thus feel more real. As a result, liveness becomes repeatable and reproducible.

The desire for a repeatable liveness in immersive theatre adumbrates a significant epistemological possibility: that we want the instantaneous to feel potentially repeatable because of our capacity to lose track of time. If we imagine the live to be repeatable, we can minimize the consequences of time passing in a very pleasurable way. From the vast world of 1950s Hollywood in *The Drowned Man*, to the entire school grounds available for roaming in *Brantwood*, part of the enjoyment for spectators seems to come from the ability to inhabit a complete, other world. Schulze articulates: "The key feature of this kind of theatre is ... always the notion of being completely immersed in the performance. In other words, audiences may well lose track of time and space while exploring. They are absorbed in the performance."[85] This results, for Machon, in an altered temporality. Describing her experience of Punchdrunk's 2007 *The Masque of Red Death* she writes, "I realized that three hours had felt like one, had gone without me being in the slightest bit aware of time passing."[86] I also had this experience, in both *Brantwood* and *The Drowned Man*. I felt shocked and saddened to find that my three-hour journey was already over. I was so utterly immersed in the world of "present-ness" – with my senses being constantly stimulated in ways that felt "in-the-moment" – that I had forgotten about the real world and the passage of real time. Confusing my sense of time, too, was my ability to see the same scene enacted over and over. For instance, at one point in my experience at *Brantwood*, I caught part of a school play in the drama classroom. Later, I caught that same school play again, in the same space. The performance acted as a time-vacuum. It defined a new relationship to the passage of time that depended upon loops and repetitions, as well as the aforementioned repeated-spontaneity.

TomorrowLove™ provides an interesting counterpoint to the kind of temporal reconfiguration possible in wholly immersive fictional worlds. An audience member articulated how she felt that she could not be entirely immersed within *TomorrowLove™*'s story world and instead was still very much aware of real time and the real world. This is how she differentiated between *Brantwood* and *TomorrowLove™*. Speaking about *Brantwood*, she described how "that was so fluid, right? Because you could choose one story line and follow it through and there was never like 'Now you choose me or you.'"[87] This is opposed to her experience with *TomorrowLove™* in which she felt that "the realism of the space is interrupted and I'm aware of the fact that they're acting as tour guide ... So I actually found that it was to me far less real, or far less immersive than [*Brantwood*], for sure."[88] She described the result of this less real experience: "I was enjoying it, but I was aware of things like the time and when I had to be back home.

And things like that. Whereas in *Brantwood*, I wasn't aware of time because I was completely immersed in what was going on. And I was acting in it, and that wasn't [what] happened here."[89] In *Brantwood*, audience members could essentially set their own pace, exploring at will. By contrast, *TomorrowLove™* imposed a pace on audiences. Enforcing a pace slow enough that no one was separated or got lost, it mediated when audience members would watch a scene.

Before automatically considering this to be some kind of failure to properly immerse audience members completely into a world, it is worth considering the structure and conceit of *TomorrowLove™* more closely. In particular, the fact that each role in the fifteen two-person scenes was memorized by both a male-identified and a female-identified performer meant that there were four possible performances of each vignette, some depicting heterosexual relationships and some depicting queer relationships. Cushman explained the impetus for this:

> I think hopefully it means you are still watching a scene between two people of different genders, or not necessarily different genders, but two people with ascribed genders, but our hope was that in the back of your mind, knowing the part could be played by other performers, you would question some of the assumptions you were making based on the people in front of you, so I think that was especially true in pieces that involve power dynamics, and also how we see relationships of different sexualities onstage ... And to me it felt current or potentially futuristic in that way, because I think we're still somewhat trapped in a theatre world or an art world where it's rare that we see people who aren't – yeah, throughout it we see – it's weird when we see something that isn't a heterosexual love story where that's not the focus of what it's about in some way or another.[90]

What Cushman seems to be suggesting is the possibility of introducing imagined alternatives and futures not just into the confined immersive world or narrative but also into the wider theatre or art worlds, and even into society at large. Cushman's goal may sound pat, and yet, it may actually be the lack of insularity in the immersion of the piece that allows for this projection onto the outside real world to occur more readily.

In her book on immersive theatre, Josephine Machon records a conversation with Pete Higgin, enrichment director at Punchdrunk. Higgin is describing work undertaken in schools when he expresses how "in such instances the immersive experience is made more intense because the storytelling environment established 'bleeds into the real world' ... ignited by the durational life of the event, whilst also lasting beyond within the imagination and body of the [audience]."[91] This comment resonates with those made by audience members at *TomorrowLove™*. For instance, one audience member brought up the notion of imagining alternative performances as a result of the mix-and-match casting of the show; the show did not entirely plunge her into a separate world such that she lost track of the real world. Instead, there was space for her to think about the real world precisely because she was not fully immersed. While *TomorrowLove™* did not create an entirely enclosed fictional world – and certainly not one solely predicated on the here-and-now of sensory engagement – it was still productive in making room for an audience to consider other times:

AUD 4e: I really like the immersive theatre thing, but also the modular element of it. Where the actors can all be mixed and matched, which, when I'm watching it makes me imagine the other actors performing the same story and how different they might interpret it. And that immediately makes me think of like anyone else performing that story and how that can change it, so it immediately makes you start thinking about each storyline from a lot of different angles while you're watching the one that is happening right now and I thought that was a really interesting element.

KJ: *Does that pull you out of the fiction at all?*

AUD 4e: I don't think so. I think it like adds different levels to it, like it just makes me start thinking that this is how these people are experiencing it and how they're interpreting it but that's not the only way this storyline can be told and the only way it can affect people. And I don't think I've ever approached a theatre performance in that way so consciously while it's being performed. Like afterwards you start thinking about how it could affect other people but me I'm like I just happened to walk into the room with this performer, instead of that performer and that shifted how like that story's being told to me right now.

KJ: *Right, right. Did that make it feel more or less real to you?*

AUD 4e: I think it made it feel more real, really made me deal with the, like, not just the content of the story but how it was being performed for me and I thought that was interesting.[92]

Whereas in *Brantwood* an audience member might imagine the other possible scenes actually playing out around the school while experiencing just one, in *TomorrowLove™* we can do that while at the same time envisioning parallel (virtual) scenes. The audience member quoted above is not explicitly describing the kind of social-good effect that Cushman articulates. However, they posit not just an awareness of alternatives but also a kind of meta-narrative: They were not simply experiencing it; they were also, simultaneously, examining *how* they were experiencing it. There is a kind of multi-temporal awareness here that, rather than simply pulling this audience member out of the fiction, was inviting greater cognitive effort and a consideration of the limits of a singular perception more broadly.

Other audience members also spoke about the ways in which *TomorrowLove™* invited mental exertion on account of its presentation of alternatives. Their descriptions provide evidence of the show's illustration of an expansion of time:

Yeah. For me I could relate to almost everything that I saw so for, like I would be thinking back to oh would I, if I were watching me and like the person that I was involved with doing this, is this how it would sound, is this how it would play out? And then also thinking because this was like multiple people, multiple roles, like if this was a guy and girl how would it play out? If this was two guys or two girls how would this go differently? Like I watched a scene with two girls, a guy and a girl, um same guy different girl so it was, it was a lot. It was a lot to process because I felt it was very real.[93]

This excerpt from an interview highlights the audience member's retrospective temporal orientation (i.e., "thinking back"). It also underscores their prospective orientation (i.e., "how would it play out"). It demonstrates how the show allows for an expansion of experience beyond what one might immediately perceive. This is not to say that conventional immersive performance prohibits the consideration of alternatives. To the contrary, when I attended *The Drowned Man* I was wholly focused on my experience even while I was conscious that I might be missing out on some key scene simultaneously happening elsewhere. To put it differently, when attending Punchdrunk performances, my sense of time was focused on the here-and-now of what was happening within the constructed immersive world, even as I imagined alternatives. After the show, I found myself comparing notes with my theatre-going companions. We considered alternative experiences but with the awareness of the show as a separate, past event. Biggin confirms this phenomenon of comparing notes with fellow audience members in her analysis of Punchdrunk fan mail: audience members might "call upon other audience members to fill them in on the 'other rooms [they] didn't find'" such that "immersive theatrical experience extends beyond the confines of in-the-moment, and beyond the individual."[94] Her words are, interestingly, indicative of potential relationship building that can occur after the show – after one has had the individuated experience as a "lone wolf."[95] What audience members of *TomorrowLove™* suggested, however, was that they were presciently aware of other people, "other times," and "other worlds" – including the real world – even while they were immersed in the story world. In this way, the notion of alternative possibilities was able to bleed into the real world. As an audience member stated,

> I think that the language they use as well is extremely realistic. Like maybe not the spaceships or the mirror thing we keep talking about, but I think that you watch it happen and you think "If I made that choice, if I was going through that" how would that have shifted my life as well. Like you think about those things.[96]

Notably, this audience member is not thinking about other possible scenes but of placing herself in a version of the scene in the real world, in her real life.

This conscious stretching of time was integrated as part of the design intention of the production, and audience members were encouraged to think about the show before and after actually attending it. Cushman described how

> Ideally it would begin even before you buy the ticket, like the first time you hear about the show, so we really tried to integrate our branding and our marketing to the feel of the show. We shot a virtual trailer for *TomorrowLove™*, because that seemed very in the nature of things, and then I've also really started thinking about

how can the experience, on the other end of things, how can the experience extend beyond when you, once you've left, and for part of the time in *TomorrowLove™*, we experimented with something where we, everyone had hung up their jackets at coat check and we put these little love poems in their pockets so that, maybe a couple of days later, you put your hand in the pocket of your jacket and you find something and it reminds you of your experience and you don't know how it got there.[97]

I found one of these love poems in my pocket a few days after attending the show, and what it flagged up for me was how the show seemed to have invaded my real world after the performance was over. The coat room at the theatre did not feel like it was part of the story world, but clearly it had been: Someone had deliberately placed the poem in my pocket. The poem made me reconsider how more of the immersive experience had bled out into my real world than I had initially thought. At the very least, this late discovery made me reflect once again on my experience as a mnemonic: I was immediately drawn into the past. The poem was also a marketing ploy, intended to make me consider attending *TomorrowLove™* again (that is, in the future). Thus, the time of *TomorrowLove™* was expanded: Not only did it present alternatives to one's present experience and future progress, but it also designed its marketing to encourage audiences to look both backward and forward.

Also notable in the *TomorrowLove™* experience was the absence of a cumulative story-world conclusion. In *Brantwood*, audience members gather in the gym for a dance, and the school is barely saved from a valedictorian-turned-bomber. In *The Drowned Man*, the majority of the audience observes a murder that concludes the storyline. The scenes in *TomorrowLove™*, however, remain unconnected to the very end: Actors adopt a new character for each scene, and the audience is discouraged from treating the various vignettes as part of a singular narrative. In fact, many threads remain unresolved. One audience member articulated: "The stories are not finished. Like they're, they're, being like, they're left alone, like unfinished. And I think that's kind of cool."[98] At the end of the show, the audience is all reassembled in the chapel, where the show had initially started. Now, however, no fictional scene is presented. Instead, the actors take turns reading aloud variations of the phrase "I love you because _____" that audience members have ostensibly filled out (e.g., "I love you because of your smile" or "I love you because you make the best sandwiches"). The finale is thus not a turn inwards to complete the story or resolve the conflict. Instead, *TomorrowLove™* turns outward, to the audience members' real worlds through a reading aloud of their work. The real world is, in this way, invited to participate in a half-finished, incomplete fictional world, and fiction and real pervade each other. The audience is compelled to think about their own world and own relationships at the close of the show, rather than bask in the tidy conclusion of a fictional journey. *TomorrowLove™* thus does not offer a complete world of immersion. Instead, it capitalizes on a unique use of space to encourage relational journeying and extensions of time, drawing the experience and its structure out of time to invoke consideration of other times: alternatives, futures, and "real" time.

6

Immersion and Exertion

Audiences, Feeling-Labour, and the Production of Real-ish-ness

I have a nearly endless list of things I have done for theatre: confessed my secrets late at night over the phone, slow-danced with a stranger, painted a huge canvas, sung an improvised song, been held, fed, caressed, cuddled, handcuffed, and even once undressed, let myself be blindfolded more times than feels appropriate, walked – and walked, and walked – through entire neighbourhoods, historic trails, huge warehouses, and tiny corridors. Much of this work is, as I have stated, "real"ly engaging insofar as there are physical requirements that sensorially make me a part of the experience. But, too, there is a level of intimacy, revelation, and of emotional sharing that is very real: to share such moments with strangers, ostensibly in service of a fictional play, is no small ask of audiences.

While in previous chapters I have described how different uses of time and space contribute to an affective real, for this final chapter I want to more closely consider the inverse possibility: real affect. This is not simply a playful rhetorical turn. The affective real and real affect are two distinct but interrelated ideas, and a deliberation over their points of convergence and divergence can facilitate an investigation into the ways in which various reals might operate in accord with one another. I consider the possibility that what I have been calling the affective real is sometimes cultivated by audience members themselves, who have invested real affect in their theatre-going experience. In other words, I examine how felt realness and real affect each may feed the other. I consider this interplay between the real and affect as a kind of feedback loop, imagining how the real feeling produced in audience members both creates and is created by an experience that feels real. In what ways are audiences asked to contribute affect-labour, to what ends, and under what kinds of contracts?

Immersive theatre is arguably the most fitting form to consider this notion of audience investment of real affect because the genre explicitly requires a variety of forms of audience participation. As argued previously, audience members are active in immersive theatre space; they are navigating, making decisions, and even forming temporary communities through a heightened awareness of relationality. Audience members are also instrumental in their own creation of experiences of liveness and personalization, as well as in their active reflection and extension of time(s) as they consider alternatives, personal pasts, and futures. This necessary work on the part of the audience thus sets the stage for an investigation of emotional investment. In particular, it calls for a consideration of how affect itself may be part of the audience participation implicitly required.

TomorrowLove™, for instance, did not necessarily generate an experience that actually felt real; rather, its real-ish-ness comes from the fact that it produced real feelings. This observation aligns nicely with Erin Hurley's argument that "feeling is the primary reason for theatre's existence [...] It is what makes theatre matter."[1] While it is obvious that immersive theatre often requires effort on the part of the audience, from walking, to tasting, to navigating, what I wish to focus on are the ways in which immersive theatre can demand another kind of participation from its audiences: affective labour. Further, I wish to emphasize the ways in which this emotional participation crafts an experience that in turn feels real. *TomorrowLove™*'s explicit use of affect in making relationships to its subject matter, as well as the implicit affect invited by the show's specific form (especially respecting audience participation) creates a heightened arena for audiences to contribute to the show affectively.

To begin, a brief personal diversion is helpful for illustrating what stimulated this idea. One of the most intense moments in an immersive theatre experience I have had occurred in a bathroom stall. A teenage girl and I were alone. She asked me for help with the bullying she was receiving. She then stood in front of a mirror and wrote on it all the things about her body she did not like, before passing a marker to me. The experience was upsetting. It forced me to revisit my own very real insecurities. At the same time, it stirred up in me a debilitating panic: I could not help this young woman because, ultimately, the bullying was fake. I knew that the show was fictional, of course, but I also knew that in the real world I was empowered to help bullied individuals: I could find resources, talk to school officials, etc. In the world of the play I was being asked for a lot, but because it was within the world of the play I also did not have much to offer, leaving me ultimately feeling powerless, deflated, and immensely insecure.[2] What exactly was I being asked for in that moment? Was my response a real affect, even as I acknowledged its constructed-ness? Did my affective response contribute to the show as a whole? Or, was the effect of my affect limited to just me, in a kind of "by me, for me" production line?

Jenn Stephenson writes that "what is real in immersive theatre ... is the real-world audience and their real-world ambivalent awareness of themselves as real."[3] She goes on to say that "caught in this parallax perspective, the self-reflexive, ontologically multiple audience is forced to negotiate between representation and their own presence enmeshed yet separate from that representation."[4] Stephenson's important investigation describes the productive potential of theatre of real to reshape and reconstruct realities. I wish to focus specifically on the affective requirements of such a "parallax perspective" on the part of the spectator, to interrogate its ethics, labour, and outcomes using the testaments of audience members themselves. Accordingly, in response to one of Stephenson's blog posts,[5] Kim Solga on 12 October 2015 described what she deemed to be the real aspects of immersive theatre:

> What's "real" is me navigating the event of the work, my primary experience is always one of immediate affective engagement. Critical thinking about my experience (hopefully) comes later, but in the moment I'm taken up with the sheer matter of experiencing, partly because my senses are so fully engaged in trying to make my way through the story/the space. What's "true" in this case are my immediate needs within the work: how to navigate it, how to calm my fears, how to cope with unexpected things popping up all over. While I know this may seem simplistic, I wonder if ultimately immersive forms offer less opportunity for critical engagement because they are so affectively overwhelming: there's little room for acts of witness, and that perhaps includes me witnessing myself ...
>
> Which makes me also think this is ultimately about *labour*: what work are audience members invited to do in each case? We talk a lot about how theatre makes us feel, but in truth there's a very different kind of affective labour in making one's way

through an immersive environment than there is in sitting in front of a traditionally crafted spectacle.

Solga suggests that we are not engaged as witnesses in immersive theatre but as labourers for whom affect takes primacy over critical thinking. If we consider the audience specifically as affect-labourers, what exactly are they contributing and how does it impact a performance's realness? I do not propose to advocate delineations or definitions of who is at work and when in immersive performance. Nevertheless, a consideration of how the realness of emotional labour acts on and is enacted by real audience members is an important aspect of the wider consideration not only of what feels real for contemporary audiences but also what real feels like. To explore this, I consider the relational work of affect as a kind of specific labour before examining how the various forms of labour demanded by *TomorrowLove™* involve relationship building. I conclude with an examination of the real-ish-ness of affect itself. If affect contributes to perceptions of realness and is – if not more powerful than critical thinking, at least precedes it – then analyzing how such affect is produced is important to broader considerations of how feelings and emotions can persuasively produce realness.

AFFECTING ME, AFFECTING YOU

Hurley cites several studies of empathy, emotion, and catharsis in theatre to argue for the foundational nature of affect in performance, including Horace's famous advisory that "Smiles are contagious; so are tears; to see / Another sobbing, brings a sob from me."[6] Horace's words point clearly to the interpersonal, communicative nature of affect, and it is this aspect of relationality in affect that I want to consider specifically here with regard to *TomorrowLove™*. This concept traces its origins from Spinoza's *Ethics* in which "Affect arises in the midst of *in-between-ness*: in the capacities to act and be acted upon."[7] This definition, which places affect between acting and being acted upon, implies co-presence and does not limit affect to a single individual experience. Instead, it places affect in some kind of system. Gilles Deleuze and Félix Guattari, following Spinoza, consider affect as an "assemblage"; it is transpersonal.[8] By this they mean that a single person is neither the origin nor the destination of affect. Massumi, translating their work *A Thousand Plateaus*, defines affection as "each such state considered as an encounter between the affected body and a second, affecting, body (with body taken in its broadest possible sense)."[9] This locates affect not within a single body but again as a between; it is an encounter or a reaction.

Theorist Sara Ahmed takes these ideas further, stating that affects "do not positively inhabit anybody or anything."[10] Instead, they exist in the "circulation between objects and signs."[11] It is thus not necessarily even something contained within the human realm insofar as bodies of any material or ideal nature can inflect affect. When considering affect then, as Erin Hurley and Sara Warner note, "the focus is not the point of origin (for there is none) but the point of impact, not the mode of expression (or repression) but the mark of the impression."[12] These scholars all imply the importance of considering affect as a concept that is persistently "between," moving amongst and through a web of relations or a system. In the case of *TomorrowLove™*, this relational system includes actors, audience members, and the entirety of the immersive experience. Interviews with audience members support the idea that affects fill the space "between" and seem to populate the performance organically. For example:

> AUD 1C: They [the performers] weren't scared to evoke emotion from other people. Like, pain, real pain.
> KJ: *From other actors, or from the audience, or?*
> AUD 1C: Um, from the audience and the actors you can see vulnerability, you can see pain. You can feel it in the air. It's very tense.[13]

This interviewee suggests that having other audience members populating the same space is crucial to the whole experience; they produce the tension that is "in the air."[14] They generate visible signs of vulnerability and pain that move between the different bodies and are felt broadly as tension. This, importantly, has the effect of sharing affect amongst the audience, as a kind of collective experience. Accordingly, Hurley and Warner in their consideration of affect in performance ask explicitly, "Which emotions are likely to marshal and mobilize spectators into collectives and communities?"[15] Their question confirms that affect is relational and in flux as it moves through a theatrical experience, with the potential to "mobilize spectators into … communities."

To further consider the potential relationality of affect that is in operation in immersive theatre, it is helpful to further consider affect as a form of labour. Hurley, citing Nicholas Ridout's *Stage Fright, Animals, and Other Theatrical Problems*, contends that theatre is an affect machine that "can't help but make us feel, even when it doesn't mean to, when it isn't particularly trying to, or when its design fails outright."[16] Ridout highlights the necessary affect production of theatre, which Hurley defines as theatre's "feeling-labour." Following Arlie Hochschild's *The Managed Heart: Commercialization of Human Feeling*, Hurley describes feeling-labour as "the work theatre does in making, managing, and moving feeling in all its types (affect, emotions, moods, sensations) in a publicly observable display that is sold to an audience for a wage."[17] Erika Fischer-Lichte articulates a feedback model in which the actors and audience simultaneously affect each other: "performances are generated and determined by a self-referential and ever-changing feedback loop."[18] Put together, we can imagine that audiences both consume and produce feeling-labour; they consume the feeling-labour of the theatrical presentation and also produce a feeling-labour that in turn is consumed by the theatrical machine. I cry at a particularly moving scene, for instance. My affect is felt by the other audience members, thereby intensifying their experience. My emotional engagement is also felt by the actors onstage. My emotional experience, in other words, circulates well beyond me and affects the performance as a whole.

One audience member at *TomorrowLove™* offered a fascinating mediation on their own contribution to the show:

> Like you'd have a break and they'd put you in the corridor and someone is making a peanut butter sandwich and you're waiting for the next scene to happen. You kind of have that moment of reflection. And you're kind of going into the scene thinking these are kind of the themes, but you're ready to open. So you kind of like – like even the end when they were just reading back and forth I was like, "I'm gonna cry" and I might actually have to leave the room. Like, it was very, very emotional, which was great.[19]

This audience member describes having a "break" from what we can possibly consider to be the "work" of the show and articulates how her affective response – in this case, crying – might require her to leave the room. Her description is interesting precisely because it highlights the emotional work she is doing: reflecting, being "ready to open," feeling, having self-awareness. She specifically highlights the show's finale ("the end where they were just reading back and forth"). In this final scene, the actors simply read aloud audience responses to the writing prompt "I love you because_____." Audience members were earlier invited to answer the prompt by filling out small slips of paper, which were returned to the actors for this final moment. The audience member quoted above describes intense emotions induced by this scene which, importantly, is entirely predicated on the literal contributions of audience members. Feeling-labour, then, is clearly in circulation as it is both consumed and produced by audience members.

In the context of the immersive nature of *TomorrowLove™*, the theatrical affect machine does not merely invite audience feeling-labour as some kind of tangent. Rather, the affect machine actually depends upon it:

> Yeah it definitely feels like you can come see the show so many times and you'd get something different every single time. Based on gender, nationality, your experience and what your, what the audience experiencing it in the room with you as well. Like what energy they create and how they respond as well.[20]

With their references to "the energy they create" and "how they respond," this audience member is explaining that the affect produced by the other audience members in the room is vital to the personalization and uniqueness of their experience. In other words, in order for the show to be fully experienced, it relies on the energy, emotions, and affect of the other audience members simultaneously experiencing it. This notion of affect as a kind of feeling-labour, insofar as the feelings and experiences of audience members craft the experience for other audience members in turn, however, prompts new and further questions. This is in part because the labour being performed, in terms of generation, moderation, and sharing of affect, comes *from* the spectator. It is spurred, certainly, from the theatrical production, but the experience is mutually intensive. The immersive theatre experience and the affect it produces eschews any form of theatre in which the spectator is solely acted upon by the machine of the theatre.

Notably, the importance of the audience to the theatre experience was only explicitly raised in the interviews I conducted at *TomorrowLove™* and not at the Trinity Pageant or *Good Fences*. This implies that there is something unique about the immersive nature of this performance and how it might prompt an awareness of the audience's affective investment. The constant highlighting of the other bodies populating (and often animating) the show in this series of audience interviews suggests individual audience members' awareness of the labour investment of the audience was specifically highlighted in this show.

HARDWORKING AUDIENCES

Feeling-labour is only one form of audience labour present in *TomorrowLove™*. The show, perhaps most obviously, also required audience members to safely move throughout the performance space and consciously choose actors to follow. But, even these less clearly affective forms of labour, such as the physical work of being ambulatory, can be considered affect-based. This is because this labour relates to relationship-building capacities. For context, I want to consider the range of labour efforts required by audiences: not just physical but also cognitive and as related to visibility, and how these might be relational forces. For instance, audience members at *TomorrowLove™* often took lengthy pauses before answering my first question – a query about what they found interesting or unique about the show. Another common response was to apologize and state that they were "Still processing, still processing"[21] or "still processing everything that happened."[22] These audience comments may seem frustratingly vague. This is because "the how of the cognitive processes that occur while audiences are watching a performance is largely out of reach to audience research that by definition takes place after the event."[23] And yet, as Ben Walmsley writes in his analysis of audience engagement, studying the evidence of such processing itself might be a rich and fruitful endeavour, with its own emotional and phenomenological insights.[24] In this case, the audience members' consistent references to processing were unique to this production; the same did not occur during my other interviews for the other productions I have analyzed in this text. Their use of the term "processing" implies both a sensory engagement (sensory-processing) and also a necessary working through (in-process); the audience labour is, in other words, still evident post-show, as the audience members continue to "process" what just happened.

Director Mitchell Cushman confirmed that he deliberately developed a production that would require mental exertion in an interview:

Another early conceit of the project was to try to do a show all about technology with as little technology as possible, and so, in almost all cases, the technology was spoken about but not demonstrated in any way, and I think there's a version of these plays that would live really well as radio pieces, like part of the joy of listening to them is the amount of detective work that the audience does. It's not all spelled out for you right away; who these people are; what the relationship is, and so the theatre kind of allows you to do that better than film where you can just be in a void and accept that and then different pieces are filled in in the audience's imagination. I think that the – we tried to make the spaces as blank as possible to allow for that.[25]

As Cushman puts it, the empty space of *TomorrowLove*™ allowed for audiences to essentially fill-in-the-blanks. This production style also required audience labour in the form of "noticeability." One interviewee articulated it as follows:

One thing, I kind of feel like I'm more part of their world. Like in the sense of, often when I'm watching a play in a regular theatre the audience is dark and as long as I don't move or make a lot of loud noises nobody will notice me. But I feel like in this I'm noticed more. Um, like in one of the shows I saw today, people, the audience, the actors would look at you and they'd say like "You could be this" and they'd say it directly to the audience member ... so it makes it more real cause you're like, that's what I am now.[26]

For this audience member, the work was related to the fact that he could not disappear. While this may not immediately appear to be a kind of labour, *being seen* can be laborious. The audience member needed to be committed to the performance insofar as he was unable to hide. That is, if he disengaged from or disrupted the scene, he might ruin the experience for himself and others; he couldn't hide in the dark and stay quiet. On account of their visibility, audience members were thus required to be attentive and involved in the production, engaged in several forms of both immediately obvious and less obvious modes of labour, including affective displays as labour.

These qualities can certainly exist in many theatrical productions – and not simply immersive theatre. I have felt the need to mentally fill-in-blanks at any number of theatrical productions or had to move through a space or have felt noticed by the artists. In fact, there has been growing recognition in audience research that arts engagement is always a process of co-creation with audiences regardless of the nature and style of that engagement. Geoffrey Crossick and Patrycja Kaszynska, in their report on a large-scale project about cultural value in arts, describe how the effects of cultural engagement are "themselves a function of the dynamic processes by which the individual, the community and the contexts affect each other."[27] What I mean to suggest in this study is that the collective effect of these forms of audience labour – physical, mental, and emotional – cumulatively demand trust, commitment, and a willingness on the part of the spectator to work, and, further, that these cumulative demands are particularly suited to the topic of *TomorrowLove™* and its exploration of the work of relationships. *TomorrowLove™* requires a less secure form of spectatorship than sitting quiet and still in the dark. Audience members need to trust that the production will not put them into dangerous situations. They need to commit to not disrupting the experience. Finally, they must recognize that engagement is required. And, these points are all true regardless of whether the audience's labour investment takes the form of following an actor down a hallway or allowing oneself to be seen.

As audience members were quick to point out, these qualities of commitment, trust, and a willingness to work are essential elements of relationships in general. They are crucial investments, and one must conscientiously decide to make them in order to establish a healthy relationship. Felix Barrett, artistic director of Punchdrunk, writes about relationship building in immersive theatre, stating that such shows allow "the body to become empowered because the audience have to make physical decisions and choices, and in doing that they make some sort of pact with the piece. They're physically involved with the piece."[28] The language of relationships he uses (e.g., "pact," "involvement") indicates that the show itself orchestrates the formation of committed relationships. The physical involvement that immersive theatre demands, as well as the general demands of trust and commitment that immersive theatre makes, craft a particular relationship between spectator and production. Notably, relationship-building not only demands affective engagement; it also creates it. As Alston observes, "it is not art objects that take precedence so much as the affective consequences of an audience's own engagement in seeking, finding, unearthing, touching, liaising, communicating, exchanging, stumbling, meandering and so on."[29] It is partially through the active establishment of a relationship, orchestrated by various forms of audience labour, that these affective consequences are made most palpable in *TomorrowLove™*. The production requires audience members to, as Alston articulates it, seek, find, communicate, and exchange.

It should be noted that my examination of *TomorrowLove™* has focused almost entirely on the frame of the production rather than the plot. The scenes themselves were presented in a more conventional theatrical mode: The audience sat and watched scenes that predominantly maintained a fourth wall and used scripted dialogue. A summary of the scenes is less useful than an acknowledgement that, in the absence of a continuous narrative, audience members were presented with short, highly emotional vignettes that treated topics such as longing, loss, abuse, paedophilia, and death. Further, the scenes presented many forms of love and relationships at various stages (e.g., an individual testifying in a court of law and drifting away from the touch of their partner; an individual wanting to entrust their extracted and materialized soul to someone who does not want it). In each case, love is presented as something to be worked on/towards/through. Without a single, clear narrative through-line, the piece offers deliberately fraught topics and emotional connections on a scene-by-scene basis, all of which take as their central focus the idea of what it means to build or maintain relationships. The production's overarching structure – its frame and formal qualities – therefore echoes the content of the scenes. This is to say, while the immersive theatre form requires audiences to form a relationship with the show itself, the content of this piece also examines how and why relationships are formed. The formal structures of what the performance demands of its audience members thus reflects and potentially intensifies the audience's experience of the performance's content.

Because of the relationship-building demands of theatre like *TomorrowLove™*, there is necessarily also the potential of negative affect: of audiences being let down or disappointed. In immersive theatre, this negative affect can expand beyond the initial disappointment. Spectators may feel that they did not work hard enough – that they failed to create relationships. Schulze writes that immersive theatre "places the burden of enjoyment onto the spectator. If you did not enjoy the piece, you probably did not work hard enough or are not smart enough for this kind of art."[30] In the case of *TomorrowLove™*, the individuated experience of choosing which actor to follow, which room to enter, or what to do during the course of the production in many ways heightens the potential pressures placed on audience members. Schulze articulates these very pressures: "This individual, tailor-made journey ... places a considerable burden on them, along the lines of: How should I behave? Am I doing this right? Did I get all the stories I was supposed to get?"[31] Arts critic Alice Jones similarly bemoans how "Too many times I have left shows only to discover that the best bit was a secret room I never found or a whispered encounter in a hidden phone box to which I was never privy."[32] I, irrationally, felt a pang of disappointment when audience members in interviews described the "Skype call scene" in *TomorrowLove™* that I had completely missed. There is also the potential for spectators to feel betrayed when they come to recognize the artifice inherent in something that felt so real: "A one-on-one performance usually tries to play it as real as possible. Afterwards, if a participant finds out that the whole event was only a show, a performance that is repeated night after night, she may rightly feel upset or even betrayed."[33] I, again, felt disappointed when I watched "my" actor from my one-to-one experience in *The Drowned Man* lead a different person away for that very same one-to-one scene. This kind of reaction suggests that I had invested considerable labour into my immersive experiences. Accordingly, Schulze describes how "The thrill and success of the performance is equal to the emotional investment and amount of risk participants put in."[34] I would add that the level of disappointment spectators may feel when they realize their one-to-one relationship was not exclusive also rivals the same spectators' emotional investment at the outset of the interaction. In the common practices of immersive theatre, then, the demand for active participation and various forms of audience labour results in the potent involvement of affect, as cultivated by the relationship-building and breaking that occurs.

It is also important here to consider the politics of accessibility – physical, intellectual, and financial – as they pertain to the creation of these labour-driven relationships. For instance, for whose bodies are these shows designed? Who is and is not permitted to build a relationship? *TomorrowLove™* did offer an "accessible route" for those with mobility issues, but choosing this route meant that one's control over one's journey was somewhat surrendered. Additionally, as there appeared to only be one accessible route, the joy in returning repeatedly to experience a new configuration of scenes was not wholly available to those with accessibility needs. In her findings related to audiences of a production called *The Persians* in Wales, Kirsty Sedgman cites John Ury's idea of "motility capital"[35] to suggest that "participatory events risk privileging able-bodied individuals in possession of the speed, shrewdness, and skill necessary to successfully hunt down spectacle."[36] One of her audience interviewees suggests that their experience would have been heightened had they not been attending with their elderly mother.[37] Punchdrunk also routinely offers those spectators who can afford more expensive tickets a more intimate, privileged experience; the reality of the power of money meant that in *The Drowned Man* you could pay more for privileged access to the "Drafting Room" where a character would direct you to go to areas where more "exciting" action was taking place. These brief examples illustrate that the effect and ethics of audience labour, especially in terms of accessibility to immersive experience, reproduce many of the same inequities as the wider real world.

WHEN IT'S ALL TOO REAL: UNWANTED AFFECT

This idea of audience labour requires a consideration of ideas of relational aesthetics, which Nicholas Bourriaud describes in part as a "set of artistic practices which take as their theoretical and practical point of departure the whole of human relations and their social context, rather than an independent and private space."[38] This notion is described by Claire Bishop as focusing too heavily on "artistic intentionality rather than issues of reception."[39] She critiques relational art as being judged on what the audience might receive from the artist, even despite its dependence on interactivity and audience participation. Matthew Reason, writing about audiences, states that "there remains a tendency to value intention over reception" in such a way that, "in Bourriaud's formulation, participation is in the offer or gift of the artist, with a lack of attention paid to the manner in which this offer is received, accepted, modified, or enacted."[40] What is striking about this is the way in which audience involvement – what I am calling audience labour – is associated with words such as "gift" or "offer": something that goes *from* the artist *to* the audience. Such a transmission implies power dynamics. Since Ranciére's *Emancipated Spectator* in 2009, critics inspired by the publication have argued that spectators in every form of theatre are active and participatory in the theatrical act. As such, the idea of participation as a gift for the audience is not only patronizing but also complicated: What happens when the gift is unwanted? What comes to pass when the gift takes an unwanted toll on audience members?

Considering the notion of "unwanted" audience labour is crucial to an examination of the relationship between affect and the real. Hurley writes about the "funny pair" of theatre and feeling – about "the strangeness of having *real* emotional responses to what are usually *unreal* … situations and characters onstage."[41] Jill Bennett, writing on affect and memory, similarly describes how "affect, properly conjured up, produces real-time somatic experience, no longer framed as representation."[42] This points to affect as operating between the real bodily response and "unreal" or representational stimulus. Of course, affective responses to proscenium or other more conventional theatre productions are possible: Historical and contemporary examples abound that illustrate the vast array and ability of theatre to provoke strong emotional and visceral responses.[43] However, the unique involvement of audiences that immersive performance demands potentially intensifies this experience of having a confusingly real response to unreal stimulus. Conventional theatre does not generally have the same sense of risk involvement. Alan Read cites the rise of the fire curtain as an example of the way in which risk decreases in conventional theatre.[44] His argument is extended by Gareth White, who suggests that immersive theatre gives an impression of real danger because it "seems to lack the heavy hands of health-and-safety and customer service"[45] evident in conventional theatre. In short, no fire curtain is visible in immersive shows, a fact which Schulze points to as a marker of increased authenticity.[46] While health and safety regulations are still applicable to immersive theatre, the impression or affectation of perceived risk or chance is created – even in the absence of real risk. For instance, as I described in the previous chapter, even though I knew that I was safe being locked in a room with a strange man, my body still produced an affective response (my heart rate increased). This does not take into account, of course, the gendered nature of my response, as a young woman.[47] As Schulze articulates, my experience is an example of when "the 'absolute fake'" nevertheless delivers the "real thing."[48] It makes the fake feel real. It is worth quoting Massumi at length to further illustrate two points: how real affect can be produced in the absence of a "really real" and how that real affect can in turn affect the "really real." He asks his reader to think of a suitcase, suspected to be full of anthrax by those who notice it at an airport.[49] Even if this suitcase is entirely harmless, Adam Alston imagines that "the affective and emotional realities produced within individuals by that suitcase, such as fear or anxiety, can bring into being their own material realities in a given environment. These 'material realities' may include SWAT teams, news helicopters, road blocks and the like."[50] What this example suggests is that the imagined or unreal can produce real affects that in turn affect reality. The real-ish-ness created by immersive theatre's unique use of audience participation can thus generate a highly affective experience that in turn makes the impression of realness feel more real.

Audience members found ways to express this perplexing real-ish status of emotional or affective response to *TomorrowLove™*:

> AUD 3b: The interactions were very authentic. Like a lot of the conversations we'd turn to each other and like "Ahhh."
> AUD 3a: "We've had this conversation!"
> AUD 3b: Too real. This is yesterday.
> AUD 3c: I thought it was really authentic, and I just watched *Hamlet* last night so this was really good.
> KJ: *So, this is something I'm having trouble with, would you equate the words authentic with real or truth with real? Or how would you sort of negotiate it?*
> AUD 3d: I don't think so. Because there were like some ideas that doesn't exist in today's world in the show, but you feel like they're real in that situation and you still connect with it. So, it feels authentic, it feels like you could experience that thing, but it's not real actually.
> AUD 3g: So the emotions are authentic?
> AUD 3d: Yeah, yeah. The interactions and the emotions are authentic but they don't have to be like real.[51]
>
> AUD 2c: I felt like the feelings evoked were real but the situations illustrated were – had no basis in reality. For the most part.[52]

The affect produced is, like the show itself, simultaneously unreal and real. It is a real kind of relationship that audience members may form with a show, or a real feeling prompted by a reflection on one's own real life that the show has inspired. The affect is also distanced from or removed from the real world precisely because it is prompted by a constructed, unreal theatrical premise. However, even if the affect produced is from an unreal proposition – a fictional story world – individual audience members are still contributing real affect. This contribution may, in turn, make the experience feel more real for both themselves and their fellow audience members. For instance, one audience member explained that they enjoyed "how in transition we were asked to like think about something or participate in something that somehow alluded to or prepared you for a scene even if you had no idea what it was. Um, like challenging yourself to think about your own relationship with love and desire and then hearing about someone else's was really nice."[53] The fictional performance, then, asked for a real reflection on the audience member's real life, which in turn enhanced the audience member's experience of the fictional show. As another example, I felt particularly emotional when I noticed that audience members in the chapel, at the end of *TomorrowLove™*, were tearful and affectionate with each other. Their real feeling-labour, which may or may not have been grounded in affect from a real-world source, did affect me in a real way.

This concept of the real-ish-ness of affect itself is not without the need for ethical investigation, however. This is particularly true when notions of the unwanted gift of relational aesthetics are invited: the stakes are raised, in other words, if this unwanted gift has potentially very real effects. Machon elaborates on the ability of some immersive theatre to "(syn)aesthetically pull the audience-immersant between the plausible and implausible ... this affects a 'dangerous' play that instills 'the doubt of what is and isn't real.'"[54] Cushman similarly described one particular emotional response from an audience member that was at best unwelcome and at worst dangerously invasive in its realness:

> I think that [scene depicting a Skype call with a dead loved one] was one of the ones that seemed to most emotionally resonate with people, and it's about a technology that may never exist, but it uses the metaphor of that, so the idea that you can Skype with a loved one after they've passed away, to just examine basically the different stages of grief and loss and what it means to try to move on after you've lost a partner. There's another piece where there's – it serves as one of the lighter pieces because it's about a

couple that argues because one of them bought a fridge that allows you to – that uses black hole technology for you to be able to hold infinite groceries, and that starts out as quite a light domestic argument between the two of them, and I think a very familiar argument to people about, "We should be consuming less. You buy too much. We don't have the space." And it ends up really getting into the realization that at least one of these partners is not satisfied in the relationship and they have this desire for more, that the other person doesn't have, and I mean, I knew pieces like the Skype scene would emotionally resonate with people. That scene, I was really caught off guard. Like we had a woman break down in tears and have to leave the play because that fridge piece connected to her so much. I think she started saying, "This is my life. This is my life," and then she had to leave.[55]

This anecdote elucidates the affective impact possible in theatrical storytelling; it underscores how theatre flirts with "real life." The "lighter scene" about an invisible fridge sparked a highly charged response in an audience member because, for her, it felt too real. She was not alone in feeling this. Another audience member explicitly stated that the show as a whole "felt way too real. I actually cried in some points. And you could see the actors getting emotional too and just even the little in-between – signing the book for the funeral or you wrote the note on the kid's lunch box and it was just like, that immersion into it made it very real."[56] This is not to say that emotional or affective experiences are unwanted by audience members. In fact, many individuals attend theatre to encounter precisely these experiences.[57] But, at what point does the emotion become "too real"? When the audience is encouraged to contribute feeling-labour to the performance (willingly or unwillingly), does it even matter to distinguish between what is real and what feels real? Especially if both real and felt real can be cultivated by and create in turn each other? Performances may become problematic at the point at which, as Reason writes, "the audience as participant becomes lost within the work and as a consequence is no longer empowered to see the work."[58] In the case of the woman crying "This is my life, this is my life," we may be compelled to ask, has she lost sight of the work? Or, has the work become hers to carry out?

To even ask these questions means to presume that affective labour in performance has a resultant effect, end goal, or outcome. While I have suggested above that the investment of real affect can make a show feel more real, I do not imagine this as a cause-and-effect relationship wherein real affect leads to realness but rather in terms of an ongoing exchange. Writing on applied theatre, James Thompson describes the importance of the "affective register."[59] He argues that "the fact that, in and of itself, affect has no point is its critical point of departure, and if the fact that there 'is no point to it' offends those who seek clear prescriptions, end goals or fixed visions the response must be that no change is possible without enthusiasm, commitment and a passionate sense of the possibility of a better life."[60] What is needed, then, is a reconsideration of what work affect is presumed to be doing. Something is certainly required of participants in the immersive theatre experiences explained herein, but it may be enough for that "thing" to be affect itself.

Kathleen Gallagher writes, "It is a powerful assessment of theatre performance that inspires political arousal by drawing productively on the senses. While such utopic notions of beauty, joy, and peace may seem to be at odds with the material world and therefore offer *an escape* from it ... the affective experience of such aesthetic states of being may, equally, *initiate* a radical process of critical engagement with the world."[61] To apply Gallagher's words to *TomorrowLove™*, the production is not an entirely consuming full immersion into "another world." Rather, it remains porous enough to allow for the outside world to occasionally leak in. As the woman's reaction to the fridge scene suggests, that entry point is often affect. It is the experience of relationships within the fictional story world that in turn cultivates an affective response about one's "real" relationships and behaviour towards others. In other words, the heightened affective experience – sensually, viscerally, and emotionally – is the gateway for the consideration of the real and one's awareness of others in the real world.

When I attended *TomorrowLove™*, I was at one point asked to write on the windows of a small, covered porch. A sentence was already on the window, and it said something like, "I desire you because ____." I was supposed to fill in the blank. I had to decide on the spot who I was going to write about and reflect on why I loved them. As such, the playing space made room for my real emotions and real individuals who were not there but whom I was now compelled to think about. Of course, the extent to which an audience member engages with this task is completely up to them. I often feel guarded in

Figure 6.1 Performer Amy Keating filling in "I Desire You Because_____" at *TomorrowLove*™, December 2016

moments when a performance enquires about or encourages my "real life" to come to the fore and am suspicious of sharing intimate emotions in a public performance. In cases where I am guarded, am I also playing a role in order to protect my real self? Am I, in the case of the above instance, finishing the end of the sentence with something adequate but not entirely true? In this instance, I made a clear and impromptu decision about to what extent I wanted to be honest. This made me very conscious that others around me may have been only partially honest in their responses. That is, they may also have been considering how "real" they wanted to be. One couple held each other close as they completed the task, and another woman was still weepy from the previous scene. I was resolute that I should not negatively affect their experience by not fully engaging in the piece. In fact, their apparent earnestness impacted my own experience and actions; I felt compelled to be as real as possible. In this way, then, the affect of the experience was productive at the very least in so far as it prompted my own hyper-awareness of others.

Another audience member described how the variety of different possible affective responses resulting from the different possible scenes of *TomorrowLove™* made him consider his fellow audience members:

> I think, there was a moment when I was watching the third scene and I sat down and I realized that everyone else in the theatre had watched two other scenes beforehand. Or maybe they had or they hadn't. Maybe they'd seen a combination of two. And I realized sort of that these people are coming into the scene with maybe completely different emotions. Maybe they saw a happy ending, maybe they saw a sad ending. Could be a different context. Maybe they followed the same actor all the way through, maybe they feel like it's the same character, maybe they feel like it's different characters.[62]

The audience member goes on to say:

> And that really just highlighted the fact that you're telling this one story, but everyone is going to see it in a completely different way. Everyone will project whatever they want onto it, whatever they feel onto it, and that, that made it feel really real. That made it feel alive. Whereas when you're looking at a photo it's the same, it's the same photo. When you're looking at this play, how your day is or whether you're cold or hot could change – could completely change how you feel about the characters.[63]

The audience member highlights the singular, individual experience enabled by the immersive nature of the show. Their awareness of this individuality presents a paradox because it also reinforces their awareness of the multi-perspective possibilities of the piece. In the audience member's comments there is a clear consideration of the other, their affective state, and where they might be coming from literally and metaphorically. Hurley writes that audience feeling-labour can indeed become "social work ... via emotional labour, theatre intervenes in how we as a society come to understand ourselves, our values, and our social world."[64] It is precisely this kind of perceptive reflection that the above audience member, and myself as I reflected on what I would write on the window, were engaged in.

Figure 6.2 Performers Damien Atkins, Paul Dunn, Amy Keating, Oyin Oladejo, and Anand Rajaram dancing in *TomorrowLove™*, December 2016

I do not think it is a stretch to say that *TomorrowLove™* generates a real affect and that that in itself is a real effect. The affect is itself a political, social outcome. This is not to say that *TomorrowLove™* expertly or even consciously set out to create a deeply impacting show for social good; in fact, the actual artistic quality of the show's content remains far less important than its formal characteristics for the purposes of this study. As Gallagher writes, "this response to the affect of art is a stimulus to collaborative work, an invitation to participate, or an engagement with others, to offer other people the same sense of pleasure, whether that be the jolt of painful awareness that new consciousness brings or the poetry of struggle."[65] Affect is not merely an outcome of the show but a tool: Affect acts as a generator of relationship building with others within and beyond the spectatorial experience. For *TomorrowLove™* this means that some of the work of perceiving the show as "good" comes from the audience themselves and how much they have invested into the experience. In the show's final scene, the audience is brought together and listens to actors read slips of paper on which, we are led to understand, audience members have written down why they love someone else: The feeling in the chapel at the end of *TomorrowLove™* is one of communion not simply because of the religious undertones of the space but also because of the sense of together-ness and temporary community-building the entire piece created.

Rather than aim for a definitive answer as to what is or is not real in immersive performance, I have argued that we are immersed in a kind of real-ish/betweenness, to borrow the equivocal descriptions I have used for the real and affect respectively. The real-ish-ness cultivated by *TomorrowLove™* is predicated on audience members forming a relationship with the show. Their contribution of feeling-labour in building this relationship and responding affectively often results in an even stronger impression of the real-ish-ness of the performance. Feeling-labour, in other words, produces a constant circulation of affective reals and real affects that inherently builds relationships. Immersive theatre is frequently highlighted as an individualistic if not narcissistic endeavour.[66] And yet, this analysis of affect and the awareness of other audience members suggested by those spectators I interviewed reveal that immersive experiences can also be deeply relational – and indeed that impressions of realness thrive in those instances when affect is shared and circulated in common.

CODA

How Real is it Anyway?

At the beginning of this text, I quoted an audience member who declared that the show they had just witnessed was seventy-four per cent real. As I noted there, this comment underscores how our current systems of appraisal do not seem adequate for considering the nebulous, difficult, and contested concept of realness. In fact, my research assistant Hannah Samuels responded to this audience quote with her own anecdote: when she was working in a museum, children would often ask her if the taxidermy was "real." The animals were indeed real, but this wasn't what the curious kids were wondering; they wanted to know if the animals were alive or not. What we seem to persistently lack is some means of articulating what, to us, realness means in different contexts, at different times. This may be because, as I suggested in the preface, Donald Trump, QAnon, anti-vaxxers, Brexit, deepfakes, social media algorithms, conspiracy theories, and more have forced a constant renegotiation of how we understand the real. Recent headlines make this contemporary crisis of the real obvious: "'Fiction is outperforming reality'" on YouTube, claims one, because its algorithm optimizes not "for what is truthful, balanced, or healthy for democracy" but instead serves up lewd, violent, or conspiratorial videos.[1] In a time of rapid information exchange, swiftly developing artificial intelligence, and sophisticated forms of technology, it has become easier to spread fake news and misinformation, to "manipulate the public's perception of reality and thought processes, resulting in the proliferation of fake news that affects our real, non-digital environment."[2] The COVID-19 pandemic forced life further online, raising even more questions of what constitutes "real" theatre, "real" interaction, and "real" experience in a world in which physical co-presence is dangerous.

Modern-day life seems to have demonstrated the futility of declaring what is, once and for all, universally real.

And yet, this has not altogether eliminated the desire for the real, and these illustrations of the indefinite nature of the term "real" do not mean that attempts to study what feels real are inconsequential or tautological. Although the term "real" may be ultimately undefinable, its centrality to and prevalence in contemporary concepts – from virtual and augmented reality, to post-truth and fake news – point to its ongoing relevance in wider discourses. Indeed, in the six years spent on this project, realness has come even more to the fore. As Daniel Schulze writes in his book on authenticity, "audiences are keen on bringing back the idea of truth, the real and authenticity, and not just as a way of performance but as a genuine human experience. While theory may have abolished truth and the real altogether, they have never ceased to play a role in peoples' lives."[3] Carol Martin writes in her study of theatre of the real that there is "a larger cultural obsession with capturing the 'real' for consumption" even as it is ceaselessly reinvented, re-applied, and re-calibrated to attend to an ever-shifting world.[4] David Shields echoes in his aptly named manifesto *Reality Hunger*: "The huge loud roar, as it returns again and again, has to do with the culture being embarrassed at how much it wants the game of reality and, within that frame, great drama."[5] It is not about accessing an essentialist real, in other words, but a desire to access something that offers an experience of the real; a seemingly paradoxical combination of the "game of reality" and "great drama."

This is not to say that there is no danger in such a poststructuralist position: To argue that nothing is real and everything is real is arguably anarchic. What I am suggesting is that the real remains a central conceit to our current ways of knowing and understanding the world but that its centrality should not be mistaken as solidity or definition. This is especially true since there are multiple and contradicting operations of facts, truths, and reals on all sides of political, social, and ethical divides. If our "reality" has neither ontological nor teleological certainty, we must be more fluid in the way we approach epistemology. We must be more willing to ask, what does it mean for something to be real? For whom does the real fail? What are the ramifications of that (failed) relationship? If, as I have argued, the real is contingent and relational, is it then also explicitly political and ideological? For what bodies then might some reals be dangerous or inadequate?

To return to the question posed in the preface, if the real is indeed in crisis, can theatre help? The theatre, as a natural merger of the fictive and real, and as a site wherein people come together to participate in a common experience, is positioned as an ideal venue for an examination of the construction of realness; the possibility of interviewing or observing multiple subjects navigating an experience full of both real and unreal moments holds potential for a wide array of reactions. In each of the theatrical productions considered herein, I have illustrated how the real operates with, and through, performance, with an eye toward what larger insights about realness in society such performances might offer. These productions cover a breadth of different instantiations of theatre of the real including documentary practice, audience participation, historical re-enactment, and immersive theatre. Together, they demonstrate how the relationship between art and reality is not unidirectional but instead is a dialectic and operates in circulation. Each performance demonstrates how particular deployments of time and space work to shape perceptions of realness by constructing affective experiences that emphasize immediacy, intimacy, locality, and presence – and this insight can be applied to the "real world" as well.

In *Good Fences*, it is the presentation of a multitude of spaces, times, and perspectives that resulted in the show feeling more real. This form of real-ish-ness, and the result of making visible the multiperspectival nature of political issues, also offers insight into echo chambers and epistemic bubbles in broader political discourse. *An Enemy of the People* toyed with political participation and how audiences might function in the creation of real-ish-ness by virtue of their invitation into performance, raising questions of "real" artistic and civic participation. This too offers some relevancy for discourse around performance of politics and political identity. The Trinity Pageant raises questions about national, historic, and cultural identity, especially in terms of how such identities come to be – or otherwise stand in for – the real. For the Newfoundland identity espoused in the pageant, what is real is in part determined by self-fulfilling cultural myths that prioritize particular life experiences and populations over others. The resonances – both the potential possibilities and dangers – of such felt truths in relation to history and historical record have much broader implications for historical truth-telling. Finally, *TomorrowLove™* offers evidence of the ways in which real sensory engagement and real feelings can inspire the perception of realness;

in other words, it examined the necessary circulation of affect and realness and the ways in which these concepts can feed each other, particularly in immersive environments in which embodied experiences take the fore. Even if affect comes from a fictional source – in this case a theatre performance, but easily transposed onto conspiracy theories, online misinformation, or falsified facts – it can have very real effect. Like Massumi's suitcase possibly full of anthrax drawing real police intervention or the false QAnon theory about the Blue Marble Jubilee forcing a real cancellation of the event, unreal things can provoke intensely real emotion and therefore have real consequences. There exist, in other words, circulations of "real feelings" that must be addressed and examined due to their potency and potential in constantly redefining and constructing the real. If affect has the potential to be effective both before and beyond conscious critical thought, it becomes even more important to consider what this visceral, bodily, reaction to perceived realness might indicate.

If, as the work herein suggests, realness is contingent, fluid, and affective – that is, if it is a feeling – then a consideration of how such real-ish-ness is produced in individuals is key to further understanding the ways in which the quality of realness is applied to contemporary culture. Regarding the real as a perceptual dimension, or as a feeling rather than fact, allows us to better understand how one's subjective perspective and experience lends weight to a particular perception of realness. Experiential phenomena – intimacy, immersion, participation, liveness and, of course, realness – are more than one-way processes of production and reception. These are processes of audience co-construction. Core to this investigation is the importance of including and centring audience perspectives. If we wish to know how productions are being felt, perceived, and valued by those that attend them, we must engage with audiences themselves.

Ultimately, it is through the theatrical that we might better understand the real precisely because the theatrical plays in the unstable realm of the real-ish, generating real emotion and affect through fiction and representation. Theatre isn't going to help establish (or re-establish) an indisputable real – or truth or fact or authenticity, for that matter – but what it might do, arguably more helpfully, is assist in revealing the epistemic frameworks through which realness is constructed. In a post-truth, post-fact, perhaps even post-real world, what theatre offers is a means of revealing the structures of feeling that produce contemporary realness.

Notes

PREFACE

1. Colbert, "Truthiness."
2. Colbert, "White House Correspondents' Dinner."
3. Sutton, Brind, and McKenzie, *The State of the Real*, 19.
4. BuzzFeedVideo. "You Won't Believe What Obama Says In This Video ;)." YouTube Video 1:12. 17 April 2018. https://www.youtube.com/watch?v=cQ54GDm1eL0.
5. Vaccari and Chadwick, "Deepfakes and Disinformation," 2.
6. BuzzFeedVideo, "You Won't Believe."
7. Kalsnes, "Fake News." Fake news itself was word of the year for Collins Dictionary in 2017.
8. Zuckerman, "QAnon and the Emergence."
9. Ibid.
10. Ibid.
11. Fisher, Cox, and Hermann, "Pizzagate: From Rumor."
12. See, for example: Thorson, "Belief echoes"; Roets, "Fake news"; Garrett, Nisbet, and Lynch, "Undermining the Corrective Effects."
13. Menegus, "Pizzagaters Aren't Giving."
14. Tan, Shin, Rindler, "American's Ugliest Days."
15. Botsman, *Who Can You Trust?*, 48.
16. Samuel, "There's a Microchip."
17. Strum and Albrecht, "Constituent Covid-19," 122.
18. Bostman, *Who Can You Trust?*, 70.
19. Hurley, *Theatre & Feeling*, 2–4.
20. Stephenson, *Insecurity*, 7.
21. Carlson, *Shattering Hamlet's Mirror*, 18.

22 Stephenson, *Insecurity*, 6.
23 Martin, *Dramaturgy of the Real*, 23.
24 Hughes, "War on Terror," 151–2.
25 Espiner, "Between the Lines."
26 Filewod, *Collective Encounters*, 14.

CHAPTER ONE

1 AUD 2e, *TM*, 2 December 2016. In this work, interviews with anonymous audience members are denoted by the number of the interview (e.g., AUD 1 was in the first interview, AUD 2 was in the second interview); order of speaking (AUD 2a was the first speaker in the second interview, AUD 2b was the second speaker in the second focus group interview); show abbreviation (e.g., GF for *Good Fences*, EP for *Enemy of the People*, TP for *Trinity Pageant*, TM for *TomorrowLove™*); and date of interview. In this case, for instance, this audience member was the fifth to speak in the second focus group interview conducted during the run of *TomorrowLove™*. The interviewer, in all cases myself, is denoted by my initials (KJ). For a full overview of the audience methodology used and all interviews conducted please see the subsection of this chapter on "Audiences."
2 Brook, *The Empty Space*, 9.
3 Hurley, "Introduction: Theatre Matters," 3.
4 Miller, "Realism."
5 Ayer, *Foundations of Empirical Knowledge*, quoted in Sutton, Brind, and McKenzie, *The State of the Real*, 4.
6 Austin, *Sense and Sensibilia*, quoted in Sutton, Brind, and McKenzie, *The State of the Real*, 5.
7 Sutton, Brind, and McKenzie, *The State of the Real*, 15.
8 Johnston, "Jacques Lacan."
9 Ballroom culture or "house/ball community" is defined by Bailey as "a community and network of Black and Latina/o women, men, and transgender women and men who are lesbian, gay, bisexual, straight, and queer. The Black and Latina/o queer members of this community use performance to create an alternative discursive terrain and a kinship structure that critiques and revises dominant notions of gender, sexuality, family, and community" (367). Houses are familial structures based on social networks rather than biological connections, usually led by "houseparents" (367). Houses compete in balls, which are competitive and celebratory performance events (368).

10 Bailey, "Gender/Racial Realness," 377.
11 Ibid., 377–8.
12 Strings and Bui, "She is Not Acting, She Is," 823.
13 McCarthy Brown, "Mimesis," 216, quoted in Bailey, "Gender/Racial Realness," 377.
14 Varga and Guignon, "Authenticity."
15 Ibid.
16 Weixler, "The Dilettantish Construction," 207.
17 Ibid., 208.
18 Pine and Gilmore, *The Experience Economy*.
19 Kim and Kim, "Destination Authenticity."
20 Cohen, "Heterogenization of Tourist Art"; Mura "Perceptions of Authenticity."
21 Funk, Groß, and Huber, "Exploring the Empty Plinth," 13.
22 Ibid.
23 Auslander, *Liveness*, 3.
24 Brandon Hunter, *Playing Real*, xviii.
25 Van Es, *The Future of Live*, 5; emphasis in original.
26 Plato, *The Republic Book X*.
27 Sutton, Brind, McKenzie, *The State of the Real*, 5.
28 Wiles, *A Short History*, 209.
29 Carlson, *Shattering Hamlet's Mirror*, 3.
30 Ibid., 7.
31 See, for instance, Sedgman, *The Reasonable AUDience*.
32 Barker and Solga, "Introduction," 2.
33 Lehmann, *Postdramatic Theatre*, 12.
34 Stephenson, *Insecurity*, 7.
35 Martin, *Theatre of the Real*, 4–5.
36 Carlson, *Shattering Hamlet's Mirror*, 15.
37 States, *Great Reckonings*, 101.
38 Binette, "Spatial Encounters," 32.
39 Ibid., 36.
40 Carlson, *Shattering Hamlet's Mirror*, 18–19.
41 Sutton, Brind, and McKenzie, *The State of the Real*, 4.
42 Funk, Huber, and Gross, "Exploring the Empty Plinth," 10.
43 Sutton, Brind, and McKenzie, *The State of the Real*, 25.
44 Gallie, *Philosophy and Historical Understanding*, 187–8, quoted in Carlson, *Performance: A Critical Introduction*, 1.
45 Forsyth and Megson, *Get Real*, 2.
46 AUD 2a and 2g, *TM*, 2 December 2016; emphasis added.

47 Hurley, *Theatre & Feeling*, 13.
48 Plantinga, *Moving Viewers*, 57.
49 Hurley, *Theatre & Feeling*, 11.
50 Plantinga, *Moving Viewers*, 57.
51 Tait, *Performing Emotions*, 16, quoted in Hurley, *Theatre & Feeling*, 19.
52 Hurley, "Introduction: Theatre Matters," 3.
53 Ibid., 4.
54 Walker, "The Text/Performance Split," 39.
55 Peters, "Witnessing," 717.
56 Van Oldenburgh, "Performing the Real," 62.
57 Artaud, *Theatre and Its Double*, 85.
58 Derrida, "The Theatre of Cruelty," 294.
59 Smyth, "Designing Embodied Interaction," 140.
60 Sutton, Brid, McKenzie, *The State of the Real*, 14.
61 Shaughnessy, *Affective Performance*, 48.
62 Clough, "Introduction," 2.
63 Heim, *Actors and Audiences*. See also Fischer-Lichte, *The Transformative Power of Performance*, 38.
64 Hurley, *Theatre & Feeling*, 17.
65 Ridout, "The Vibratorium Electrified," 215.
66 Brennan, "The Transmission of Affect," 20.
67 Ibid., 68.
68 Gregg and Seigworth, "An Inventory of Shimmers," 1; emphasis in original.
69 Van Oldenborgh, "Performing the Real," 63; emphasis in original.
70 Freshwater, *Theatre & Audience*; Park-Fuller, "Audiencing the Audience"; Reinelt, "What UK Spectators Know."
71 Freshwater, *Theatre & Audience*, 3–4.
72 Ibid.
73 Freshwater, *Theatre & Audience*, 29.
74 Sedgman, "Audience Experience," 307.
75 Tomlin, *Political Dramaturgies*, 25.
76 Freshwater, *Theatre & Audience*, 6, quoted in Sedgman, "Audience Experience," 318.
77 Bennet, *Theatre Audiences*, 226–8, quoted in Sedgman, *Locating the Audience*, 7.
78 Reinelt, "What UK Spectators," 338.
79 Philip, "Who's Listening," 8–10.
80 See also Paul Kosidowski, "Thinking Through the Audience," *Theatre Topics* 13, no. 1 (2003): 83–6 (84).

81 Barker, "I Have Seen," 131.
82 There are some notable exceptions, including the work of Wilmar Sauter (see Sauter, "Thirty Years of Reception Studies," and "Who Reacts When, How and upon What"); Martin Barker (see Barker, "Crash, Theatre Audiences, and the Idea of 'Liveness'"); John Tulloch (see Tulloch, *Shakespeare and Chekhov*); and Rebecca Scollen (see Scollen, "Talking Theatre").
83 Walmsley, "Engagement," 299, 301.
84 Reason and Sedgman, "Editors' introduction," 117.
85 I was able to conduct audience interviews at *Good Fences*, the Trinity Pageant, and *TomorrowLove™*. I did not conduct audience interviews at *An Enemy of the People* but was able to attend and observe post-show talkbacks.
86 Gallagher, Balt, Valve, "Vulnerability, Care, Hope," 4–6.
87 Wallendorf and Brucks, "Introspection," 341.
88 Orona, "Temporality and Identity," quoted in Walmsley, "Deep Hanging Out," 276.
89 Walmsley, "Deep Hanging Out," 277.
90 Sedgman, "On Rigour," 467.
91 Ang, *Living Room Wars*, 37.
92 Sedgman, "On Rigour," 476.
93 Johanson and Glow, "A Virtuous Circle," cited in Walmsley, "Deep Hanging," 284.
94 Schrøder et al., *Researching Audiences*, 17.
95 Alvarez, *Immersions Cultural Difference*, 4; emphasis in original.
96 Duggan, *Trauma-Tragedy*, 74.

CHAPTER TWO

1 Ellen Close, interview with the author, 28 March 2015.
2 Filewod, *Collective Encounters*, 182.
3 Beginning in the company's 2008–09 season, almost each year of Downstage's seasons has included a piece developed by the Downstage Creation Ensemble. These include *In the Wake*, about geo-engineering, oceans and fisheries, and eco-terrorism, and *Bus(t)*, which explored debt and economic collapse through mask performance.
4 Filewod, *Collective Encounters*, 182.
5 "Oil and gas," Invest Alberta, Government of Alberta, accessed 20 June 2020, https://investalberta.ca/industry-profiles/oil-and-gas.
6 Economic figures reinforce the assertions related to Alberta's longstand-

ing relationship with non-renewable energy resources: In 2015, the mining and oil and gas extraction industries made up 27.4 per cent of Alberta's gross domestic product according to Alberta Learning Information Service website ("Mining and Oil and Gas Extraction," Alberta Learning Information Service, Government of Alberta, accessed 18 December 2017, https://alis.alberta.ca/occinfo/industry-profiles/mining-and-oil-and-gas-extraction/o). Comparatively, oil and gas and mining contributed only 13.5 per cent of Texas's gross domestic product in the same time period ("Texas Oil and Gas," Economic Development & Tourism Division, Office of the Texas Governor, accessed 5 May 2017, gov.texas.gov/files/ecodev/TXOil.pdf). Agriculture, including ranching, comprised only 1.2 per cent of Alberta's GDP in 2015 ("Agriculture," Alberta Learning Information Service, Government of Alberta, accessed 12 June 2017, https://alis.alberta.ca/occinfo/industry-profiles/agriculture).

7   The consequence of the boom and bust cycles inherent to the industry is that citizens oscillate between periods of prosperity and relative poverty. In short, their livelihood is dependent on the rise and fall of global oil and gas prices. A sharp decline in the oil industry in 2015 saw an estimated 31.3 per cent drop in conventional oil and gas investment, a 24.5 per cent decline in oil sands spending, and a 36.3 per cent fall in spending by the oil and gas services extraction industry, which had drastic effects on the industry ("Economic Results," Alberta, Government of Alberta, 24 May 2016, http://www.albertacanada.com/about-alberta/economic-results.html). This trend continued, and from 2014–19 there was an overall estimated 58.2 per cent drop in capital spending in the oil industry and 64.6 per cent drop in capital spending in the oil sands (Hussey, "Future of Alberta's Oil Sands"). In terms of employment, this extraction industry directly employed 135,800 people in 2016, which was a decrease of 12.6 per cent or 19,500 jobs from the previous year ("Mining and Oil and Gas Extraction," Alberta Learning Information Service, Government of Alberta, accessed 18 December 2017, https://alis.alberta.ca/occinfo/industry-profiles/mining-and-oil-and-gas-extraction). This drop in employment figures continued in following years, with an overall estimated loss of 53,000 jobs from 2014 to 2019 (Hussey, "Future of Alberta's Oil Sands").

8   Also in-performance, they emphasize that all six of the major sponsors of the festival were oil and gas companies. Interestingly, however, *Good Fences* most recently received a funding award from the environment branch of the Calgary Foundation. In many ways, then, *Good Fences*'s

engagement with oil is what makes it appealing to its funders, even from those who oppose certain industry practices.
9 Close, interview with the author, 28 March 2015.
10 Knapp, "Shooter Feared for His Life."
11 MacArthur, "Farmers Establish Trust Fund."
12 Knapp, "Shooter Feared for His Life."
13 *Global News*, "Oilpatch Bomber."
14 Nguyen, "Echo Chambers," 141.
15 Botsman, *Who Can You Trust?*, 46.
16 Nguyen, "Echo Chambers," 141.
17 Botsman, *Who Can You Trust?*, 46.
18 Nguyen, "Echo Chambers," 142.
19 See, for instance Eli Pariser, *The Filter Bubble: What the Internet Is Hiding From You* (London: Penguin UK, 2011).
20 As mentioned in the preface, in the example of Pizzagate, the fact that no secret child-trafficking ring was found at the pizza restaurant did not deter believers: members of the online forum instead took the event as a sign of the liberal control of mainstream media and the gunman's admission that there was no trafficking as evidence that he was a paid actor.
21 Obama, "Farewell Address."
22 Mallett, interview with the author, 28 March 2015.
23 *Good Fences* performance, 25 March 2015.
24 Ibid.
25 Silverman et al., "Hyperpartisan Facebook Pages."
26 Nicholson, Holdsworth, and Milling, *The Ecologies of Amateur Theatre*, 4.
27 Ibid.
28 Ibid., 11.
29 Ibid., 13.
30 States, *Great Reckonings*, 8.
31 In his mixed-methods spectatorship research (2020), Scott Mealey has noted audience resistance to obviously didactic theatre. Rather than being receptive to the message being imparted, some audience members actually become more resistant if they sense that the show is deliberately instructive. Specifically, his research demonstrates that an increased level of education in spectators attending a Boalian-style performance was correlated with a low level of felt importance of practical messaging (206–7).
32 AUD 6a, *GF*, 28 March 2015.
33 Close, interview with the author, 28 March 2015.

34 See, for instance, Malzacher and Dreyesse, *Experts of the Everyday* (2008), and Davidson "Amateur Actors" (1987).
35 Rugoff, "Other Experts," 14.
36 Close and Mallett, interview with the author, 28 March 2015.
37 AUD 2a and 2b, *GF*, 25 March 2015.
38 Stephenson, *Upsurges of the Real*.
39 AUD 3, *GF*, 27 March 2015.
40 Bachelard, *The Dialectic of Duration*, 44.
41 Rabey, *Theatre, Time and Temporality*, 54.
42 Ibid., 55.
43 Ibid.
44 Bachelard, *The Dialectic of Duration*, 108.
45 Adam, *Timescapes of Modernity*, 55.
46 Rabey notably begins his first chapter of *Theatre, Time and Temporality: Melting Clocks and Snapped Elastics* with a contemplation of the slippery and multitudinous nature of both time and theatre: "When we consider both time and theatre, we are brought into contact with issues of perception, speculation and action, which are fundamental – and fundamentally contentious. The significantly mercurial qualities of time and theatre make them difficult to discuss, either separately or in combination. Any attempt to establish a single authoritative perspective on, or arising from, either time or theatre will rightly be suspect. Both time and theatre provide forms of definition, which are also indefinite; time and theatre both intrinsically indicate alternatives and adjacencies, even as we perceive their moments of highest precision" (11).
47 Bogart, *What's the Story*, 80.
48 Rabey, *Theatre, Time and Temporality*, 70.
49 Arstila and Lloyd, *Subjective Time*, 320.
50 Limon, *Chemistry of the Theatre*, 18.
51 Ibid.; emphasis in original.
52 Rabey, *Theatre, Time and Temporality*, 13.
53 Stephenson, "Winning and/or Losing," 216.
54 Ibid., 215.
55 Crumlish and Malone, *Designing Social Interfaces*, 291.
56 Ibid.
57 Stephenson, *Insecurity*, 45.
58 Ibid., 46.
59 Rabey, *Theatre, Time, and Temporality*, 21.
60 Lehmann, *Postdramatic Theatre*, 186.
61 Schroeder, *The Presence of the Past*, 12.

62 AUD 6a, *GF*, 28 March 2015.
63 States, *Great Reckonings*, 50.
64 Rabey, *Theatre, Time and Temporality*, 27.
65 Wagner, *Shakespeare, Theatre, and Time*, 12.
66 Stephenson, *Insecurity*, 18.
67 MacAloon, *Rite, Drama, Festival, Spectacle*, 1.
68 Bennett, "3-D A/B," 41.
69 Stephenson, *Performing Autobiography*, 106.
70 Ibid., 105.
71 If we return to Rabey's suggestion to think of theatre as a quantum art, this multiplicity of possible futures might be similar to the idea of a quantum superposition, most commonly explicated in the thought experiment nicknamed "Schrodinger's Cat" in which a cat in a box with radioactive material may be thought of as simultaneously dead and alive until the very moment in which the box is opened. Schrodinger was attempting to discredit such blurred models of reality by pointing to their implausibility: the cat is either dead or alive logically, but his experiment illustrates how potent unknowing can allow for simultaneous states of being.
72 Mallett, interview with the author, 28 March 2015.
73 Hawking, *A Brief History of Time*, 33.
74 Mallett, interview with the author, 28 March 2015.
75 Nicholson, "A Good Day Out," 250.
76 Ibid.
77 Ibid.
78 Ibid.
79 Vattimo, "Dialectics, Difference," 40, quoted in Lavery, "Performance and Ecology," 230.
80 Vattimo, "Dialectics, Difference," 40.
81 Lavery, "Performance and Ecology," 230.
82 Ridout, *Passionate Amateurs*, 124.
83 Ibid.
84 Heritage, "Taking Hostages," 100.
85 Massey, "Geographies of Responsibility," 6.
86 Cohen-Cruz, "The Stranger Within," 123.
87 AUD 5a and 5b, *GF*, 28 March 2015.
88 Cohen-Cruz, *Local Acts*, 184–5.
89 Mallett, interview with the author, 28 March 2015.
90 Bacon, Yuen, and Korza, *Animating Democracy*, 12, quoted in Cohen-Cruz, *Local Acts*, 95.

91 Kennelly, "Acting Out," 551.
92 AUD 1, *GF*, 27 March 2015.
93 AUD 2a, *GF*, 27 March 2015.
94 Stephenson, "Winning and/or Losing," 219.
95 AUD 5a, *GF*, 28 March 2015.
96 Mallett, interview with the author, 28 March 2015.
97 AUD 2b, *GF*, 27 March 2015.
98 AUD 1, *GF*, 27 March 2015.
99 Mouffe, *Agonistics*, cited in Tomlin, *Political Dramaturgies*, 74.
100 Ibid.
101 AUD 4, *GF*, 28 March 2015.
102 Salverson, "Transgressive Storytelling," 39.
103 Ibid.
104 AUD 1, *GF*, 27 March 2015.
105 Col Cseke, interview with the author, 28 March 2015.
106 Lehmann, *Postdramatic Theatre*, 12.
107 Stephenson, *Insecurity*, 34–5.
108 Martin, *Dramaturgy of the Real*, 22.
109 Ibid.

CHAPTER THREE

1 White, *Audience Participation*, 1.
2 Heim, "Argue with us!," 189. Heim specifically lists New York theatres to illustrate her claim, but a brief online search similarly reveals that as of 2020 the following Toronto theatres offer regular or occasional talkbacks: Tarragon Theatre, Canadian Stage, Young People's Theatre, Factory Theatre, Theatre Passe Muraille, Alumnae Theatre, Nightwood Theatre, Native Earth Performing Arts, Theatre Centre, Soulpepper Theatre.
3 Heim, "Argue with us!," 189.
4 Reason, "*Participations* on Participation," 272.
5 Rancière, *Emancipated Spectator*, 2.
6 Ibid., 7.
7 Ibid., 13.
8 Ibid., 16.
9 Reason, "*Participations* on Participation," 272.
10 Freshwater, *Theatre & Audience*, 3.
11 Collini, "On Variousness," 67.
12 Jansen, "Public Enemies," *An Enemy of the People* Tarragon Theatre program, 2014.

13 Lavery, "Performance and Ecology," 229.
14 I am indebted to Maria Milisavljevic, the Toronto and Berlin-based translator of the Tarragon production who provided access to the unpublished scripts and generously answered script-related queries. Then artistic director Richard Rose was also very helpful in providing access to an archival recording of the production.
15 In the 2014 production at Tarragon Theatre, the role of Doctor Stockmann was played by male-identified actor Joe Cobden. In the 2015 production, the role was played by female-identified actor Laura Condlln. I have thus chosen to use gender-neutral pronouns.
16 This manifesto, *The Coming Insurrection*, was published in 2005 and translated into English in 2009. It was written anonymously by the "Invisible Committee" and is a broad condemnation of globalization, neoliberalism, and capitalism.
17 Audience Talkback, 15 October 2015.
18 "Walkerton" refers to an *E. coli* outbreak resulting from the contamination of the drinking water supply of Walkerton, Ontario in 2000. There were more than 2,000 cases of *E. coli* reported (almost half of the community's population at the time), and seven deaths. ("Inside Walkerton," 2010).
19 Borchmeyer, *An Enemy of the People*, 66.
20 Audience Talkback, 15 October 2015.
21 Audience Talkback, 17 October 2015.
22 Maria Milisavljevic, personal communication with the author, 25 May 2020.
23 Ouzounian, "An Enemy of the People."
24 Jansen and Syme, "Tarragon Lecture Series."
25 Nestruck, "An Enemy of the People."
26 Milisavljevic, personal communication with the author, 25 May 2020.
27 Milisavljevic, *An Enemy of the People*, 2.
28 Ouzounian, "An Enemy of the People."
29 Woods, "Recently Banned"; Yuqing and Fan, "China Cancels Ibsen."
30 Jansen and Syme, "Tarragon Lecture Series."
31 Ouzounian, "An Enemy of the People."
32 For a thorough examination of audience behaviour and etiquette, including its classist, racist implications, see Sedgman, *The Reasonable Audience*.
33 Collini, "On Variousness," 67.
34 Jansen, "Public Enemies," *An Enemy of the People Tarragon Theatre* program, 2014.

35 Tomlin, *Political Dramaturgies*, 50.
36 Žižek, *Mapping Ideology*, 15–16.
37 Audience Talkback, 17 October 2015.
38 White, *Audience Participation*, 48.
39 Borchmeyer, *An Enemy of the People*, 73.
40 Ibsen, *An Enemy of the People*, 66.
41 This change in name, from Thomas to Tommi (short for Thomasina) for Doctor Stockmann, was made to accompany the change in performer gender from Joe Cobden in 2014 to Laura Condlln in 2015.
42 Wood, "Who is the Enemy."
43 Nestruck, "An Enemy of the People."
44 Borchmeyer, *An Enemy of the People*, 72.
45 Zhulina, "Invisible Stage Hand," 401.
46 Ibsen, *An Enemy of the People*, 58.
47 Ibid., 59; emphasis in original.
48 Borchmeyer, *An Enemy of the People*, 72.
49 Ibid., 73.
50 Collini, "On Variousness," 67.
51 Audience Talkback, 17 October 2015.
52 Audience Talkback, 15 October 2015.
53 Cushman, "Theatre Review."
54 Miessen, *The Nightmare of Participation*, 14.
55 We may consider here how racism, gender inequality, capitalism, etc. are held up and/or reinforced by dominant hegemonic structures, systems, and institutions in wider society.
56 Breed and Prentki, "General Introduction," 5.
57 Borchmeyer, *An Enemy of the People*, 72.
58 Bishop, *Artificial Hells*, 2.
59 Stephenson, "Assembling the Audience-Citizen," 164.
60 Tomlin, *Political Dramaturgies*, 17.
61 Kohn, "Homo spectator," 480.
62 Tomlin, *Political Dramaturgies*, 18.
63 Ibid., 163–4.
64 boyd, "Social Network Sites," 43.
65 Goffman, *Presentation of Self*, 22, quoted in Hogan, "Presentation of Self," 377.
66 Vittadini and Pasquali, "Virtual Shadowing," 161 citing, boyd, *Taken out of Context*.
67 Sundén, *Material Virtualities*, 3.
68 Abercrombie and Longhurst, *Audiences*, 72.

69 Lonergan, *Theatre & Social Media*, 2.
70 Wood, "Language in Digital Activism."
71 For more on performative allyship, see Kalina, "Performative Allyship"; Hesford, "Reading the Signs"; Jennings, "Who are the black squares"; and Phillips, "Performative Allyship is Deadly."
72 Kelleher, review of Alan Read's *Theatre, Intimacy & Engagement: The Last Human Venue*, 182.
73 Ibid.
74 Kelleher, *Theatre & Politics*, 24.
75 Audience Talkback, 15 October 2015.
76 Robinson, *Hungry Listening*, 218.
77 Ibid., 230–1.
78 Ibid., 218.
79 Thomas Ostermeier, "Iconic Artist Talk," with Branden Jacobs-Jenkins, 12 October 2017, Brooklyn Academy of Arts, Brooklyn, NY, quoted in Zhulina, "Invisible Stage Hand," 403.
80 Wood, "Who is the Enemy."

CHAPTER FOUR

1 AUD 3a and 3b, *TP*, 27 August 2016.
2 AUD 4a, *TP*, 31 August 2016.
3 "Census Profile, 2016 Census," *Statistics Canada*, accessed 4 August 2020, https://www12.statcan.gc.ca/census-recensement/2016/dp-pd/prof/details/page.cfm?Lang=E&Geo1=CSD&Code1=1007015&Geo2=CD&Code2=1007&Data=Count&SearchText=trinity&SearchType=Begins&SearchPR=01&B1=All&TABID=1.
4 Rising Tide Theatre, 2016 Season Brochure.
5 Butt, interview with the author, 31 August 2016.
6 "Rising Tide Theatre," reviews, *TripAdvisor*, accessed 13 July 2020, https://www.tripadvisor.ca/Attraction_Review-g499208-d2236194-Reviews-Rising_Tide_Theatre-Trinity_Newfoundland_Newfoundland_and_Labrador.html. There were 221 reviews of Rising Tide Theatre as of June 2020. Of these, 165 are 5-star, 42 are 4-star, 11 are 3-star, and 3 are 2-star.
7 AUD 1b and 1d, *TP*, 21 August 2016.
8 AUD 3a, *TP*, 27 August 2016.
9 AUD 4b, *TP*, 31 August 2016.
10 Interview with Trinity Pageant audience member, 27 August 2016.
11 Overton, "The Real Newfoundland," 115.

12 Ibid., 119.
13 Seifert, *Rewriting Newfoundland*, 24.
14 Omner, "Rosie's Cove," 20.
15 See Parsons, "Branded Newfoundland," and Chafe, "Only an Artist," for further analysis of these tourism efforts.
16 Overton, "The Real Newfoundland," 133.
17 Ibid.
18 Government of Newfoundland and Labrador, *The Newfoundland Adventure*, 25, quoted in Overton, *Making a World of Difference*, 121.
19 Pitt, "Trinity."
20 Ibid.
21 Butt, interview with the author, 28 November 2015.
22 Ahmed, *The Cultural Politics of Emotion*, 90–3, quoted in Riedner, "Review of *The Cultural Politics of Emotion*," 701.
23 Ahmed, "Affective Economies," 119.
24 Austin, *How to Do Things with Words*.
25 Mackey and Whybrow, "Taking Place," 2–3; emphasis in original.
26 Ahmed, *The Cultural Politics of Emotion*, 130–1.
27 Overton, "The Real Newfoundland," 129.
28 Lehmann, *Postdramatic Theatre*, 36.
29 Ibid., 37.
30 Ibid.
31 Hurley, *National Performance*, 22.
32 Schneider, *Performing Remains*, 35.
33 Overton, "'A Future in the Past'?," 64.
34 Schneider, *Performing Remains*, 37.
35 Rising Tide Theatre Program, 2016.
36 AUD 1f, *TP*, 20 August 2016.
37 AUD 2c, *TP*, 24 August 2016.
38 Magelssen, *Simming*, 5.
39 Ibid., 186.
40 Ibid., 185.
41 I attended a walking tour of Trinity on 29 August 2016 led by local historian Kevin Toope, M.Ed, and he graciously verified the reference for this court case afterwards via email correspondence.
42 AUD 4a, *TP*, 31 August 2016.
43 AUD 4b, *TP*, 31 August 2016.
44 AUD 1a, *TP*, 24 August 2016.
45 Geertz, *The Interpretation of Cultures*.
46 Gordon, *Time Travel*, 15.

47 Magelssen, *Living History Museums*, 22.
48 Notably, Sedgman's analysis of Welsh audiences attending a similarly promenade-style performance dealt in similarly complex and unstable notions of what is real: "the 'realness' of the event – the physical fact of being there in the town, walking its streets and coming across performers along the way – was felt to be an important aspect of the experience, its 'authenticity' (what is portrayed about the 'truth' of the location) did not seem to figure in any meaningful way." Sedgman, *Locating the Audience*, 105.
49 Gordon, *Time Travel*, 15.
50 Trinity Pageant performance, Trinity, NL, 21 August 2016.
51 Butt, interview with the author, 28 November 2015.
52 AUD 4b, *TP*, 31 August 2016.
53 AUD 4c, *TP*, 31 August 2016.
54 Trinity Pageant performance, 27 August 2016.
55 Overton, "'The Real Newfoundland,'" 122.
56 Bousquet, "Poet and the Roots," 189.
57 Reinelt, "Theatre on the Brink of 2000," 127.
58 Bousquet, "Poet and the Roots," 189–90.
59 Alvarez, *Immersions in Cultural Difference*, 165.
60 AUD 1a, *TP*, 24 August 2016.
61 Handler and Gable, *The New History in an Old Museum*, 71.
62 Magelssen, *Living History Museums*, xvii.
63 Schneider, *Performing Remains*, 11, 45.
64 AUD 4c, *TP*, 31 August 2016.
65 Butt, interview with the author, 31 August 2016.
66 Harvey, "Make What You Need," 44.
67 Butt, interview with the author, 28 November 2015.
68 Overton, "The Real Newfoundland," 119.
69 Bennett, *Performing Ireland*, 30.
70 54obirenea, review "Don't Miss This," 17 September 2016.
71 Redfield, "The Folk Society," quoted in Narváez, "The Folklore," 129.
72 Narváez, "The Folklore," 128.
73 Ibid., 129.
74 Massey, *Space, Place, and Gender*, 147.
75 Butt, interview with the author, 31 August 2016.
76 Massey, *Space, Place, and Gender*, 151.
77 Morash and Richards, *Mapping Irish Theatre*, 21.
78 Tuan, *Space and Place*, 4–6.
79 Morash and Richards, *Mapping Irish Theatre*, 75.

80 Overton, *Making a World of Difference*, 17.
81 Massey, *Space, Place, and Gender*, 151–2.
82 Pearson and Shanks, *Theatre/Archaeology*, 23.
83 Rebellato, "Playwriting and Globalisation," 103; Morash and Richards, *Mapping Irish Theatre* 154–6.
84 Morash and Richards, *Mapping Irish Theatre*, 156.
85 AUD 1a, 1b, 1g, *TP*, 20 August 2016.
86 AUD 2b, *TP*, 24 August 2016
87 Massey, *Space, Place, and Gender*, 151.
88 AUD 3b, 3e, 3c, *TP*, 27 August 2016.
89 AUD 4a and 4c, *TP*, 31 August 2016.
90 AUD 4b, *TP*, 31 August 2016.
91 AUD 4a, *TP*, 31 August 2016.
92 McAuley, *Space in Performance*, 11.
93 AUD 2b, *TP*, 24 August 2016.
94 Trinity Pageant performance, 24 August 2016.
95 Hurley, *National Performance*, 23.
96 Bennett and Polito, "Thinking Site," 8.
97 Ibid., 8–9.
98 AUD 4b, *TP*, 31 August 2016.
99 AUD 4d, *TP*, 31 August 2016.
100 Massey, *Space, Place, and Gender*, 154.
101 McLucas, "Brith Gof," 2.
102 Houston, "Collaborating with Audiences," 3.
103 Sedgman, *Locating the Audience*, 36; emphasis in original.
104 Butt, interview with the author, 28 November 2015.
105 McAuley, "Introduction," 17.
106 Butt, interview with the author, 28 November 2015.
107 McAuley, "Introduction," 17.
108 Schneider, *Performing Remains*, 35; emphasis in original.
109 Ibid., 37; emphasis in original.
110 Ibid., 36; emphasis in original.
111 Massey, *Space, Place, and Gender*, 155.
112 Butt, interview with the author, 31 August 2016. Mark Turner also describes how "Rising Tide has embedded itself in the province as a cultural institution, responsible for developing and sustaining an infrastructure upon which multiple generations of theatre artists, musicians and an entire community (Trinity) have come to rely" ("Rising Tide," 20).
113 Ibid.

114   Morash and Richards, *Mapping Irish Theatre*, 8.
115   Massey, *For Space*, 76, 9.
116   AUD 3c, *TP*, 27 August 2016.
117   Ahmed, "Happy Objects," 11; Schneider, *Performing Remains*, 36; emphasis in original.
118   Harvie, *Staging the UK*, 42.
119   AUD 4a, *TP*, 31 August 2016.
120   Schneider, *Performing Remains*, 37.
121   AUD 2c, *TP*, 24 August 2016.
122   AUD 4c, *TP*, 31 August 2016.
123   AUD 2b, *TP*, 24 August 2016.
124   Schneider, *Performing Remains*, 37; emphasis in original.
125   Trinity Pageant performance, 24 August 2016.
126   Ibid.
127   Dolan, "Performance, Utopia, and the 'Utopian Performance,'" 476–7, quoted in Magelssen, *Simming*, 9.
128   AUD 4c, *TP*, 31 August 2016.
129   Kirshenblatt-Gimblett, "Afterlives," 2.
130   Massey, *Space, Place, and Gender*, 151.
131   Overton, "'The Real Newfoundland,'" 129.
132   Ibid.
133   Schneider, *Performing Remains*, 6.

CHAPTER FIVE

1   AUD 1a, *TM*, 1 December 2016.
2   For example, one audience member described, "The choose your own adventure bit. Like the 'follow me or follow me.' Isn't that like the books, the novel? 'Go to page 47'" (AUD 5a, *TM*, 4 December 2016). This is a reference to a popular novel series from the 1970s and 80s written from the second-person point of view in which the reader takes on the role of the protagonist. Every few pages, the reader is faced with a decision and must make a choice by turning to a page that will determine the protagonist's actions and survival. The series was pioneered by Edward Packard in his first novel, *Sugarcane Island*, in 1976. The *Choose Your Own Adventure* series now spans 180 books and sold more than 250 million books in 38 languages between 1979 and 1998 (Lodge, "Chooseco Embarks on Its Own Adventure").
3   Nestruck, "TomorrowLove™ is an Amorous Adventure."
4   White, "On Immersive Theatre," 221.

Notes to pages 149–62

5 Cavendish, "Punchdrunk: Plunge into a World of Extraordinary Theatre."
6 Machon, *Immersive Theatres*, 60.
7 White, "On Immersive Theatre," 221.
8 Higgins, "Immersive Theatre: Tired and Hackneyed Already?"
9 Ramos et al., "The Post-Immersive Manifesto."
10 Sedgman, "Ladies and Gentlemen Follow Me," 160.
11 Reason, "*Participations* on Participation," 275.
12 Alston, *Beyond Immersive Theatre*, 3–4.
13 AUD 1a, *TM*, 1 December 2016.
14 Mandell, "Immersive Theatre Defined."
15 McGonigal, *Reality is Broken*, 104.
16 Ibid.
17 Oddey and White, "Introduction: Visions Now: Life is a Screen," 8.
18 Ibid.
19 Mitchell Cushman, interview with the author, 24 February 2017.
20 Schulze, *Authenticity in Contemporary Theatre and Performance*, 67.
21 Machon, "On Being Immersed," 42.
22 Ibid, 40.
23 Ibid, 42.
24 Iezzi, "Punchdrunk's Felix Barrett."
25 Alston, "Audience Participation and Neoliberal Value."
26 National Theatre, "The Drowned Man: A Hollywood Fable: Presented by Punchdrunk and the National Theatre," *National Theatre*, accessed 14 August 2017, https://archive.is/JqnC8.
27 Beret, "Throw the Rose." The disturbing implication of wanting to be "molested" is particularly troubling given the spate of sexual harassment and assault reported at Punchdrunk's New York production, *Sleep No More*. See Jamieson, "Performers and Staffers" (2018).
28 Rose Biggin has written extensively on fan relationship and response to Punchdrunk. See her article "Reading Fan Mail: Communicating Immersive Experience in Punchdrunk's *Faust* and *The Masque of the Red Death*" and her book *Immersive Theatre and Audience Experience*.
29 Alston, "Audience Participation and Neoliberal Value," 133.
30 Zaiontz, "Narcissistic Spectatorship," 410.
31 Mitchell Cushman, interview with the author, 24 February 2017.
32 Ibid.
33 Nestruck, "TomorrowLove™ is an Amorous Adventure."
34 Karen Jacobson, in communication with the author, 30 May 2014.
35 AUD 3g and 3c, *TM*, 3 December 2016.

36　AUD 5b, *TM*, 4 December 2016.
37　Ibid.
38　AUD 5c, *TM*, 4 December 2016.
39　AUD 3a, 3b, 3d and 3e, *TM*, 3 December 2016.
40　AUD 5a and 5b, *TM*, 4 December 2016.
41　Biggin, *Immersive Theatre*, 101–3.
42　AUD 2c, *TM*, 2 December 2016.
43　AUD 3g, *TM*, 3 December 2016.
44　AUD 3b and 3d, *TM*, 3 December 2016.
45　Pons, "*Outdoors:* A Rimini Protokoll Theatre-Maze," 119.
46　AUD 3g, *TM*, 3 December 2016.
47　Raynaud, *Landscape Theatre/Théatre de Paysage*, 13–14, quoted in Machon, *Immersive Theatres*, 73.
48　AUD 3d, *TM*, 3 December 2016.
49　AUD 2e, *TM*, 2 December 2016.
50　Lavery, "Participation, Ecology, Cosmos," 305.
51　Schulze, *Authenticity in Contemporary Theatre and Performance*, 67.
52　Michelle Yagi, interview with the author, 8 February 2017.
53　Mitchell Cushman, interview with the author, 24 February 2017.
54　AUD 2g and 2a, *TM*, 2 December 2016.
55　Schulze, *Authenticity in Contemporary Theatre and Performance*, 153.
56　Foucault, "Of Other Spaces," 26.
57　Ibid., 24.
58　Schulze, *Authenticity in Contemporary Theatre and Performance*, 153.
59　Ibid.
60　White, "Odd Anonymized Needs: Punchdrunk's Masked Spectator," 228.
61　Schulze, *Authenticity in Contemporary Theatre and Performance*, 157.
62　Gardner, "I Didn't Know Where to Look."
63　AUD 5c, *TM*, 4 December 2016.
64　Machon, *Immersive Theatres*, 77.
65　Fuchs, *The Death of Character*, 132.
66　Alston, "Audience Participation and Neoliberal Value," 129.
67　Fuchs, *The Death of Character*, 134.
68　Pine and Gilmore, *Experience Economy*.
69　Ibid.
70　Phelan, *Unmarked*, 146.
71　Scarry, *The Body in Pain*, 197.
72　Machon, *Immersive Theatres*, 43.
73　Phelan, *Unmarked*, 148.
74　See for instance, Gail Bishop's blog

(https://gailebishop.wordpress.com/tag/drowned-man), *At the Gates Guarded by the Horses,* (http://templestudios.tumblr.com/post/65913090844/trust-me-ninth-journey), and *The Bloody Business* (https://www.thebloodybusiness.tumblr.com/post/74730811538/on-my-tenth-visit-i-may-have-stolen-an-itty-bitty#notes).

75 Burton also states that she knows at least two people who have seen *Sleep No More* upwards of 250 times. Burton, "Losing Sleep with the Superfans of 'Sleep No More.'"
76 Biggin, *Immersive Theatre,* 110.
77 AUD 1a, 1c, 1g, TM, 1 December 2016.
78 AUD 3b, TM, 3 December 2016.
79 Auslander, *Liveness,* 52.
80 Phelan, *Unmarked,* 149.
81 Barker, "*Crash,* Theatre Audiences, and the Idea of 'Liveness,'" 28.
82 Ibid.
83 Biggin, *Immersive Theatre,* 103.
84 Auslander, *Liveness,* 62.
85 Schulze, *Authenticity in Contemporary Theatre and Performance,* 132.
86 Machon, *Immersive Theatres,* 43.
87 AUD 2a, TM, 2 December 2016.
88 Ibid.
89 Ibid.
90 Mitchell Cushman, interview with the author, 24 February 2017. It is important to note that more recent discussions on representation, especially those on colour-conscious as opposed to colour-blind casting, would trouble any utopic interpretations of the actors' interchangeability.
91 Machon, *Immersive Theatres,* 87.
92 AUD 4e, TM, 4 December 2016.
93 AUD 4b, TM, 4 December 2016.
94 Biggin, *Immersive Theatre,* 105.
95 Ibid. In fact, in my experiences attending Punchdrunk's *The Drowned Man* and *The Burnt City* I would deliberately try to run away from my theatre-going companions – who reported doing the same – to try to "preserve" the sense of immersion into another world.
96 AUD 1a, TM, 1 December 2016.
97 Mitchell Cushman, interview with the author, 24 February 2017.
98 AUD 3e, TM, 3 December 2016.

CHAPTER SIX

1. Hurley, *Theatre & Feeling*, 4.
2. The scene described here is from *Learning Curve*, produced by Albany Theatre Projects in Chicago, IL. It ran from 31 July 2016 until 17 December 2016.
3. Stephenson, *Insecurity*, 173.
4. Ibid.
5. Stephenson, "The Theatrical Affect of Haunted Houses."
6. Horace, "The Art of Poetry," 73.
7. Gregg and Seigworth, "An Inventory of Shimmers," 1; emphasis in original.
8. Deleuze and Guattari, *A Thousand Plateaus*, 90.
9. Ibid., xvi.
10. Ahmed, *The Cultural Politics of Emotion*, 46.
11. Ahmed, "Affective Economies," 120.
12. Hurley and Warner, "Affect/Performance/Politics," 105.
13. AUD 1C, *TM*, 1 December 2016.
14. This is interesting to note in light of Caroline Heim's analysis of the audience-actor interaction in her book titled *Actors and Audiences: Conversations in the Electric Air*.
15. Hurley and Warner, "Affect/Performance/Politics," 99.
16. Hurley, *Theatre & Feeling*, 8.
17. Ibid., 9.
18. Fischer-Lichte, *The Transformative Power of Performance*, 38.
19. AUD 1d, *TM*, 1 December 2016.
20. AUD 1a, *TM*, 1 December 2016.
21. AUD 4b, *TM*, 4 December 2016.
22. AUD 4a, *TM*, 4 December 2016.
23. Reason and Reynolds, "Kinesthesia, empathy," 71.
24. Walmsley, "Deep Hanging Out," 287.
25. Mitchell Cushman, interview with the author, 24 February 2017.
26. AUD 4c, *TM*, 4 December 2016.
27. Crossick and Kaszynska, "Understanding the Value," 157.
28. Quoted in Machon, *(Syn)aesthetics*, 89.
29. Alston, *Beyond Immersive Theatre*, 7–8.
30. Schulze, *Authenticity in Contemporary Theatre and Performance*, 161.
31. Ibid., 151.
32. Jones, "Is Theatre Becoming Too Immersive?"
33. Schulze, *Authenticity in Contemporary Theatre and Performance*, 115.

34 Ibid., 120.
35 Ury, *Mobilities*.
36 Sedgman, "Ladies and Gentlemen," 166.
37 Ibid., 165.
38 Bourriaud, *Relational Aesthetics*, 112–13.
39 Bishop, "Antagonism and Relational Aesthetics," 62.
40 Reason, "*Participations* on Participation," 275.
41 Hurley, *Theatre & Feeling*, 7; emphasis in original.
42 Bennett, *Empathic Vision*, 23.
43 For instance, a series of articles describes audience response to the Broadway production of *1984* by directors Robert Icke and Duncan Macmillan: "Why Broadway's '1984' Audiences Are Fainting, Vomiting and Getting Arrested" by Ashley Lee for the *Hollywood Reporter* (24 June 2017) and "Broadway's '1984' Is Making Audience Members Puke, Faint And Fight" by Priscilla Frank for *Huffington Post* (26 June 2017).
44 Read, *Theatre and Everyday Life*, 218–21.
45 White, "Odd Anonymized Needs," 220.
46 Schulze, *Authenticity in Contemporary Theatre and Performance*, 140.
47 See also Laura Levin's *Performing Ground: Space, Camouflage and the Art of Blending In* (2014) for a consideration of the gendered nature of Punchdrunk's *Sleep No More*.
48 Schulze, *Authenticity in Contemporary Theatre and Performance*, 140.
49 Massumi, "The Future Birth of the Affective Act," 57.
50 Alston, "Politics in the Dark," 224.
51 AUD 3a, 3b, 3c, 3d, TM, 3 December 2016.
52 AUD 2c, TM, 2 December 2016.
53 AUD 1e, TM, 1 December 2016.
54 Machon, *Immersive Theatres*, 109.
55 Cushman, interview with the author, 24 February 2017.
56 AUD 3c, TM, 3 December 2016.
57 Hurley, *Theatre & Feeling*, 1.
58 Reason, "*Participations* on Participation," 277.
59 Thompson, *Performance Affects*, 116.
60 Ibid., 128.
61 Gallagher, "Politics and Presence," 78.
62 AUD 1f, TM, 1 December 2016.
63 Ibid.
64 Hurley, *Theatre & Feeling*, 10.
65 Gallagher, "Politics and Presence," 79.

66 Zaiontz, "Narcissistic Spectatorship," and Alston, "Audience Participation and Neoliberal Value."

CODA

1 Lewis, "Fiction is Outperforming."
2 Gu, Kropotov, and Yarochkin, "Fake News Machine," 3.
3 Schulze, *Authenticity in Contemporary Theatre*, 36.
4 Martin, "Introduction: Dramaturgy of the Real," 1.
5 Shields, *Reality Hunger*, 35.

Bibliography

A., Irene (@54obirenea). "Don't Miss This." TripAdvisor review, 17 September 2016. https://www.tripadvisor.ca/ShowUserReviews-g499208-d2236194-r1419518437-Rising_Tide_Theatre-Trinity_Newfoundland_Newfoundland_and_Labrador.html.

Abercrombie, Nicholas, and Brian Longhurst. *Audiences: A Sociological Theory of Performance and Imagination*. London, UK: SAGE Publications, 1998.

Adam, Barbara. *Timescapes of Modernity: The Environment and Invisible Hazards*. London, UK: Routledge, 1998.

– *Timewatch: The Social Analysis of Time*. Cambridge, MA: Polity Press, 1995.

Ahmed, Sara. "Affective Economies." *Social Text* 22, no. 2 (2004): 117–39.

– *The Cultural Politics of Emotion*. 2nd edition. Edinburgh: Edinburgh University Press, 2014.

– "Happy Objects." In *The Affect Theory Reader*, edited by Melissa Gregg and Gregory J. Seigworth, 29–51. Durham, NC: Duke University Press, 2010.

Alston, Adam. "Audience Participation and Neoliberal Value: Risk, Agency and Responsibility in Immersive Theatre." *Performance Research* 18, no. 2 (April 2013): 128–38.

– *Beyond Immersive Theatre: Aesthetics, Politics and Productive Participation*. London, UK: Palgrave Macmillan, 2016.

– "Politics in the Dark: Risk Perception, Affect and Emotion in Lundahl & Seitl's Rotating in a Room of Images." In *Affective Performance and Cognitive Science: Body, Brain and Being*, edited by Nicola Shaughnessy, 217–27. London, UK: Bloomsbury, 2013.

Alter, Jean. *A Sociosemiotic Theory of Theatre*. Philadelphia: University of Pennsylvania Press, 1990.

Alvarez, Natalie. "Affect Management and Militarism in Alberta's Mock Afghan Villages: Training the 'Strategic Corporal.'" In *Theatres of Affect*,

edited by Erin Hurley, 14–37. Toronto: Playwrights Canada Press, 2014.
— *Immersions in Cultural Difference: Tourism, War, Performance.* Ann Arbor, MI: University of Michigan Press, 2018.
Anderson, Benedict. *Imagined Communities: Reflections on the Origin and Spread of Nationalism.* Revised edition. London, UK: Verso, 2006.
Ang, Ien. *Living Room Wars: Rethinking Media Audiences.* London, UK: Routledge, 2006.
Arstila, Valtteri, and Dan Lloyd. "Subjective Time: From Past to Future." In *Subjective Time: The Philosophy, Psychology, and Neuroscience of Temporality,* edited by Dan Lloyd and Valtteri Arstila, 309–22. Cambridge, MA: MIT Press, 2014.
Artaud, Antonin. *The Theatre and Its Double.* 1938. New York, NY: Grovepress, 1958.
Aston, Elaine. *An Introduction to Feminism and Theatre.* London, UK: Routledge, 1995.
Auslander, Philip. *Liveness: Performance in a Mediatized Culture.* 2nd edition. London, UK: Routledge, 2008.
Austin, J.L. *How to Do Things with Words.* Cambridge, MA: Harvard University Press, 1962.
Ayckborn, Alan. *The Crafty Art of Playmaking.* London, UK: Faber and Faber, 2002.
Ayer, Alfred J. *The Foundations of Empirical Knowledge.* 1940. Reprint, London, UK: Palgrave Macmillan, 1964.
Bachelard, Gaston. *The Dialectic of Duration.* Translated by Mary McAllester James. Manchester, UK: Clinamen Press, 2000.
Bacon, Barbara Schaffer, Cheryl Yuen, and Pam Korza. *Animating Democracy: The Artistic Imagination as a Force in Civic Dialogue.* Washington, DC: Americans for the Arts, 1999.
Badiou, Alain. *The Century.* Translated by Alberto Toscano. Cambridge, UK: Polity Press, 2007.
Bailes, Sara Jane. *Performance Theatre and the Poetics of Failure: Forced Entertainment, Goat Island, Elevator Repair Service.* London, UK: Routledge, 2011.
Bailey, Marlon M. "Gender/Racial Realness: Theorizing the Gender System in Ballroom Culture." *Feminist Studies* 37, no. 2 (2011): 365–86.
Banes, Sally, and André Lepecki, eds. *The Senses in Performance.* London, UK: Routledge, 2007.
Barish, Jonas. *The Antitheatrical Prejudice.* Berkeley: University of California Press, 1985.

Barker, Martin. "*Crash*, Theatre Audiences, and the Idea of 'Liveness.'" *Studies in Theatre and Performance* 23, no. 1 (January 2003): 21–39.
– "I Have Seen the Future and it is Not Here Yet …; Or, on Being Ambitious for Audience Research." *The Communication Review* 9, no. 2 (2006): 123–41.
Barker, Roberta, and Kim Solga, eds. "Introduction: Reclaiming Canadian Realisms, Part Two." In *New Canadian Realisms*, edited by Roberta Barker and Kim Solga, 1–15. Vol. 2 of *New Essays on Canadian Theatre*, edited by Ric Knowles. Toronto, ON: Playwrights Canada Press, 2012.
Barthes, Roland. "The Reality Effect." In *The Rustle of Language*, edited by François Wahl, translated by Richard Howard, 141–8. Berkeley, CA: University of California Press, 1969.
Baudrillard, Jean. *Simulacra and Simulation*. Translated by Sheila Faria Glaser. Ann Arbor, MI: University of Michigan Press, 1994.
Bennett, Jill. *Empathic Vision: Affect, Trauma, and Contemporary Art*. Stanford, CA: Stanford University Press, 2005.
Bennett, Susan. "3-D A/B." In *Theatre and AutoBiography: Writing and Performing Lives in Theory and Practice*, edited by Sherrill Grace and Jerry Wasserman, 33–48. Vancouver, BC: Talon Books, 2006.
– "Performing Ireland: Tourism and the Abbey Theatre." *Canadian Journal of Irish Studies* 30, no. 2 (Fall 2004): 30–7.
– *Theatre Audiences*. London, UK: Routledge, 1997.
Bennett, Susan, and Mary Polito. "Thinking Site: An Introduction." In *Performing Environments: Site-Specificity in Medieval and Early Modern English Drama*, edited by Susan Bennett and Mary Polito, 1–13. London, UK: Palgrave Macmillan, 2014.
Beret, Raspberry. "Throw the Rose: Dreams from Temple Studios." Tumblr. 17 May 2014. http://throwtherose.tumblr.com/post/86002401016/the-premiumexecutive-entrance-spoilers-there.
Berlant, Lauren. *Cruel Optimism*. Durham, NC: Duke University Press, 2011.
Biggin, Rose. *Immersive Theatre and Audience Experience: Space, Game and Story in the Work of Punchdrunk*. Basingstoke, UK: Palgrave Macmillan, 2017.
– "Reading fan mail: Communicating immersive experience in Punchdrunk's Faust and The Masque of the Red Death." *Participations*, 12, no. 1 (2015): 301–17.
Binette, Melanie. "Spatial Encounters: Spectatorship in Immersive Performances." Master's thesis, Concordia University, 2014. https://spectrum.library.concordia.ca/978496/1/Binette_MA_S2014.pdf.
Bishop, Claire. "Antagonism and Relational Aesthetics." *October* 110 (Fall 2004): 51–80.

- *Artificial Hells: Participatory Art and the Politics of Spectatorship.* London, UK: Verso, 2012.
Bogart, Anne. *What's the Story: Essays about Art, Theater and Storytelling.* London, UK: Routledge, 2014.
Borchmeyer, Florian. *An Enemy of the People.* Adapted from the original text by Henrik Ibsen, translated by Maria Milisavljevic. Unpublished script, 2014.
Botsman, Rachel. *Who Can You Trust?: How Technology Brought Us Together and Why It Might Drive Us Apart.* London, UK: Penguin, 2017.
Bottoms, Stephen. "Authorizing the Audience: The Conceptual Drama of Tim Crouch." *Performance Research* 14, no. 1 (March 2009): 65–76.
Bourdieu, Pierre. *The Rules of Art: Genesis and Structure of the Literary Field.* Translated by Susan Emanuel. Stanford, CA: Stanford University Press, 1996.
Bourriaud, Nicolas. *Relational Aesthetics.* Translated by Simon Pleasance and Fronza Woods. Dijon, FR: Les Presse du Réel, 2002. http://artsites.ucsc.edu/sdaniel/230/Relational%20Aesthetics_entire.pdf.
Bousquet, David. "Poet and the Roots: Authenticity in the Works of Linton Kwesi Johnson and Benjamin Zephaniah." In *The Aesthetics of Authenticity: Medial Constructions of the Real*, edited by Wolfgang Funk, Irmtraud Huber, and Florian Groß, 187–206. Bielefeld: Transcript Verlag, 2014.
Boyd, Shelley. *Garden Plots: Canadian Women Writers and Their Literary Plots.* Montreal, QC, and Kingston, ON: McGill-Queen's University Press, 2014.
boyd, danah. "Social Network Sites as Networked Publics." In *A Networked Self: Identity, Community, and Culture on Social Network Sites*, edited by Zizi Papacharissi, 39–58. New York, NY: Routledge, 2010.
- *Taken out of Context: American Teen Sociality in Networked Publics.* Doctoral thesis, University of California, 2008. http://www.danah.org/papers/TakenOutOfContext.pdf.
Breed, Ananda, and Tim Prentki. "General Introduction." In *Performance and Civic Engagement*, edited by Ananda Breed and Tim Prentki, 1–16. Basingstoke, UK: Palgrave Macmillan, 2018.
- "Introduction to Politicising Communities." In *Performance and Civic Engagement*, edited by Ananda Breed and Tim Prentki, 19–24. Basingstoke, UK: Palgrave Macmillan, 2018.
Brennan, Teresa. *The Transmission of Affect.* Ithaca, NY: Cornell University Press, 2004.
Brook, Peter. *The Empty Space.* New York, NY: Touchstone, 1968.

Buck, Ross, and Stacie Renfro Powers. "Emotion, Media, and the Global Village." In *The Routledge Handbook of Emotions and Mass Media*, edited by Katrin Döveling, Christian von. Scheve, and Elly Konijn, 181–94. London, UK: Routledge, 2011.

Burton, Tara Isabella. "Losing Sleep with the Superfans of 'Sleep No More.'" *Narratively*, 9 September 2015. http://narrative.ly/losing-sleep-with-the-superfans-of-sleep-no-more.

Carlson, Marvin. *Performance: A Critical Introduction*. London, UK: Routledge, 1996.

– *Shattering Hamlet's Mirror: Theatre and Reality*. Ann Arbor, MI: University of Michigan Press, 2016.

Carson, Anne. *Eros the Bittersweet*. McLean, IL: Dalkey Archive Press, 1998.

Case, Sue-Ellen. "Towards a Butch-Femme Aesthetic." In *The Lesbian and Gay Studies Reader*, edited by Henry Abelove, 294–306. New York, NY: Routledge, 1993.

Cavell, Stanley. "The Fact of Television." *Daedalus* 111, no. 4 (September 1982): 75–96.

Cavendish, Dominic. "Punchdrunk: Plunge Into a World of Extraordinary Theatre." *The Telegraph*, 20 June 2013. https://www.telegraph.co.uk/culture/theatre/theatre-features/10127892/Punchdrunk-plunge-into-a-world-of-extraordinary-theatre.html.

CBC *News*. "Roberts Says He Shot Oil Executive in Self-Defence." 8 November 2000. www.cbc.ca/news/canada/roberts-says-he-shot-oil-executive-in-self-defence-1.242513.

Chafe, Paul. "'Only an Artist Can Measure Up to Such a Place': Place and Identity in Contemporary Newfoundland Fiction." PhD dissertation, Memorial University of Newfoundland, 2008.

Clough, Patricia Ticineto. "Introduction." In *The Affective Turn: Theorizing the Social*, edited by Patricia Ticineto Clough and Jean Halley, 1–33. Durham, NC: Duke University Press, 2007.

Cohen, Erik. "The heterogeneization of a tourist art." *Annals of Tourism Research* 20, no. 1 (1993): 138–63.

Cohen-Cruz, Jan. *Local Acts: Community-Based Performance in the United States*. New Brunswick, NJ: Rutgers University Press, 2005.

– "The Stranger Within." *Performance Research* 9, no. 4 (2004): 123–5. http://doi.org/10.1080/13528165.2004.10872063.

Colbert, Stephen. "Truthiness." *The Colbert Report*. Comedy Central Video, 2:40. 17 October 2005. http:// www.cc.com/video-clips/63ite2/the-colbert-report-the-word–truthiness.

- "White House Correspondents' Dinner 20016." YouTube video, CNN, 29 April 2016. https://www.youtube.com/watch?v=IJ-a2KeyCAY.
Collini, Stefan. "On Variousness, and on Persuasion." *New Left Review* 27 (2004): 65–97.
Coveney, Michael. "Stage directions: Immersive Theatre" *Prospect*. 19 August 2010, https://www.prospectmagazine.co.uk/magazine/you-me-bum-bum-train-one-on-one-theatre.
Crossick, Geoffrey, and Patrycja Kaszynska. *Understanding the Value of Arts & Culture: The AHRC Cultural Value Project*. Swindon, UK: Arts and Humanities Research Council, 2016.
Crumlish, Christian, and Erin Malone. *Designing Social Interfaces: Principles, Patterns and Practices for Improving the User Experience*. Sebastopol, CA: O'Reilly Media, 2009.
Cubitt, Sean. "Laurie Anderson: Myth, Management and Platitude." In *Art Has No History!: The Making and Unmaking of Modern Art*, edited by John Roberts, 278–96. London, UK: Verso, 1994.
Cushman, Robert. "Theatre Review: Tarragon Elevates a 'Lesser' Ibsen in One of the Great Plays about Sibling Rivalry." *National Post*, Postmedia Network, 8 October 2014. https://nationalpost.com/entertainment/theatre/theatre-review-tarragon-elevates-a-lesser ibsen-in-one-of-the-great-plays-about-sibling-rivalry.
Davidson, Clifford. "'What hempen home-spuns have we swagg'ring here?' Amateur Actors in *A Midsummer Night's Dream* and the Coventry Civic Plays and Pageants." *Shakespeare Studies* 19 (January 1987): 87–99.
Davis, Tracy C. "Performative Time." In *Representing the Past: Essays in Performance Historiography*, edited by Charlotte M. Canning and Thomas Postlewait, 142–67. Iowa City, IA: University of Iowa Press, 2010.
Dawson, Gary Fisher. *Documentary Theatre in the United States: An Historical Survey and Analysis of Its Content, Form, and Stagecraft*. Westport, CT: Greenwood Publishing Group, 1999.
Day, Graham. *Community and Everyday Life*. London, UK: Routledge, 2006.
Debord, Guy. "Introduction to a Critique of Urban Geography." Translated by Ken Knabb. *Les Lévres Nues* 6 (September 1955): 23–7. https://www.cddc.vt.edu/sionline/presitu/geography.html.
Deleuze, Gilles. *Proust and Signs: The Complete Text*. Translated by Richard Howard. Minneapolis, MN: University of Minnesota Press, 2003.
Deleuze, Gilles, and Félix Guattari. *A Thousand Plateaus: Capitalism and Schizophrenia*. Translated by Brian Massumi. Minneapolis, MN: University of Minnesota Press, 1987.
Derrida, Jacques. "Structure, Sign and Play in the Discourse of the Human

Sciences." In *Writing and Difference*, translated by Alan Bass, 352–70. London, UK: Routledge, 1978.

– "The Theatre of Cruelty and the Closure of Representation." In *Writing and Difference*, translated by Alan Bass, 292–316. London, UK: Routledge, 1978.

Devine, Michael. "Cultural Evolution in Newfoundland Theatre: The Rise of the Gros Morne Theatre Festival." *Theatre Research in Canada/Recherches théâtrales Au Canada* 25, no.1 (Spring/Fall 2004): 67–88.

Diamond, Elin. *Unmaking Mimesis: Essays on Feminism and Theater*. London, UK: Routledge, 1997.

Di Benedetto, Stephen. "Guiding Somatic Responses within Performative Structures: Contemporary Live Art and Sensorial Perception." In *The Senses in Performance*, edited by Sally Barnes and André Lepecki, 124–34. London, UK: Routledge, 2007.

"Digital Wildfires in a Hyperconnected World," *World Economic Forum Report 2016*, https://reports.weforum.org/global-risks-2013/risk-case-1/digital-wildfires-in-a-hyperconnected-world.

Dolan, Jill. "Performance, Utopia, and the 'Utopian Performance.'" *Theatre Journal* 53, no. 3 (October 2001): 455–79. http://doi.org/10.1353/tj.2001.0068.

– *Utopia in Performance: Finding Hope at the Theater*. Ann Arbour, MI: University of Michigan Press, 2005.

Doubrovsky, Serge. *Fils*. Paris: Gallimard, 1977.

Downstage Creation Ensemble (Ellen Close, Ethan Cole, Col Cseke, Anton DeGroot, Nicola Elson, Braden Griffiths, and Simon Mallet). *Good Fences*. Unpublished script, 3 March 2015.

Dreysse, Miriam, and Florian Malzacher, eds. *Experts of the Everyday: The Theatre of Rimini Protokoll*. Berlin: Alexander Verlag, 2008.

Duggan, Patrick. "Others, Spectatorship, and the Ethics of Verbatim Performance." *New Theatre Quarterly* 29, no. 2 (May 2013): 146–58. https://doi.org/10.1017/S0266464X13000250.

– *Trauma-Tragedy: Symptoms of Contemporary Performance*. Manchester, UK: Manchester University Press, 2012.

Dundes, Alan. *Interpreting Folklore*. Bloomington, IN: Indiana University Press, 1980.

Dustagheer, Sarah. "Shakespeare and the 'Spatial Turn.'" *Literature Compass* 10, no. 7 (July 2013): 570–81. https://doi.org/10.1111/lic3.12068.

Eagleton, Terry. "Pork Chops and Pineapples." Review of *Mimesis*, by Eric Auerbach. *London Review of Books*, 23 October 2003. https://www.lrb.co.uk/the-paper/v25/n20/terry-eagleton/pork-chops-and-pineapples.

Ermarth, Elizabeth Deeds. *Sequel to History: Postmodernism and the Crisis of Representational Time*. Princeton, NJ: Princeton University Press, 1992.

Eco, Umberto. "Travels in Hyperreality." In *Travels in Hyper Reality: Essays*, translated by William Weaver, 1–58. San Diego, CA: Harcourt Brace Jovanovich, 1983.

Enns, Anthony, and Shelley Trower. "Introduction." In *Vibratory Modernism*, edited by Anthony Enns and Shelley Trower, 1–29. Basingstoke, UK: Palgrave Macmillan, 2013.

Espiner, Mark. "Between the lines." *The Guardian*, 22 May 2004. https://www.theguardian.com/arts/features/story/0,,1222402,00.html.

Filewod, Alan. *Collective Encounters: Documentary Theatre in English Canada*. Toronto, ON: University of Toronto Press, 1987.

– "The Mummers Troupe, The Canada Council, and the Production of Theatre History." *Theatre Research in Canada/Recherches théâtrales Au Canada* 19, no. 1 (January 1998): 3–34. https://journals.lib.unb.ca/index.php/TRIC/article/view/7116.

– "National Theatre/National Obsession." In *Canadian Theatre History: Selected Readings*, edited by Don Rubin, 424–31. New York, NY: McGraw-Hill, 1996.

Fischer-Lichte, Erika. "Shared bodies, shared spaces: the bodily co-presence of actors and spectators." In *The Transformative Power of Performance*, 46–82. London, UK: Routledge, 2008.

Fisher, Marc, John Woodrow Cox, and Peter Hermann. "Pizzagate: From rumor, to hashtag, to gunfire in D.C." *The Washington Post*, 6 December 2016.

Forsyth, Alison, and Chris Megson, eds. *Get Real: Documentary Theatre Past and Present*. Basingstoke, UK: Palgrave Macmillan, 2009.

Foucault, Michel. "Of Other Spaces." Translated by Jay Miskowiec. *Diacritics* 16, no. 1 (Spring 1986): 22–7. http://doi.org/10.2307/464648.

Freshwater, Helen. *Theatre & Audience*. Basingstoke, UK: Palgrave Macmillan, 2009.

Frye, Northrop. *The Bush Garden: Essays on the Canadian Imagination*. Toronto, ON: House of Anansi Press, 1971.

Fuchs, Elinor. *The Death of Character: Perspectives on Theater after Modernism*. Bloomington IN: Indiana University Press, 1996.

Funk, Wolfgang, Florian Groß, and Irmtraud Huber. "Exploring the Empty Plinth: The Aesthetics of Authenticity." In *The Aesthetics of Authenticity: Medial Constructions of the Real*, edited by Wolfgang Funk, Florian Groß, Irmtaud Huber, 9–21. Bielefeld: Transcript Verlag, 2012.

Gallagher, Kathleen. "Politics and Presence: A Theatre of Affective Emotions." In *In Defense of Theatre: Aesthetic Practices and Social Interventions*, edited by Kathleen Gallagher and Barry Freeman, 67–82. Toronto, ON: University of Toronto Press, 2016.

– *Why Theatre Matters: Urban Youth, Engagement, and a Pedagogy of the Real*. Toronto, ON: University of Toronto Press, 2014.

Gallagher, Kathleen, Christine Balt, and Lindsay Valve. "Vulnerability, care and hope in audience research: theatre as a site of struggle for an intergenerational politics." *Studies in Theatre and Performance*, vol. 41, no. 1 (2021): 1–19. http://doi.org/10.1080/14682761.2020.1862998.

Gallagher, Kathleen, Scott Mealey, and Kelsey Jacobson. "Accuracy and Ethics, Feelings and Failures: Youth Experimenting with Documentary Practices of Performing Reality." *Theatre Research in Canada/Recherches théâtrales Au Canada* 39, no. 1 (Spring 2018): 58–76.

Gallie, W.B. *Philosophy and the Historical Understanding*. New York, NY: Schoken Books, 1964.

Garde, Ulrike, and Meg Mumford. "Postdramatic Reality Theatre and Productive Insecurity: Destabilizing Encounters with the Unfamiliar in Theatre from Sydney and Berlin." In *Postdramatic Theatre and the Political: International Perspectives on Contemporary Performance*, edited by Karen Jürs-Munby, Jerome Carroll, and Steven Giles, 147–64. New York, NY: Bloomsbury Publishing, 2013.

Gardner, Lyn. "I Didn't Know Where to Look." *The Guardian*, 3 March 2005. https://www.theguardian.com/stage/2005/mar/03/theatre2.

– "In Theatre, Fiction is Being Underrated." *The Guardian*, 26 May 2014. https://www.theguardian.com/stage/theatreblog/2014/may/26/verbatim-theatre-fiction-stories-london-road.

Garrett, R. Kelly, Erik C. Nisbet, and Emily K. Lynch. "Undermining the Corrective Effects of Media-Based Political Fact Checking? The Role of Contextual Cues and Naïve Theory." *Journal of Communication* 63, no. 4 (2013): 617–37.

Geertz, Clifford. *The Interpretation of Cultures: Selected Essays*. New York, NY: Basic Books, 1973.

Gilmore, Rachel. "Fake news on Facebook: 18 million posts containing COVID-19 misinformation removed." *Global News*, 19 May 2021. https://globalnews.ca/news/7876321/covid-19-misinformation-social-media-facebook-instagram.

Giroux, Henry, Jason Stanley, and Kathleen Higgins. "The Truth About Post-Truth." Interview by Paul Kennedy. *Ideas*, CBC, 18 January 2017. Audio,

54:00. https://www.cbc.ca/radio/ideas/the-truth-about-post-truth-1.3939958.

Global News. "Oilpatch bomber Wiebo Ludwig, warrior to some, terrorist to others, dead at 70." *The Canadian Press*, 9 April 2012. https://globalnews.ca/news/231986/oilpatch-bomber-wiebo-ludwig-warrior-to-some-terrorist-to-others-dead-at-70.

Goffman, Erving. *The Presentation of Self in Everyday Life.* London, UK: Penguin Books, 1990.

Gordon, Alan. *Time Travel: Tourism and the Rise of the Living History Museum in Mid-Twentieth Century Canada.* Vancouver: University of British Columbia Press, 2016.

Government of Newfoundland and Labrador. *The Newfoundland Adventure.* St John's: Department of Industrial Development, 1975.

Gregg, Melissa, and Gregory J. Seigworth. "An Inventory of Shimmers." In *The Affect Theory Reader*, edited by Melissa Gregg and Gregory J. Seigworth, 1–25. Durham, NC: Duke University Press, 2010.

Gu, Lion, Vladimir Kropotov, and Fyodor Yarochkin. "The Fake News Machine: How Propagandists Abuse the Internet and Manipulate the Public." *TrendLabs Research Paper*, 2017. https://documents.trendmicro.com/assets/white_papers/wp-fake-news-machine-how-propagandists-abuse-the-internet.pdf.

Handler, Richard, and Eric Gable. *The New History in an Old Museum: Creating the Past at Colonial Williamsburg.* Durham, NC: Duke University Press, 1997.

Harvey, Dustin Scott. "Make What You Need." In *In Defense of Theatre: Aesthetic Practices and Social Interventions*, edited by Kathleen Gallagher and Barry Freeman, 35–48. Toronto, ON: University of Toronto Press, 2016.

Harvie, Jen. *Staging the UK.* Manchester, UK: Manchester University Press, 2005.

Hawking, Stephen. *A Brief History of Time.* London, UK: Bantam Books, 1988.

Heathcote, Dorothy. *Dorothy Heathcote on Education and Drama: Essential Writings.* Edited by Cecily O'Neill. London, UK: Routledge, 2015.

Heim, Caroline. *Actors and Audiences: Conversations in the Electric Air.* London, UK: Routledge, 2020.

– "'Argue with us!': Audience Co-creation Through Post-Performance Discussions." *New Theatre Quarterly* 28, no. 2 (May 2012): 189–97. http://doi.org/10.1017/S0266464X12000279.

– *Audience as Performer: The Changing Role of Theatre Audiences in the Twenty-First Century.* London, UK: Routledge, 2016.

Heritage, Paul. "Taking Hostages: Staging Human Rights." *TDR: The Drama Review* 48, no. 3 (Fall 2004): 96–106. http://doi.org/10.1162/105420 4041667695.

Hesford, Wendy S. "Reading the signs: Performative white allyship." *Quarterly Journal of Speech* 107, no. 2 (2021): 239–44.

Higgins, Charlotte. "Immersive Theatre: Tired and Hackneyed Already?" *The Guardian*, 7 December 2009. https://www.theguardian.com/culture/charlottehigginsblog/2009/dec/07/theatre-punchdrunk.

Higgins, Jenny. "Cod Moratorium." Heritage Newfoundland and Labrador, 2009. http://www.heritage.nf.ca/articles/economy/moratorium.php.

Hochschild, Arlie Russell. *The Managed Heart: Commercialization of Human Feeling*. Berkeley, CA: University of California Press, 1983.

Hogan, Bernie. "The presentation of self in the age of social media: Distinguishing performances and exhibitions online." *Bulletin of Science, Technology & Society* 30, no. 6 (2010): 377–86.

Hoile, Christopher. "An Enemy of the People." *Stage Door*, 25 September 2014. http://www.stage-door.com/Theatre/2014/Entries/2014/9/25_An_Enemy_of_the_People.html

Holdsworth, Nadine, Jane Milling, and Helen Nicholson. "Theatre, Performance, and the Amateur Turn." *Contemporary Theatre Review* 27, no. 1 (April 2017): 4–17. http://doi.org/10.1080/10486801.2017.1266229.

Horace. "The Art of Poetry." In *Theatre/Theory/Theatre: The Major Critical Texts from Aristotle and Zeami to Soyinka and Havel*, edited by Daniel Gerould, translated by John Conington, 68–83. 1st Century BC. New York, NY: Applause, 2000.

Houston, Andy. "Collaborating with Audiences in the Creation of Site-Specific Performance, or, Transgression, Endurance, and Collaboration in *Windblown / Rafales*." Unpublished paper, 2013.

Hughes, Jenny. "Theatre, Performance, and the 'War on Terror': Ethical and Political Questions arising from British Theatrical Responses to War and Terrorism." *Contemporary Theatre Review* 17, no. 2 (May 2007): 149–64.

Hunter, Lindsay Brandon. *Playing Real: Mimesis, Media, and Mischief*. Evanston, IL: Northwestern University Press, 2021.

Hurley, Erin. "Introduction: Theatre Matters." In *Theatres of Affect*, edited by Erin Hurley, 1–11. Vol. 4 of *New Essays on Canadian Theatre*, edited by Ric Knowles. Toronto, ON: Playwrights Canada Press, 2014.

– *National Performance: Representing Quebec from Expo 67 to Céline Dion*. Toronto, ON: University of Toronto Press, 2010.

– *Theatre and Feeling*. Basingstoke, UK: Palgrave Macmillan, 2010.

Hurley, Erin, and Sara Warner. "Special Section: 'Affect/Performance/

Politics.'" *Journal of Dramatic Theory and Criticism* 26, no. 2 (Spring 2012): 99–107. http://doi.org/10.1353/dtc.2012.0000.

Hussey, Ian. "The Future of Alberta's Oil Sands Industry." *Parkland Institute, University of Alberta*, 10 March 2020. https://www.parklandinstitute.ca/the_future_of_albertas_oil_sands_industry.

Ibsen, Henrik. *An Enemy of the People*. Mineola, NY: Dover Publications, 1999.

Iezzi, Teressa. "Punchdrunk's Felix Barrett Drops You in His Theater with No Directions Home." *Fast Company*, 8 October 2011. https://www.fastcompany.com/1772599/punchdrunks-felix-barrett-drops-you-his-theater-no-directions-home.

Irigaray, Luce. *Speculum of the Other Woman*. Ithaca, NY: Cornell University Press, 1985.

Jackson, Shannon. *Social Works: Performing Art, Supporting Publics*. London, UK: Routledge, 2011.

Jacobson, Kelsey. "Really Sell it to Me: Immersive Theatre as Ideal Commodity." *Etudes* 2, no. 2 (December 2016): 1–23.

Jamieson, Amber. "Performers and Staffers at 'Sleep No More' Say Audiences Members Have Sexually Assaulted Them." *Buzzfeed*, 6 February 2018. https://www.buzzfeednews.com/article/amberjamieson/sleep-no-more.

Jansen, David, and Holger Syme. "Tarragon Lecture Series – Dr. Holger Syme and David Jansen discuss An Enemy of the People." *Tarragon Theatre*, 30 October 2015. YouTube Video, 1:01:00. https://www.youtube.com/watch?v=wG7M_L1iAZE.

Jauss, Hans Robert, and Elizabeth Benzinger. "Literary History as a Challenge to Literary Theory." *New Literary History* 2, no. 1 (Autumn 1970): 7–37. http://doi.org/10.2307/468585.

Jennings, Rebecca. "Who are the black squares and cutesy illustrations really for?" *VOX*, 6 June 2020. https://www.vox.com/the-goods/2020/6/3/21279336/blackout-tuesday-black-lives-matter-instagram-performative-allyship.

Johanson, Katya, and Hilary Glow. "A Virtuous Circle: The Positive Evaluation Phenomenon in Arts Audience Research." *Participations* 12, no. 1 (2015): 254–70.

Johnson, Tracy. "Just How Many Jobs Have Been Cut in the Oilpatch?" *CBC News*, 6 July 2016, www.cbc.ca/news/canada/calgary/oil-patch-layoffs-how-many-1.3665250.

Johnston, Adrian. "Jacques Lacan." In *The Stanford Encyclopedia of Philosophy*, edited by Edward N. Zalta, 2013. https://plato.stanford.edu/archives/win2016/entries/lacan.

Johnston, Caleb, and Geraldine Pratt. "Taking *Nanay* to the Philippines: Transnational Circuits of Affect." In *Theatres of Affect*, edited by Erin Hurley, 192–212. Toronto: Playwrights Canada Press, 2014.

Jones, Alice. "Is Theatre Becoming Too Immersive?" *The Independent*, 6 March 2013. http://www.independent.co.uk/arts-entertainment/theatre-dance/features/is-theatre-becoming-too-immersive-8521511.html.

Kalina, Peter. "Performative Allyship." *Technium Social Sciences Journal* 11, (2020): 479–81.

Kalsnes, Bente. "Fake News." In *Oxford Research Encyclopedia of Communication*, edited by Jon F. Nussbaum. New York, NY: Oxford University Press, 2018.

Kant, Immanuel. "On the Form and Principles of the Sensible and the Intelligible World [Inaugural Dissertation]." In *Theoretical Philosophy, 1755–1770*, edited by David Walford and Ralf Meerbote, 373–416. Cambridge, UK: Cambridge University Press, 2016.

Kaye, Nick. *Site-Specific Art: Performance, Place and Documentation*. London, UK: Routledge, 2000.

Kelleher, Joe. "Review of *Theatre, Intimacy & Engagement: The Last Human Venue* by Alan Read." *The Drama Review* 54, no. 2 (2010): 181–3.

– *Theatre & Politics*. London, UK: Red Globe Press, 2009.

Kennelly, Jacqueline. "'Acting Out' in the Public Sphere: Community Theatre and Citizenship Education." *Canadian Journal of Education/Revue canadienne de l'éducation* 29, no. 2 (2006): 541–62.

Kim, Minseong, and Jihye Kim. "Destination Authenticity as a Trigger of Tourists' Online Engagement on Social Media." *Journal of Travel Research* 59, no. 7 (2020): 1238–52.

Kirshenblatt-Gimblett, Barbara. "Afterlives." *Performance Research* 2, no. 2, (September 1997): 1–9. http://doi.org/10.1080/13528165.1997.10871545.

Knaller, Susan. "Authenticity as an Aesthetic Notion: Normative and Non-Normative Concepts in Modern and Contemporary Poetics." In *The Aesthetics of Authenticity: Medial Constructions of the Real*, edited by Wolfgang Funk, Florian Groß, Irmtaud Huber, 25–40. Bielefeld: Transcript Verlag, 2012.

Knapp, Shelley. "Shooter Feared for His Life: Oil Company Official Charged Him, Accused Says." *Calgary Herald*, 9 November 2000, B5.

Knowles, Ric. "Documemory, Autobiology, and the Utopian Performative in Canadian Autobiographical Solo Performance." In *Theatre and Autobiography: Writing and Performing Lives in Theory and Practice*, edited by Sherrill Grace and Jerry Wasserman, 49–71. Vancouver, BC: Talonbooks, 2006.

Kohn, Margaret. "Homo spectator: Public Space in the Age of the Spectacle." *Philosophy & Social Criticism* 34, no. 5 (2008): 467–86.

Kroker, Arthur. "The Cultural Imagination and the National Questions." *Canadian Journal of Political and Social Theory* 6, nos. 1–2 (Winter 1982): 5–11.

Kwon, Miwon. *One Place After Another: Site-Specific Art and Locational Identity*. Cambridge, MA: MIT Press, 2004.

Lavery, Carl. "Introduction: Performance and Ecology – What Can Theatre Do?" *Green Letters* 20, no. 3 (2016): 229–36. http://doi.org/10.1080/14688 417.2016.1206695.

– "Participation, Ecology, Cosmos." In *Reframing Immersive Theatre: The Politics and Pragmatics of Participatory Performance*, edited by James Frieze, 303–16. London, UK: Palgrave Macmillan, 2016.

Lederman, Marsha. "Alberta Theatre Projects Launches 'Urgent' Fundraising Campaign." *Globe and Mail*, last modified 21 March 2018. www.theglobeandmail.com/arts/theatre-and-performance/alberta-theatre-projects-launches-urgent-fundraising-campaign/article34188921.

Lefebvre, Henri. *The Production of Space*. Translated by Donald Nicholson-Smith. Oxford, UK: Blackwell Publishers, 1991.

Lehmann, Hans-Thies. *Postdramatic Theatre*. Translated by Karen Jürs-Munby. Abingdon, UK: Routledge, 2006.

Lewis, Paul. "'Fiction is outperforming reality': how YouTube's algorithm distorts truth." *The Guardian*, 2 February 2018. https://www.theguardian.com/technology/2018/feb/02/how-youtubes-algorithm-distorts-truth.

Limon, Jerzy. *The Chemistry of the Theatre: Performativity of Time*. Basingstoke, UK: Palgrave Macmillan, 2010.

Little, Edward. "When you're up to your ass in alligators." In *In Defense of Theatre: Aesthetic Practices and Social Interventions*, edited by Barry Freeman and Kathleen Gallagher, 49–64. Toronto, ON: University of Toronto Press, 2016.

Lodge, Sally. "Chooseco Embarks on Its Own Adventure." *Publisher's Weekly*, 18 January 2007. https://www.publishersweekly.com/pw/by-topic/childrens/childrens-book-news/article/209-chooseco-embarks-on-its-own-adventure.html.

Loneran, Patrick. *Theatre & Social Media*. Basingstoke, UK: Palgrave Macmillan, 2015.

MacAloon, John. "Introduction: Cultural Performances, Cultural Theory." In *Rite, Drama, Festival, Spectacle: Rehearsal Towards a Theory of Cultural Performance*, edited by John J. MacAloon, 1–15. Philadelphia: Institute for the Study of Human Issues, 1984.

MacArthur, Mary. "Farmers Establish Trust Fund." *The Western Producer*, 12 November 1998. www.producer.com/1998/11/farmers-establish-trust-fund.

Machon, Josephine. *Immersive Theatres: Intimacy and Immediacy in Contemporary Performance*. Basingstoke, UK: Palgrave Macmillan, 2013.
- "On Being Immersed: The Pleasure of Being: Washing, Feeding, Holding." In *Reframing Immersive Theatre: The Politics and Pragmatics of Participatory Performance*, edited by James Frieze, 29–42. London, UK: Palgrave Macmillan, 2016.
- *(Syn)aesthetics: Redefining Visceral Performance*. Basingstoke, UK: Palgrave Macmillan, 2009.

Mackey, Sally, and Nicolas Whybrow. "Taking Place: Some Reflections on Site, Performance and Community." *Research in Drama Education: The Journal of Applied Theatre and Performance* 12, no. 1 (January 2007): 1–14.

Magelssen, Scott. *Living History Museums: Undoing History Through Performance*. Lanham, MD: Scarecrow Press, 2007.
- *Simming: Participatory Performance and the Making of Meaning*. Ann Arbor, MI: University of Michigan Press, 2014.

Mandell, Jonathan. "Immersive Theatre, Defined: Five Elements in *Sleep No More*, *Then She Fell*, and More." *Howlround*, 9 February 2016. http://howlround.com/immersive-theatre-defined-five-elements-in-sleep-no-more-then-she-fell-and-more

Martin, Carol. "Bodies of Evidence." *TDR: The Drama Review* 50, no. 3 (Fall 2006): 8–15. https://www.muse.jhu.edu/article/201932.
- "Introduction: Dramaturgy of the Real." In *The Dramaturgy of the Real on the World Stage*, edited by Carol Martin, 1–14. Basingstoke, UK: Palgrave Macmillan, 2010.
- *Theatre of the Real*. Basingstoke, UK: Palgrave Macmillan, 2013.

Massey, Doreen. *For Space*. London, UK: SAGE Publications, 2005.
- "Geographies of Responsibility." *Geografiska Annaler. Series B, Human Geography* 86, no. 1 (2004): 5–18.
- "Places and Their Pasts." *History Workshop Journal* 39, no. 1 (Spring 1995): 182–92.
- *Space, Place, and Gender*. Minneapolis, MN: University of Minnesota Press, 1994.

Massumi, Brian. "The Future Birth of the Affective Act: The Political Ontology of Threat." In *The Affect Theory Reader*, edited by Melissa Gregg and Gregory J. Seigworth, 52–70. Durham, NC: Duke University Press, 2010.
- *Parables for the Virtual: Movement, Affect, Sensation*. Durham, NC: Duke University Press, 2002.

McAuley, Gay. "Introduction." In *Unstable Ground: Performance and the Politics of Place*, edited by Gay McAuley, 15–24. Brussels: Peter Lang, 2006.

– *Space in Performance: Making Meaning in the Theatre*. Ann Arbor, MI: University of Michigan Press, 1999.
McCarthy Brown, Karen. "Mimesis in the Face of Fear: Femme Queens, Butch Queens, and Gender Play in the House of Greater Newark Public Policy." In *Passing: Identity and Interpretation in Sexuality, Race, and Religion*, edited by María Carla Sánchez and Linda Schlossberg, 208–27. New York, NY: New York University Press, 2001.
McGonigal, Jane. *Reality is Broken: Why Games Make Us Better and How They Can Change the World*. New York, NY: Penguin Press, 2011.
Mealey, Scott. "Recollection of an Audience: Style, Experience, and Change in the Study of Theatre Spectatorship." Doctoral thesis, University of Toronto, 2020. Unpublished.
Menegus, Bryan. "Pizzagaters Aren't Giving This Shit Up." *Gizmodo*, 5 December 2016. https://gizmodo.com/pizzagaters-arent-giving-this-shit-up-1789692422.
Miessen, Markus. *The Nightmare of Participation (Crossbench Praxis as a Mode of Criticality)*. Cambridge, MA: MIT Press, 2011.
Milisavljevic, Maria. *An Enemy of the People*, based on the original text by Henrik Ibsen, with Richard Rose. Unpublished script, 2016.
Miller, Alexander. "Realism." In *The Stanford Encyclopedia of Philosophy*, edited by Edward N. Zalta, Winter 2021. https://plato.stanford.edu/archives/win2021/entries/realism.
Morash, Chris, and Shaun Richards. *Mapping Irish Theatre: Theories of Space and Place*. Cambridge, UK: Cambridge University Press, 2013.
Mouffe, Chantal. *Agonistics: Thinking the World Politically*. London, UK: Verso Books, 2013.
Muñoz, José Esteban. *Cruising Utopia: The Then and There of Queer Futurity*. New York: New York University Press, 2009.
Mura, Paolo. "Perceptions of authenticity in a Malaysian homestay – a narrative analysis." *Tourism Management* 51 (2015): 225–33.
Muse, John H. "Performance and the Pace of Empathy." *Journal of Dramatic Theory and Criticism* 26, no. 2 (2012): 173–88. http://doi.org/10.1353/dtc.2012.0019.
Narváez, Peter. "The Folklore of 'Old Foolishness.'" *Canadian Literature* 108 (Spring 1986): 125–43.
Nestruck, J. Kelly. "An Enemy of the People: This take on Ibsen is the next best thing to a classic." *The Globe and Mail*, 26 September 2014. https://www.theglobeandmail.com/arts/theatre-and-performance/theatre-reviews/an-enemy-of-the-people-this-take-on-ibsen-is-the-next-best-thing-to-a-classic/article20800275.

- "TomorrowLove™ is an Amorous Adventure That's Hard to Fall in Love With." *The Globe and Mail*, 25 November 2016. https://www.theglobeandmail.com/arts/theatre-and-performance/theatre-reviews/tomorrowlove-is-an-amorous-adventure-thats-hard-to-fall-in-love-with/article33051327.
Nguyen, C. Thi. "Echo Chambers and Epistemic Bubbles." *Episteme* 17, no. 2 (2020): 141–61.
Nicholson, Helen. "A Good Day Out: Applied Theatre, Relationality and Participation." In *Critical Perspectives on Applied Theatre*, edited by Jenny Hughes and Helen Nicholson, 248–68. Cambridge, UK: Cambridge University Press, 2016.
Nicholson, Helen, Nadine Holdsworth, and Jane Milling. *The Ecologies of Amateur Theatre*. London, UK: Palgrave Macmillan, 2018.
Nikiforuk, Andrew. *Saboteurs: Wiebo Ludwig's War Against Big Oil*. Vancouver, BC: Greystone Books, 2014.
Obama, Barack. "Farewell Address." *White House Archives*, 10 January 2017. https://obamawhitehouse.archives.gov/farewell.
Oddey, Alison, and Christine White. "Introduction: Visions Now: Life is a Screen." In *Modes of Spectating*, edited by Alison Oddey and Christine White, 7–14. Bristol, UK: Intellect, 2009
O'Dea, Shane. "Culture and Country: The Role of the Arts and Heritage in the Nationalist Revival in Newfoundland." *Newfoundland and Labrador Studies* 19, no. 2 (Fall 2003): 378–86.
Omasta, Matt. "Artist intention and audience reception in theatre for young audiences." *Youth Theatre Journal* 25, no. 1 (2011): 32–50.
Omner, Rosemary. "Rosie's Cove: Settlement Morphology, History, Economy, and Culture in a Newfoundland Outport." In *Fishing Places, Fishing People: Traditions and Issues in Canadian Small-Scale Fisheries*, edited by Dianne Newell and Rosemary E. Ommer, 17–31. Toronto, ON: University of Toronto Press, 1999.
Orona, Celia J. "Temporality and identity loss due to Alzheimer's disease." In *The Qualitative Researcher's Companion*, edited by Michael Huberman and Matthew B. Miles, 367–92. London, UK: SAGE Publications, 2002.
Ouzounian, Richard. "An Enemy of the People loses something in translation." *The Star*, 26 September 2014. https://www.thestar.com/entertainment/stage/2014/09/26/an_enemy_of_the_people_loses_something_in_translation.html.
Overton, James. "Coming Home: Nostalgia and Tourism in Newfoundland." *Acadiensis* 14, no. 1 (October 1984): 84–97.
- "'A Future in the Past'? Tourism Development, Outport Archaeology, and

the Politics of Deindustrialization in Newfoundland and Labrador in the 1990s." *Urban History Review* 35, no. 2 (Spring 2007): 60–74.
- *Making a World of Difference: Essays on Tourism, Culture and Development in Newfoundland.* Essex, UK: Institute of Social and Economic Research, 1996.
- "A Newfoundland Culture?" *Journal of Canadian Studies/Revue d'Études Canadiennes* 23, no.1 (Spring/Summer 1988): 5–22.
- "Promoting 'The Real Newfoundland' Culture as Tourist Commodity." *Studies in Political Economy* 4, no. 1 (March 1980): 115–37.

Paget, Derek. "Acts of Commitment: Activist Arts, the Rehearsed Reading, and Documentary Theatre." *New Theatre Quarterly* 26, no. 2 (May 2010): 173–93.

Park-Fuller, Linda M. "Audiencing the Audience: Playback Theatre, Performative Writing, and Social Activism." *Text and Performance Quarterly* 23, no. 3 (July 2003): 288–310. http://doi.org/10.1080/1046293031 0001635321.

Parsons, Jonathan. "Branded Newfoundland: Lisa Moore's Alligator and Consumer Capitalism." *Newfoundland and Labrador Studies* 28, no. 1 (Spring 2013): 5–27.

Pearson, Mike. *"In Comes I": Performance, Memory and Landscape.* Exeter, UK: University of Exeter Press, 2006.

Pearson, Mike, and Michael Shanks. *Theatre/Archaeology.* London, UK: Routledge, 2001.

Peters, John Durham. "Witnessing." *Media, Culture & Society* 23, no. 6 (2001): 707–23.

Phelan, Peggy. *Unmarked: The Politics of Performance.* London, UK: Routledge, 1993.

Philip, M. NourbeSe. "Who's Listening? Artists, Audiences, and Language." *New Contexts of Canadian Criticism* (1997): 1–14.

Phillips, Holiday. "Performative Allyship is Deadly (Here's What to do Instead." *Forge*, 9 May 2020. https://forge.medium.com/performative-allyship-is-deadly-c900645d9f1f.

Pine, B. Joseph, II, and James H. Gilmore. *The Experience Economy: Work Is Theater & Every Business a Stage.* Boston, MA: Harvard Business School Press, 1999.

Pitt, Janet E.M. "Trinity." In *The Canadian Encyclopedia* from *Historica Canada*. 2012. http://www.thecanadianencyclopedia.ca/en/article/trinity.

Plantinga, Carl. *Moving Viewers: American Film and the Spectator's Experience.* Berkeley: University of California Press, 2009.

Plato. *The Republic.* Edited by G.R.F. Ferrari and translated by Tom Griffith. Cambridge, UK: Cambridge University Press, 2000.

Pons, Esther Belvis. "*Outdoors:* A Rimini Protokoll Theatre-Maze." In *Reframing Immersive Theatre: The Politics and Pragmatics of Participatory Performance*, edited by James Frieze, 119–28. London, UK: Palgrave Macmillan, 2016.

Potolsky, Matthew. *Mimesis*. New York, NY: Routledge, 2006.

Power, Cormac. *Presence in Play: A Critique of Theories of Presence in the Theatre*. Amsterdam: Editions Rodopi, 2008.

Pywell, Geoff. *Staging Real Things: The Performance of Ordinary Events*. Lewisburg, PA: Bucknell University Press, 1994.

Rabey, David Ian. *Theatre, Time and Temporality: Melting Clocks and Snapped Elastics*. Bristol, UK: Intellect, 2016.

Radbourne, Jennifer, Hilary Glow, and Katya Johanson. *The Audience Experience: A Critical Analysis of Audiences in the Performing Arts*. Bristol, UK: Intellect, 2013.

Ramos, Jorge Lopes, Joseph Dunne-Howrie, Persis Jadé Maravala, and Bart Simon. "The Post-Immersive Manifesto." *International Journal of Performance Arts and Digital Media* (2020): 1–17. http:doi.org/10.1080/14794713.2020.1766282.

Ranciére, Jacques. *The Emancipated Spectator*. London, UK: Verso, 2009.

Raynaud, Savine. "Landscape Theatre/Théâtre de paysage." *Le Voyage d'Orphée en Europe avec Bill Mitchell et la Compagnie WildWorks*. Montpellier, FR: L'Entretemps, 2008.

Rayner, Alice. *Ghosts: Death's Double and the Phenomena of Theatre*. Minneapolis, MN: University of Minnesota Press, 2006.

Read, Alan. *Theatre and Everyday Life: An Ethics of Performance*. London, UK: Routledge, 1995.

– *Theatre, Intimacy & Engagement: The Last Human Venue*. New York, NY: Palgrave Macmillan, 2008.

Reason, Matthew. "Introduction to Part 2: *Participations* on Participation: Researching the 'Active' Theatre Audience." *Participations* 12, no. 1 (May 2015): 271–80.

– *The Young Audience: Exploring and Enhancing Children's Experiences of Theatre*. Stoke-on-Trent, UK: Trentham Books, 2010.

Reason, Matthew, and Dee Reynolds. "Kinesthesia, empathy, and related pleasures: an inquiry into audience experiences of watching dance." *Dance Research Journal* 42, no. 2 (2010): 49–75.

Reason, Matthew, and Kirsty Sedgman. "Editors' Introduction: Themed Section on Theatre Audiences." *Participations* 12, no. 1 (May 2015): 117–22.

Rebellato, Dan. "Playwriting and Globalisation: Towards a Site-Unspecific Theatre." *Contemporary Theatre Review* 16, no. 1 (February 2006): 97–113.

Redfield, Robert. "The Folk Society." *American Journal of Sociology* 52, no. 2 (January 1947): 293–308. https://www.jstor.org/stable/2771457.

Reinelt, Janelle. "Theatre on the Brink of 2000: Shifting Paradigms." *Theatre Research International* 20, no. 2 (Summer 1995): 123–31. https://doi.org/10.1017/S0307883300008361.

– "Toward a Poetics of Theatre and Public Events." *TDR: The Drama Review* 50, no. 3 (Fall 2006): 69–87.

– "What UK Spectators Know: Understanding How We Come to Value Theatre." *Theatre Journal* 66, no. 3 (October 2014): 337–61.

Reinelt, Janelle, David Edgar, Chris Megson, Dan Rebellato, Julie Wilkinson, and Jane Woddis. *Critical Mass: Theatre Spectatorship and Value Attribution.* Swindon, UK: Arts & Humanities Research Council, 2015. http://britishtheatreconference.co.uk/wp-content/uploads/2014/05/Critical-Mass-10.7.pdf.

Ridout, Nicholas. *Passionate Amateurs: Theatre, Communism, and Love.* Minneapolis, MN: University of Michigan press, 2013.

– *Stage Fright, Animals, and Other Theatrical Problems.* Cambridge, UK: Cambridge University Press, 2006.

– "The Vibratorium Electrified." In *Vibratory Modernism*, edited by Anthony Enns and Shelley Trower, 215–26. Basingstoke, UK: Palgrave Macmillan, 2013.

Robinson, Dylan. *Hungry Listening: Resonant Theory for Indigenous Sound Studies.* Minneapolis, MN: University of Minnesota Press, 2020.

Robinson, KiMi. "How an Arizona couple helped fuel the Wayfair sex trafficking theory." *Azcentral*, 11 August 2020. https://www.azcentral.com/story/entertainment/life/2020/07/15/wayfair-human-trafficking-conspiracy-arizona-couple-spread-instagram-rumors/5429146002.

Roets, Arne. "'Fake news': Incorrect, but hard to correct. The role of cognitive ability on the impact of false information on social impressions." *Intelligence* 65 (2017): 107–10.

Rugoff, Ralph. "Other Experts." In *Amateurs*, 9–14. San Francisco: California College of the Arts Wattis Institute for Contemporary Arts, 2008.

Salter, Denis. "The Idea of a National Theatre." In *Canadian Canons: Essays in Literary Value*, edited by Robert Lecker, 71–90. Toronto, ON: University of Toronto Press, 1991.

Salverson, Julie. "Transgressive Storytelling or an Aesthetic of Injury: Performance, Pedagogy and Ethics" *Theatre Research in Canada/Recherches théâtrales Au Canada* 20, no. 1 (April 1999): 35–51.

Samuel, Danica. "There's a microchip, it will make me infertile, alter my DNA: The roots and truth about COVID-19 vaccine myths." *The Toronto Star*,

4 February 2021. https://www.thestar.com/news/gta/2021/02/04/theres-a-microchip-it-will-make-me-infertile-alter-my-dna-the-roots-and-truth-about-covid-19-vaccine-myths.html.

Sauter, Willmar. *The Theatrical Event: Dynamics of Performance and Perception.* Iowa City, IA: University of Iowa Press, 2000.

— "Thirty Years of Reception Studies: Empirical, Methodological and Theoretical Advances." *About Performance*, no. 10 (2010): 241–63.

— "Who Reacts When, How and upon What: From Audience Surveys to the Theatrical Event." *Contemporary Theatre Review* 12, no. 3 (2002): 115–29.

Scarry, Elaine. *The Body in Pain: The Making and Unmaking of the World.* Oxford, UK: Oxford University Press, 1985.

Schechner, Richard. *Performance Studies: An Introduction.* Abingdon, UK: Routledge, 2002.

Schneider, Rebecca. *Performing Remains: Art and War in Times of Theatrical Reenactment.* Abingdon, UK: Routledge, 2011.

Schrøder, Kim, Kirsten Drotner, Stephen Kline, and Catherine Murray. *Researching Audiences.* London, UK: Bloomsbury Academic, 2003.

Schroeder, Patricia R. *The Presence of the Past in Modern American Drama.* Cranbury, NJ: Associated University Presses, 1989.

Schulze, Daniel. *Authenticity in Contemporary Theatre and Performance.* London, UK: Bloomsbury Publishing, 2017.

Scollen, Rebecca. "Talking Theatre: Developing Audiences for Regional Australia." *The International Journal of the Arts in Society* 3, no. 3 (2008): 103–14.

Sedgman, Kirsty. "Audience Experience in an Anti-expert Age: A Survey of Theatre Audience Research." *Theatre Research International* 42, no. 3 (October 2017): 307–22.

— "Ladies and Gentlemen Follow, Please Put on Your Beards: Risk, Rules, and Audience Reception in National Theatre Wales." *Contemporary Theatre Review* 27, no. 2 (2017): 158–76.

— *Locating the Audience: How People Found Value in National Theatre Wales.* Bristol, UK: Intellect, 2016.

— "On Rigour in Theatre Audience Research." *Contemporary Theatre Review* 29, no. 4 (2019): 462–79.

— *The Reasonable Audience: Theatre Etiquette, Behaviour Policing, and the Live Performance Experience.* Basingstoke, UK: Palgrave Macmillan, 2018.

Sedgwick, Eve Kosofsky. *Touching Feeling: Affect, Pedagogy, Performativity.* Durham, NC: Duke University Press, 2003.

Seifert, Martina. *Rewriting Newfoundland Mythology: The Works of Tom Dawe.* Berlin: Galda + Wilch Verlag, 2002.

Shaughnessy, Nicola, ed. *Affective Performance and Cognitive Science: Body, Brain and Being*. London, UK: Bloomsbury Methuen Drama, 2013.
– *Applying Performance: Live Art, Socially Engaged Theatre and Affective Practice*. Basingstoke, UK: Palgrave Macmillan, 2012.
Shields, David. *Reality Hunger: A Manifesto*. New York: Alfred A. Knopf, 2010.
Silverman, Craig. "This Analysis Shows How Viral Fake Election News Stories Outperformed Real News on Facebook." *BuzzFeed News*, 16 November 2016. https://www.buzzfeednews.com/article/craigsilverman/viral-fake-election-news-outperformed-real-news-on-facebook.
Silverman, Craig, Lauren Strapagiel, Hamza Shaban, Ellie Hall, and Jeremy Singer-Vine. "Hyperpartisan Facebook Pages Are Publishing False and Misleading Information At An Alarming Rate." *BuzzFeed News*, 20 October 2016. https://www.buzzfeednews.com/article/craigsilverman/partisan-fb-pages-analysis.
Smyth, Michael. "Designing for Embodied Interaction: Experiencing Artefacts with and Through the Body." In *The State of the Real: Aesthetics in the Digital Age*, edited by Damian Sutton, Susan Brind, and Ray McKenzie, 140–50. London, UK: I.B. Tauris, 2007.
Snyder-Young, Dani. "Ownership, Expertise, and Audience Research: Developing Collaborative, Artist-Centric Methods for Studying Reception." *Theatre Topics* 30, no. 1 (2020): 31–40.
– *Privileged Spectatorship: Theatrical Interventions in White Supremacy*. Evanston, IL: Northwestern University Press, 2020.
– "Studying the Relationship Between Artistic Intent and Observable Impact." *Performance Matters* 5, no. 2 (2019): 150–5.
Solon, Olivia. "Facebook's Failure: Did Fake News and Polarized Politics get Trump elected?" *The Guardian*, 10 November 2016. https://www.theguardian.com/technology/2016/nov/10/facebook-fake-news-election-conspiracy-theories.
States, Bert O. *Great Reckonings in Little Rooms: On the Phenomenology of Theater*. Berkeley: University of California Press, 1985.
Steele, Donald H., Raoul Andersen, and J.M. Green. "The Managed Commercial Annihilation of Northern Cod." *Newfoundland and Labrador Studies* 8, no. 1 (January 1992): 34–68. https://journals.lib.unb.ca/index.php/nflds/article/view/919/1272.
Stephenson, Jenn. "Assembling the Audience-Citizen (Or, Should Each Person Be Responsible for Their Own Paté?)" *Performance Matters* 5, no. 2 (2019): 162–8.

- *Insecurity: Perils and Products of Theatres of the Real.* Toronto, ON: University of Toronto Press, 2019.
- *Performing Autobiography: Contemporary Canadian Drama.* Toronto, ON: University of Toronto Press, 2013.
- "The Theatrical Affect of Haunted Houses." *Upsurges of the Real: A Performance Research Blog,* Wordpress, 7 October 2015. https://realtheatre.blog/2015/10/07/the-theatrical-affect-of-haunted-houses.
- *Upsurges of the Real: A Performance Research Blog.* https://realtheatre.blog.
- "Winning and/or Losing: The Perils and Products of Insecurity in Postdramatic Autobiographical Performance." *Theatre Journal* 68, no. 2 (May 2016): 213–29. http://doi.org/10.1353/tj.2016.0046.

Sturm, Tristan, and Tom Albrecht. "Constituent Covid-19 apocalypses: contagious conspiracism, 5G, and viral vaccinations." *Anthropology & Medicine* 28, no. 1 (2021): 122–39.

Straub, Julia. 2012. "Introduction: The Paradoxes of Authenticity." In *Paradoxes of Authenticity: Studies on a Critical Concept*, edited by Julia Straub, 9–32. Bielefeld: Trancscipt Verlag.

Strings, Sabrina, and Long T. Bui. "She Is Not Acting, She Is." *Feminist Media Studies* 14, no. 5 (2014): 822–36.

Sundén, Jenny. *Material Virtualities: Approaching Online Textual Embodiment.* New York, NY: Peter Lang, 2003.

Sutton, Damian, Susan Brind, and Ray McKenzie. *The State of the Real: Aesthetics in the Digital Age.* London, UK: I.B. Tauris, 2007.

Tait, Peta. *Performing Emotions: Gender, Bodies, Spaces in Chekhov's Drama and Stanislavski's Theatre.* Aldershot, UK: Ashgate, 2002.

Tan, Shelly, Youjin Shin, and Danielle Rindler. "How one of America's ugliest days unraveled inside and outside the Capitol." *The Washington Post,* 9 January 2021. https://www.washingtonpost.com/nation/interactive/2021/capitol-insurrection-visual-timeline.

Thompson, James. *Performance Affects: Applied Theatre and the End of Effect.* Basingstoke, UK: Palgrave Macmillan, 2009.

Thorson, Emily. "Belief echoes: The persistent effects of corrected misinformation." *Political Communication* 33, no. 3 (2016): 460–80.

Thrift, Nigel. *Non-Representational Theory: Space, Politics, Affect.* Abingdon, Oxon, UK: Routledge, 2008.

Tomlin, Liz. *Acts and Apparitions: Discourses on the Real in Performance Practice and Theory, 1990–2010.* Manchester, UK: Manchester University Press, 2013.
- *Political Dramaturgies and Theatre Spectatorship: Provocations for Change.* London, UK: Methuen Drama, 2019.

Tormey, Jane. "Photographic Practice, Postmodernism and the 'Irreal.'" In *The State of the Real: Aesthetics in the Digital Age*, edited by Damian Sutton, Susan Brind, and Ray McKenzie, 28–37. London, UK: I.B. Tauris, 2007.

"Trust Me: Ninth Journey." *At the Gates Guarded by Horses* (blog), Tumblr. 3 November 2013. http://templestudios.tumblr.com/post/65913090844/trust-me-ninth-journey.

Tuan, Yi-Fu. *Space and Place: The Perspective of Experience.* Minneapolis: University of Minnesota Press, 1977.

Tulloch, John. *Shakespeare and Chekhov in Production and Reception: Theatrical Events and Their Audiences.* Iowa City: University of Iowa Press, 2009.

Turner, Mark. "The Cognitive Study of Art, Language, and Literature." *Poetics Today* 23, no. 1 (Spring 2002): 9–20.

– "Rising Tide Theatre: Communication and Paradigm." *Canadian Theatre Review* 140 (Fall 2009): 20–5.

Ubersfeld, Anne. *Reading Theatre.* Toronto, ON: University of Toronto Press, 1999.

Ury, John. *Mobilities.* Cambridge, UK: Polity Press, 2007.

Vaccari, Cristian, and Andrew Chadwick. "Deepfakes and Disinformation: Exploring the Impact of Synthetic Political Video on Deception, Uncertainty, and Trust in News." *Social Media + Society* 6, no. 1 (2020): 1–13.

Van Es, Karin. *The Future of Live.* Hoboken, NJ: Wiley and Sons, 2016.

Van Oldenborgh, Lennaart. "Performing the Real." In *The State of the Real: Aesthetics in the Digital Age*, edited by Damian Sutton, Susan Brind, and Ray McKenzie, 62–72. London, UK: I.B. Tauris, 2007.

Varga, Somogy, and Charles Guignon. "Authenticity." *Stanford Encyclopedia of Philosophy*, edited by Edward N. Zalta, Spring 2020. https://plato.stanford.edu/archives/spr2020/entries/authenticity.

Vattimo, Gianni. "Dialectics, Difference, Weak Thought." In *Weak Thought*, edited by Gianni Vattimo and P.A. Rovatti and translated by Peter Carravetta, 39–52. New York, NY: SUNY, 2012.

Vermeulen, Timotheus, and Robin van den Akker. "Notes on Metamodernism." *Journal of Aesthetics and Culture* 2, no. 1 (January 2010): 5677. http://doi.org.10.3402/jac.v2i0.5677.

Vittadini, Nicoletta, and Francesca Pasquali. "Virtual Shadowing, Online Ethnographies and Social Networking Studies." In *Audience Research Methodologies: Between Innovation and Consolidation*, edited by Geoffrey Patriarche, Helena Bilandzic, Jakob Linaa Jensen, and Jelena Jurišić, 160–73. New York, NY: Routledge, 2013.

Vogt, P.J., and Alex Goldman. "Voyage Into Pizzagate." *Reply All Podcast*, Gimlet Media, 2016. https://gimletmedia.com/shows/reply-all/emhwl5.

W., Mila (@CalgaryMila). "Excellent, Excellent, Excellent!" TripAdvisor review, 13 September 2016. https://www.tripadvisor.ca/ShowUserReviews g499208-d2236194-r418273923-Rising_Tide_Theatre-Trinity _Newfoundland_Newfoundland_and_Labrador.html.

Wagner, Matthew D. *Shakespeare, Theatre, and Time*. New York, NY: Routledge, 2012.

Walker, Julia. "The Text/Performance Split Across the Analytic/Continental Divide." In *Staging Philosophy: Intersections of Theater, Performance, and Philosophy*, edited by David Krasner and David Z. Saltz, 19–40. Ann Arbor, MI: University of Michigan Press, 2006.

Wallendorf, Melanie, and Merrie Brucks. "Introspection in Consumer Research: Implementation and Implications." *Journal of Consumer Research* 20, no. 3 (1993): 339–59.

Walmsley, Ben. *Audience Engagement in the Performing Arts: A Critical Analysis*. London, UK: Palgrave Macmillan, 2019.

– "Deep hanging out in the arts: an anthropological approach to capturing cultural value." *International Journal of Cultural Policy* 24, no. 2 (2018): 272–91.

– "Engagement: The New Paradigm for Audience Research." *Participations* 18, no. 1 (2021): 299–16.

Weixler, Antonius. "The Dilettantish Construction of the Extraordinary and the Authenticity of the Artificial: Tracing Strategies for Success in German Popular Entertainment Shows." In *The Aesthetics of Authenticity: Medial Constructions of the Real*, edited by Wolfgang Funk, Florian Groß, Irmtaud Huber, 207–36. Bielefeld: Transcript Verlag, 2012.

White, Gareth. *Audience Participation in Theatre: Aesthetics of the Invitation*. Basingstoke, UK: Palgrave Macmillan, 2013.

– "Odd Anonymized Needs: Punchdrunk's Masked Spectator." In *Modes of Spectating*, edited by Alison Oddey and Christine White, 219–30. Bristol, UK: Intellect, 2009.

– "On Immersive Theatre." *Theatre Research International* 37, no. 3 (October 2012): 221–35.

Wickstrom, Maurya. "Thinking About Temporality and Theatre." *The Journal of American Drama and Theatre* 28, no. 1 (Winter 2016): 1–3. https://www.jadt journal.org/2016/03/23/thinking-about-temporality-and-theatre.

Wiles, David. *A Short History of Western Performance Space*. Cambridge, UK: Cambridge University Press, 2003.

Williams, Kirk. "Anti-Theatricality and the Limits of Naturalism." In *Against Theatre: Creative Destructions on the Modernist Stage*, edited by Alan Ackerman and Martin Puchner, 95–111. Basingstoke, UK: Palgrave Macmillan, 2007.

Wood, Eric Emin. "Who is the Enemy of the People? It's up to you and me." *Streeter*, 18 October 2015. https://streeter.ca/central-toronto/views/column/who-is-the-enemy-of-the-people-its-up-to-you-and-me.

Wood, Marissa K. "Language in digital activism: exploring the performative functions of #MeToo Tweets." *Diggit Magazine*, 1 November 2018. https://www.diggitmagazine.com/academic-papers/language-digital-activism-exploring-performative-functions-metoo-tweets.

Woodruff, Paul. *The Necessity of Theater: The Art of Watching and Being Watched*. Oxford, UK: Oxford University Press, 2008.

Woods, Byron. "Recently Banned in China, A Leading German Theatre Company Is Making Ibsen Dangerous Again." *Indy Week*, 3 October 2018. https://indyweek.com/culture/stage/recently-banned-in-china-a-leading-german-theater-company-is.

Yuqing, Wing, and Yang Fan. "China Cancels Ibsen's 'Enemy of the People' Amid Ever Widening Censorship," translated by Lussietta Mudie. *Radio Free Asia*, 13 September 2018. https://www.rfa.org/english/news/china/censorship-09132018124920.html.

Zaiontz, Keren. "Narcissistic Spectatorship in Immersive and One-on-One Performance." *Theatre Journal* 66, no. 3 (October 2014): 405–25.

Zhulina, Alisa. "The Invisible Stage Hand; or, Henrik Ibsen's Theatre of Capital." *Theatre Survey* 59, no. 3 (2018): 386–408.

Žižek, Salvoj. *Mapping Ideology*. London, UK: Verso, 1994.

– *Welcome to the Desert of the Real: Five Essays on September 11 and Related Dates*. London, UK: Verso, 2002.

Zola, Émile. "Preface to Thérèse Raquin." In *Theatre/Theory/Theatre: The Major Critical Texts from Aristotle and Zeami to Soyinka and Havel*, edited by Daniel C. Gerould, 353–67. Montclair, NJ: Applause Books, 2000.

Zuckerman, Ethan. "QAnon and the Emergence of the Unreal." *Journal of Design and Science* 6. https://doi.org/10.21428/7808da6b.6b8a8.

Index

9/11. *See* terrorism
1930s Federal Theatre Project (US), 10
1984, 236n43

Abercrombie, Nicholas, 99
accessibility, 200–1
Adam, Barbara, 50–1
Aesthetics of Authenticity, 7
affect, 192–6, 192–210; as concept, 193; definition of, 15, 192–3; impact on audience feelings of realness, 16; and relationship building, 209–10; social purpose of, 15–16
affective experiences, 13; leading to increased feelings of real, 15; and relational dimension, 15
affective labour, 15, 189–91, 205–6
"affective register," 206
Ahmed, Sara, 113; on affect, 193; analysis of "affective economy," 111–12; on the "stickiness" of affect, 141
Albany Theatre Projects, 235n2
Alberta (Canada), 29–76 *passim*, 76; conflicts between oil and gas industry, and ranching industry, 33; economy of, 31–3, 219–20n6, 220n7; oil and gas industry of, 22, 26, 29, 31, 32, 35, 40–1, 50, 60–3, 69, 85, 219–20n6, 220n7; politics of, 70; ranching industry of, 27, 29, 31–2, 35, 40–1, 57, 60–1, 220n6
alienation, 10
Alston, Adam, 151–2, 198–9, 203; definition of immersive theatre, 175
Alvarez, Natalie, 25–6, 123–4
amateur theatre, 37–9
American Civil War, re-enactments of, 115, 125
Ang, Ien, 24
Animating Democracy, 70
anti-vaxxers, xii–xiii
Arbour Lake Community Centre, 39
Arstila, Valtteri, 52–3
Artaud, Antonin, 10, 14; *Theatre of Cruelty*, 14
Arts Commons (Calgary), 39
audience, 39; behaviour of, 225n32; belief structures of, 25–6, 36–7;

bias of, 41, 87–8; as capitalist market force, 18; characteristics of, 17–18; as collective, 15; desire for ideological grounding, 97–8; emotional response of, 192–210 *passim*; etiquette of, 9; as experts, 17–18; and perceived realness, 16–25; perception, 11; perception of cultural value by, 23; political reflections by, 72–3; role of, 16–17, 55–6; scholarship on, 16–19, 21–4; and spectatorship, 16–17

audience labour, 28, 196–210; as unwanted, 202–10. *See also* immersive theatre

audience participation, 76–102, 93–100, 153–4, 190; as active, 103–4, 135–6; as biased, 89; conventional models of, 94–5; definition of, 96; evolution of, 78–9; as passive, 79; politics of, 79–80; and power, 93–100; and real-ishness, 96–7. *See also* immersive theatre

audience research. *See* audience: scholarship on

Auslander, Philip, 7, 14, 180–1

Austin, J.L., 5–6, 112

authenticity, 6–7, 14, 119; as cultivated by a community, 124; definition of, 6–7; as it relates to what is real, 7. *See also* historical re-enactment: and authenticity

avant-garde theatre, 38

Ayer, A.J., 4

Bacon, Barbara Schaffer, 69–70
Bailey, Marlon M., 5–6, 216n9. *See also* ballroom culture

ballroom culture, 5–6; definition of, 216n9. *See also* Bailey, Marlon M.

Balt, Christine, 21

Barish, Jonas A., 8–9

Barker, Martin, 18, 180

Barker, Roberta, 9. *See also New Canadian Realisms*

Barrett, Felix, 157, 198

Bennett, Susan, 18, 61, 126, 135

Beothuk, 110

Berlant, Lauren; on affect, 15

bias. *See* audience: bias of

Biden, Joe (president), xii

Biggin, Rose, 166, 177, 180–1, 186; on Punchdrunk, 231n28

binarism, 90, 95

Binet, Robert, 147

Binette, Melanie, 10

Bishop, Claire, 96, 201. *See also* participation

Bogart, Anne, 51–2. *See also* chronos; kairos

Borchmeyer, Florian, 80–2, 92–3. See also *An Enemy of the People*: Schaubühne (Berlin) production of

Botsman, Rachel, 33–4; on dispersed trust, xi; *Who Can You Trust?*, xi

Bourriaud, Nicholas, 201

Bousquet, David; on authenticity, 122–3

Bowie, David; "Changes," 81

boyd, danah, 98

Boyle, Sir Cavendish, 112

Brantwood, 156, 160, 162, 178, 182, 185; audience participation in, 153–4; conclusion of, 187–8; one-to-one experience, 181; use

of former school as site, 171–2, 174; use of wandering in, 164–7, 175. *See also* Cushman, Mitchell; Tepperman, Julie
Brecht, Bertolt, 10
Brechtian theatre, 38
Breed, Ananda, on civic engagement, 95
Brennan, Teresa, on affect, 15
Brind, 5
Brind, Susan, 11; *The State of the Real: Aesthetics in the Digital Age*, x
Brook, Peter, definition of theatre, 3
Brooklyn Academy of Arts, 101
Brucks, Merrie, 22
Bui, Long T. See *RuPaul's Drag Race*
Bullock, Rev. William, 136
Burnt City, The, 234n95
Burton, Tara Isabella, 177, 234n75
Bush, George W. (former president), ix–x
Bus(t). *See* Downstage theatre company: Downstage Creation Ensemble
Butt, Donna, 106–7, 120–1, 125–7, 135, 137–8; aim for Trinity Pageant, 110–11; introductory remarks at Trinity Pageant, 143; on place of the Trinity Pageant, 139–40

capitalism, 18, 87, 225n16, 226n55
Carlson, Marvin, xiv, 8–9; *Performance: A Critical Introduction*, 12; *Shattering Hamlet's Mirror*, 10–11
Centre for Spectatorship and Audience Research, xviii, 19
child trafficking. *See* Pizzagate

China, People's Republic of. See *An Enemy of the People*
chronos; as concept, 51–2
Clinton, Hilary, xii
Close, Ellen, 29–33, 35, 42, 44–5, 53, 55–8 *passim*, 89; baby shower for, 50–2, 54; on "invitations," 66; real pregnancy of, 61–2
Clough, Patricia Ticineto, on affect, 15
Cobden, Joe, 225n15, 226n41
Cohen-Cruz, Jan, 68–9
Colbert, Stephen, ix–x, xv; at Correspondents' Dinner (2005), xiii; use of the term "truthiness," ix–x
Cole, Ethan, 29
Collini, Stefan, definition of politics, 79, 87, 93–4
colonial structures, influence on history, 108–9, 124–5, 127, 129
colonization. *See* Newfoundland (Canada): colonization of
Come From Away, representation of Newfoundland in, 109
Comey, James, xi–xii
Coming Insurrection, The, 225n16
community theatre, 37
community-based performance, 68–70. *See also* Cohen-Cruz, Jan
Condlln, Laura, 225n15, 226n41
consumerism, 175–6
creators-as-actors, 62
Crossick, Geoffrey, 198
Crumlish, Christian, 55
Cseke, Col, 29, 42, 58–9, 65, 71; baby shower for, 50–1, 54, 60–1; on realness as humanizing, 75
cultural engagement, 24, 198
cultural narratives, 111–12

cultural performance. *See* MacAloon, John
Cushman, Mitchell, 94, 147, 152, 154–5, 162, 170–1, 183, 185–7, 196–7, 204–5, 234n90; on first-person perspective in immersive theatre, 154–6; *Mr. Marmalade*, 155; *Vitals*, 160. See also *Brantwood*; *TomorrowLove*™

de Groot, Anton, 29
Deavere-Smith, Anna: *Fires in the Mirror*, 10; *Twilight: Los Angeles, 1992*, 10
deepfakes, ix, xi, 14, 211
Deleuze, Gilles, 192
democracy, 79, 88–9, 94, 96, 101–2; under threat by misinformation, xii–xiii
Derrida, Jacques, 5, 14, 115
didactic theatre, audience resistance to, 221n31
Discourse and Discovery of the New Founde Lande, A. *See* Whitbourne, Sir Richard
documentary theatre, xv, 8–9, 12, 26, 29–76 *passim*; in Canada, 31–2
Dolan, Jill, 143
Downstage theatre company, 29–76; Downstage Creation Ensemble, 29, 219n3; mandate of, 63; use of documentary practices, 31–2; use of "invitations," 65–6. See also *Good Fences*
Drotner, Kirsten, *Researching Audiences*, 24
Drowned Man, The, 161–2, 171–4, 177, 182, 185–6, 200–1, 234n95; conclusion of, 187–8; intimacy of, 157; one-to-one experience, 181; use of wandering in, 164–7. *See also* Punchdrunk (London)
Duggan, Patrick; on "mimetic shimmering," 26; *Trauma-Tragedy: Symptoms of Contemporary Performance*, 26

echo chambers, 33–4, 36, 55, 73
elections: Canadian federal (2015), 82, 87, 91; Toronto mayoral (2014), 77, 83; United States (2020), xii
Elson, Nicola, 29, 57, 61–2
emotional investment. *See* immersive theatre: emotional investment in
"Enbridge playRites Festival of New Canadian Plays" (2012), 32, 220n8
Enemy of the People, An, 26, 27, 219n85; China production of, 86; England production of, 86; as forum for debate, 90; on identity, 99–100; localness in, 85–8; and "the majority," 93, 100; original text (1882), 80; participation in, 100–2; plot of, 77, 81–2; political participation in, 213; Québec production of, 86; *real-ish-ness* of, 213; role of Doctor Stockmann as mobilizing character, 81–3, 89–92 *passim*, 225n15; Saint John Theatre Company production of, 86; Schaubühne (Berlin) production of, 80–1, 85–7, 92; Tarragon Theatre production of, 80–1; town-hall scene, 79–80; use of post-show talkbacks in, 88, 90, 100–1; use of time and space in,

83–4. *See also* "politi-real theatre";
Tarragon Theatre
environmental issues, 86, 91. *See also* Alberta (Canada): oil and gas industry of
epistemic bubbles, 34, 73
escapism, xiv, 128
Espiner, Mark, xv
Experience Economy, The: Work Is Theatre & Every Business a Stage, 175–6

Facebook, 34
fake news, ix, xii, xiv, 73–4, 211–12
"feeling-labour," 194–210; inequities of, 201. *See also* Hurley, Erin
fiction, 9–11, 26, 28, 30, 40–4 *passim*, 52–3, 70, 75–7, 82–4, 91, 95, 97–8, 102, 104, 115, 169, 172–4, 182, 184, 187–8, 204, 211–12, 214; tension with real, x, xii–xiii, 41, 43–4
Filewod, Alan, xv, 31–2
Fischer-Lichte, Erika, 193
Ford, Rob, 85
Forsyth, Alison, rejection of defining theatre of the real, 12
Foucault, Michel, 172. *See also* heterotopia
fourth wall, xiv, 9, 27, 30, 38, 42, 47–8, 57–8, 65–6, 70, 72, 75, 77, 81–3, 151, 199
fragmentation, 127–8
framing, 56–7, 83–4; as facilitator of audience experience, 40–1
Freshwater, Helen, on audience scholarship, 16–17; on spectatorship as relates to political action, 79
Fuchs, Eleanor, 175–6, 180; and "shopping theatre," 175

Funk, Wolfgang, 7–8, 11. *See also Aesthetics of Authenticity*
future haunting, 59–63. *See also Good Fences*

Gable, Eric, 124–5
Gallagher, Kathleen, 21, 206
Gallie, W.B., *Philosophy and the Historical Understanding*, 12
gaming. *See* video games
Garde, Ulrike, on "productive insecurity," 54
Garland, John Bingley, 113
Geertz, Clifford, on "thick description," 119
gender, 216n9, 226n55
geography, as relates to community-based theatre, 68–9
Ghost River Theatre (Alberta), *An Eye for an Eye*, 33
Gilmore, James, on the experience economy, 175–6
globalization, 127–8
Glow, Hilary, 19; on audience research, 25
Gof, Brith, 136–7
Goffman, Erving: *The Presentation of Self in Everyday Life*, 98; on valuing the real, 8
Good Fences, 22, 26, 29–76, 78, 219n85; 2015 tour, 36–46 *passim*, 61–2; "amateur aesthetic" in, 37–8; attendance at land stewardship community meetings, 52; blurring of time in, 83; Calgary Foundation funding of, 220–1n8; "Community Tour" (2015), 29; conflict in, 65, 67–74; conversation in, 63–76; design features of, 36–46; "ethico-political" engage-

ment in, 56–7; as forum for debate, 90; fragmentation of, 57; lack of resolution, 59–60; local politics in, 87; negative pedagogy of, 66–7; oil and gas industry, 27; political agenda of, 35, 56–7; production style, 40–1; *real-ish-ness* of, 213; realness of, 45; and relationality, 64–5; relationship to place, 36, 85; role of the non-expert in, 43–6; script changes in, 51; talkbacks, 30–2, 43–8 *passim*, 55–6, 62–3, 67, 69, 70, 75, 77; on the uncertainties of the future, 59–63; use of interviews, 29–30; use of multiple truths, 54–5; use of the real, 30–1, 36–46; use of time, 46–59. *See also* Alberta (Canada): oil and gas industry of; spaces: community-based

Grass Valley Charter School Foundation, xii

Great Comet, The, 150

Gregg, Melissa; on affect, 15–16

Griffiths, Braden, 29, 40, 42, 52–3, 65, 71; and the sharing of time, 55

Groß, Florian, 7–8, 11. *See also Aesthetics of Authenticity*

grounded theory, 23

Guattari, Félix, 192

Guignon, Charles, 6. *See also* authenticity

Handler, Richard, 124–5

Harvey, Dustin Scott, 126

Harvie, Jen, 141

hegemonic structures, 226n55

Heim, Caroline, 15, 78, 224n2, 235n14

Heritage, Paul, on "impossible encounters," 68

heterotopia, 172–3; definition of, 172. *See also* Foucault, Michel

Higgin, Pete, 183–4

Higgins, Charlotte, 150

Higgins, Kathleen, xiii

historical re-enactment, 27, 103–46; and authenticity, 6–7, 119–25; constructivist approaches to, 124–5; as marker or maker of real cultural identity, 107; as "mimetic" or "progressive realism," 124–5; and real feelings, 104; realist approaches to, 124–5

history, as "embroidered," 118–19

Hochschild, Arlie, 193

Hogan, Bernie, 98

Hoile, Christopher, 82

Holdsworth, Nadine, 38–9

Horace, 192

"house/ball community." *See* ballroom culture

Houston, Andy, 136–7

Huber, Irmtaud, 7–8, 11. *See also Aesthetics of Authenticity*

Hughes, Jenny, xv

Hunter, Lindsay Brandon, 7

Hurley, Erin, 13, 15, 190, 192–4, 208; definition of "feeling-labour," 193

Husserl, Edmund, 4

Ibsen, Henrik, 77, 80, 84. *See also An Enemy of the People*: original text (1882)

Icke, Robert, 236n43

identity, politics of, 138

illusion, 10

immersive theatre, 117; audience

empowerment effect, 155; audience labour in, 28, 194–210; definition of, 149–50, 175; emotional investment in, 28, 152, 173; as genre, 154–5, 175, 190; and hard materiality, 14; intimacy of, 155–62, 173–4; multi-sensory experience in, 174–6, 178–9; need for post-immersive manifesto, 150; relationship-building in, 198–200; and risk, 202–3; use of space, 152

In the Wake. *See* Downstage theatre company: Downstage Creation Ensemble

inclusion; politics of, 138

Indigenous peoples, 44, 86, 110, 112; and reconciliation, 101. *See also* Beothuk; Mi'kmaq

inequality, 226n55

International Network for Audience Research in the Performing Arts (iNARPA), 19

intimacy. *See* immersive theatre: intimacy of

intimate theatre, definition of, 155–6

"Invisible Committee," 225n16

Irish theatre, and notions of Irishness, 129

Jain, Ravi, *A Brimful of Asha*, 43
Jansen, David, 79–80, 85, 87
Johanson, Katya, 19; on audience research, 25
Jones, Alice, 200

kairos, as concept, 51
Kalsnes, Bente, on fake news, xi
Kant, Immanuel, 4
Kaszynska, Patrycja, 198

Kaufman, Moises, *The Laramie Project*, 10
KB Resources, 32
Keidan, Lois, 173–4
Kelleher, Joe: definition of politics, 79; on real effects of political theatre, 100
Kennedy, John F. (former president), xi
Kennelly, Jacqueline, 70
Kent, Patrick, 32
Kline, Stephen, *Researching Audiences*, 24
knowledge, diverse systems of, 18
Kohn, Margaret, 97
Korza, Pam, 70

Lacan, Jacques, 5
Lavery, Carl, 66–8; on audience participation, 170. *See also An Enemy of the People*
Learning Curve, 235n2
Lehmann, Hans-Thies, 56–7; definition of mimesis, 113–14; on post-dramatic theatre, 75; *Postdramatic Theatre*, 114
Levin, Laura, 236n47
Limon, Jerzy, 53
Live Arts Development Agency, 173–4
liveness, 14; as affective quality, 181–2; of immersive theatre, 176–7, 180–1; as it relates to what is real, 7–8
living history museums, 117, 119
Living Newspapers. *See* 1930s Federal Theatre Project (US)
Lloyd, Dan, 52–3
logocentrism, 5. *See also* Derrida, Jacques

Lonergan, Patrick, *Theatre & Social Media*, 99
Longhurst, Brian, 99
Longview (Alberta), 57
Longview Community Hall, 37
Ludwig, Wiebo, 33; as "eco-warrior," 33; as "industry-terrorist," 33

MacAloon, John, on cultural performance, 60–1
Machon, Josephine, 156–7, 175–7, 183–4, 204; on changing definition of immersive theatre, 149–50; definition of the epic, 156; and temporality, 182
Mackey, Sally, 112–13
Macmillan, Duncan, 236n43
Magelssen, Scott, 117–21 *passim*, 143. See also "simming"
Mallett, Simon, 29, 33–4, 38, 44, 64; on conversation, 63; on "invitations," 66; on staged conflict, 67–72
Malone, Erin, 55at
Mandell, Jonathan, 153
Martin, Carol, 76, 212; description of theatre of the real, xiii–xv; *Theatre of the Real*, 13–14
Masque of Red Death, The, 182. See also Punchdrunk (London)
Massey, Doreen, 127–8, 132, 136, 140; on localism, 68; *Space, Place, and Gender*, 129
Massumi, Brian, 192–3, 203, 214; *A Thousand Plateaus*, 192
mazes, 167–8. See also Pons, Esther Belvis
McAuley, Gay, 138; on local and located theatre, 134
McGonigal, Jane, definition of an epic environment, 153–4, 156
McKee, Carly, 42, 57, 61–2
McKenzie, Ray, 11; *The State of the Real: Aesthetics in the Digital Age*, x
McLucas, Cliff, 136–7
"McTheatre." See Rebellato, Dan
Mealey, Scott; on audience resistance to didactic theatre, 221n31
Megson, Chris, rejection of defining theatre of the real, 12
metatheatre, 38–40, 50, 84–5
Miessen, Markus, *The Nightmare of Participation*, 94–5. See also audience participation: conventional models of
Mi'kmaq, 110
Milisavljevic, Maria, 33, 80–1, 84–5, 225n14. See also Tarragon Theatre: *Peace River Country*
Miller, Alexander, on realism, 4
Milling, Jane, 38–9
mimesis, 10–11, 14, 113–16; and "mimetic shimmering," 27
misinformation, ix–xii, 73, 211, 214
Mitchell, Bill, 168
Morash, Chris, 128–31, 140
Moscow Art Theatre, 86. See also *An Enemy of the People*
"motility capital," 201. See also Ury, John
Mouffe, Chantal, *Agonistics: Thinking the World Politically*, 73
Mr. Burns, A Post-electric Play, 152
Mumford, Meg, on "productive insecurity," 54
Murray, Catherine, *Researching Audiences*, 24
Muskrat Falls, 115

Narváez, Peter, on outport culture, 126–7
National Film Board, *Wiebo's War*, 33
national identity, construction of, 27. *See also* Newfoundland (Canada); Trinity Pageant
National Theatre, 157
National Theatre Wales, 19, 150, 157
Nazism, 10
neoliberalism, 85, 225n16; potential impact on immersive theatre, 157–9, 163, 173
Nestruck, J. Kelly, 91, 160
"networked publics," 98–9
New Canadian Realisms, 9
Newfoundland (Canada), 26–7, 103–46; cod-fishing industry of, 120; colonization of, 112, 138; culture of, 105–8, 112–13, 127, 144; discovery of, 105, 122; identity of, 109–10, 114, 139; nation-building in, 109–10; outport history of, 110–11, 126, 137, 144; and the "Real Newfoundland," 27, 109–12, 115, 120–1, 126–7, 133–4, 144–5, 213; tourism industry of, 109, 115–16, 129, 133–4, 144–5, 228n15. *See also* Trinity Pageant
Nguyen, C. Thi, 34, 36, 73. *See also* echo chambers; epistemic bubbles
Nicholson, Helen, 38–9
Nikiforus, Andrew, *Saboteurs: Wiebo Ludwig's War Against Big Oil*, 33
Norway, 83, 85
nostalgia, 112–13; as unreal, 113

Obama, Barack (former president), x–xi, 34
Oddey, Allison, *Modes of Spectating*, 154
oil and gas industry. *See* Alberta (Canada): oil and gas industry of
Omasta, Matt, audience research in relation to young people, 19
"original" history, 117
Orona, Celia J., 23
Ostermeier, Thomas, 80–2, 101
Outside the March, 147–88. See also *Mr. Burns, A Post-electric Play*; *TomorrowLove*™
Ouzounian, Richard, 84–6
Overton, James, 109–10, 115, 126, 129, 144–5. *See also* Newfoundland (Canada): and the "Real Newfoundland"

Packard, Edward, *Sugarcane Island*, 231n2
Pankiw, Bill, 32
"parallax perspective," 191
Parkdale Community Association, 39–40, 64
participation. *See* audience participation
Pasquali, Francesca, 98
patriarchal structures, influence on history, 124–5
Pearson, Mike, 135–7; on site-specific performances, 130
Peele, Jordan, xi
performative allyship, 227n71
Persians, The, 201
Peters, John Durham, 13
Phelan, Peggy, 180; *Unmarked: The Politics of Performance*, 176–7
Philip, M. NourbeSe, 18

"physical fabric." *See* spaces: community-based
Pine, B. Joseph, II, on the experience economy, 175–6
Pitt, Janet, 110
Pizzagate, xii, 221n20
Plantinga, Carl, on feeling, 13
Plato, 8
Plotinus, 8
political silos, 27, 33, 55
politics: Canadian, 77; in theatre, 77–102. *See also* "politi-real theatre"
"politi-real theatre," 77–102, 79; definition of, 78; effects of, 100–2
Polito, Mary, 135
Pons, Esther Belvis, 167
postmodernism, 11
poststructuralism, 14. *See also* realness: poststructural view of
"post-truth," ix–xiv *passim*, 73, 212, 214; definition of, xiii
Prentki, Tim, on civic engagement, 95
Presentation of Self in Everyday Life, The, 8
promenade performance. *See* Trinity Pageant: "walkabout" style of
Punchdrunk (London), 27–8, 149, 152, 172–3, 178–9, 181, 183–4, 186, 198; *The Burnt City*, 149; *The Drowned Man*, 149, 153–4; *Sleep No More*, 149; use of anonymizing masks, 164, 173; use of space, 152–4. *See also Sleep No More*; *The Masque of Red Death*

QAnon, xi–xii, xii; and the Blue Marble Jubilee, 214
queer theory, 5–6

Rabey, David Ian: on theatre as a quantum art, 223n71; theatre as *intersubjective*, 53–4; *Theatre, Time and Temporality: Melting Clocks and Snapped Elastics*, 222n46
race, 216n9
racism, 226n55
Radbourne, Jennifer, 19
ranching industry. *See* Alberta (Canada): ranching industry of
Rancière, Jacques, *Emancipated Spectator*, 78–9, 202
Read, Alan, 202
real affect, 61, 102, 116–19, 134, 189–91, 203–4, 206, 209–10
real history, 111, 114–17, 124, 132, 134, 172, 174
real-ish-ness, 25–8, 123–4, 203, 214; 170; construction of, 26; definition of, 11–12
realism, xiv–xv, 9–13 *passim*, 116, 129, 132, 182; and "mimetic" realism, 124; and "progressive" realism, 124
reality television, 6
realness, 211–14; connection with affect, 13; crisis of, 211–12; definition of, 3–4, 28; feeling as assessment of realness, 12–13; poststructuralist view of, 5; as potentially deceptive, 6; sensory perception of, 4–5; valuing of, 8
real/representation binarism, 9–10
Reason, Matthew, 19, 78–9, 150, 201; *Participations*, 19
Rebellato, Dan, 130
Red Deer College, 64, 69
Redfield, Robert, on "folk society," 126
Reinelt, Janelle, 18; on authenticity

Index

in "localized" theatre, 122–3;
   work with UK audiences, 19
relationality, 18, 27, 55, 64–5, 69–70, 74, 122, 130–8, 139, 161, 169, 174, 179, 190, 192–3. See also *TomorrowLove*™
representation, xiv, 8–9, 14, 234n90;
   under threat by the real world, 9
representation binary, 8, 11
Richards, Shaun, 128–31, 140
Ridout, Nicholas: *Fright, Animals, and Other Theatrical Problems*, 193; *Passionate Amateurs: Theatre, Communism and Love*, 67; "The Vibratorium Electrified," 15
Rimini Protokoll, use of "experts of the everyday," 43
Rising Tide Theatre, 103–4, 106–7, 126, 132, 227n6; cultural role of, 230n112. See also Trinity Pageant
Roberts, Eifion Wyn (Wayne), trial of, 32–3
Roberts, Rick, 85–6, 90
Robinson, Dylan, 101
Romanticism, 8–9
Rose, Richard, 85, 225n14
RuPaul's Drag Race, 6

Saint John Theatre Company (New Brunswick), 86
Salverson, Julie, 74
Sauter, Willmar, 19, 219n82
Scarry, Elaine, and "presence," 176
Schaubühne. See *An Enemy of the People:* Schaubühne (Berlin) production of
Schneider, Rebecca, 115–16, 121, 125, 139, 141–2, 145–6
Schrøder, Kim, 25; *Researching Audiences*, 24

"Schrodinger's Cat," 223n71
Schulze, Daniel, 170, 172–3, 182, 199–200, 202–3; on authenticity, 212; on intimate theatre, 155–6
Scollen, Rebecca, 219n82
sealing. See Trinity Bay Disaster (1892)
Sedgman, Kirsty, 17–19, 150, 201; on *locating* Welsh audiences, 137; *Participations*, 19; on promenade-style performance, 229n48; on self-reflexivity in audience research, 24–5
Sedgwick, Eve Kosofsky, on affect, 15
Seigworth, Gregory J., on affect, 15–16
sentimentalism, 143
sexuality, 216n9
Shakespeare, William, 59
Shanks, Michael, 130
Shattering Hamlet's Mirror. See Carlson, Marvin
Shaughnessy, Nicola, on authenticity, 14
Shields, David, *Reality Hunger*, 212
"simming," 117–18, 143. See also Magelssen, Scott
site-specific performance, 27, 103–46
Sleep No More, 177, 234n75; gendered nature of, 236n47; sexual harassment and assault reports, 231n27. See also Punchdrunk (London)
Small, Rosamund, 147, 160
Smyth, Michael, 14
Snyder-Young, Dani, audience research relating to white supremacy, 19

social media, 73; affects of filters in, 33–4; curated identities on, 98–9; on facts and truths, 36; and political issues, 36; public conversations on, 55
Solga, Kim, 9; on real aspects of immersive theatre, 191–2. See also *New Canadian Realisms*
spaces: community-based, 36–46 *passim*; malfunctions of, 42; use of real world in production, 36
spectators. *See* audience; audience participation
Spinoza, Baruch, *Ethics*, 192
St John's (Newfoundland), 126
St Paul's Anglican Church (Trinity, NL), 103, 136; as site of Trinity Pageant, 106
Stark, Jim, as "superfan," 177
State of the Real, 5
States, Bert O., 10; on "binocular vision," 40; *Great Reckonings in Little Rooms*, 58
Stephenson, Jenn, xiv; on the "audience-citizen," 96; on past bodily experiences, 61; on "productive insecurity," 54, 56, 60; *Productive Insecurity: perils and products of theatres of the real*, xiv, 25–6; on theatre of the real, 25–6, 54, 70–1, 76, 191
Strings, Sabrina. *See RuPaul's Drag Race*
subjective *times*, 52–3
Sundén, Jenny, 99
Sutton, Damian, x, 5, 11

Tait, Peta, 13
talkbacks, 29, 30, 43–6, 80, 88–9, 224n2. *See also Good Fences*

Tamara, 175
Tarragon Theatre, 80, 84, 86, 90, 225n14, 225n15; *Peace River Country*, 33; use of talkbacks, 81; video lecture series by, 85. *See also An Enemy of the People*
technology, 14
temporal blending, 142–6, 182
Tepperman, Julie, 152. *See also Brantwood*
terrorism, 109
Texas, 220n6
"real, the": and lack of definition, 11; as notion in the context of performance, 12; as philosophical construct, 11; as provocative, xiv
theatre: antecedents of, 8–9; as art form, xiii–xiv, 53; children's experiences of, 19; definition of, 3; duality of, 40; as genre, 9–10, 16; as manipulator of the real world, 9; as meeting place, 63–4; orientation to the fictive, xiii–xiv; political engagement in, 98–9; and role of expressing truth, xv; and "weak theatre," 67
theatre history, 8–10
theatre of the real, xv; as genre, xiv, 9–10, 14
Theatre of the Real. See Martin, Carol
Thompson, James, 206
timescape. *See* Adam, Barbara
Tomlin, Liz, 17, 73, 97–8; on spectatorship, 97–8
TomorrowLove™, 26, 28, 147–88, 193, 196–9, 219n85; absence of conclusion, 187–8; affect-labour of, 190–6 *passim*, 203–4; audience

decision-making in, 167; audience insecurity in spaces, 168; audience proximity to performers in, 162–3; audience relationship-building in, 163–7, 174, 179–80; finale as non-fiction experience, 188; "first-person player" perspective in, 172; framing of, 199; friction due to funeral home site, 170–2; on futuristic relationships, 149; gamification of, 178–9; group navigation in, 167–70; intimacy of, 161–2; invitation for audience to think about alternatives, 185–6; meta-narrative in, 185; moving through spaces as a follower in, 164–7; personalization of, 179; real affect of, 206–10; *real-ish-ness* of, 210, 213–14; repeatability paradox, 177–8; sexuality in, 183; use of affect, 193; use of blank aesthetic in, 159–63, 173–4, 188, 197; use of conscious stretching of time, 185–7; use of love poems, 187; use of pacing the audience, 183; use of vignettes, 149. See also Cushman, Mitchell

Toope, Kevin, 117–18, 228n41

Toronto, 85, 86

Trickle Creek (Alberta), 33

Trinity Bay (Newfoundland), 117; historic tour of, 117–18, 228n41; outport history of, 110–11, 126; restoration efforts in, 110–11. See also Newfoundland (Canada); Trinity Pageant

Trinity Bay Disaster (1892), 103

Trinity Pageant, 26, 27, 103–46 *passim*, 106–7, 151, 219n85; affect in, 113; audience acceptance of, 123–4; audience as fictional characters in, 103–4; as "authentic experience," 119; authenticity of, 107–8, 122–3; church scene, 112, 132–3, 135–6, 139, 140–1; class representation (historical) in, 111; as constructionist history, 125, 127; departures from realism in, 116–17; Dwyer's pig (farcical) scene, 118–19; election (1832) scene, 113, 130; establishment of the "Real Newfoundland" in, 114, 124; as exclusionary history, 111–13; as fiction making real a fiction, 115; fish flake scene as illustration of authenticity versus real, 120–1, 132, 139; fishing industry "truck system" scene, 116–17; fluidity of, 115; incitement of "true Newfoundlanders," 113; Indigenous representation in, 111; marketing of, 130–1, 144–5; mimesis in, 114; plot of, 106; real-ish history in, 116–19; realness of, 106–7, 114, 119–20, 213; site-specific performance, 104–5, 125–38; temporality of, 142–5; use of costume in, 103; use of Lester-Garland house as place, 130; "walkabout" style of, 104–6, 229n48. See also Rising Tide Theatre

Trump, Donald (former president), x–xi, xii

truth, 13, 93; historical, 107. See also audience; "post-truth"

Tuan, Yi-Fu, definition of "space," 129

Tulloch, John, 219n82

Turner, Mark, 230n112
Twitter, 34

Unitarian Church of Calgary, 39, 64
Ury, John, 201

Valve, Lindsay, 21
van Es, Karin, 7–8
Van Oldenborgh, Lennaart, 14, 16
Varga, Somogy, 6. *See also* authenticity
Vattimo, Gianni, 67
video games, 154
Vikings, 122
Vittadini, Nicolette, 98

Wagner, Matthew, 59
Walker, Julia, 13
Walkerton (Ontario), 85; *E. coli* outbreak (2000), 83, 85, 91, 225n18
Wallendorf, Melanie, 22
Walmsley, Ben, 23, 25; on audience engagement, 19, 196
war propaganda, 10
Warner, Sara, 193

Washburn, Anne, 152. See also *Mr. Burns, A Post-electric Play*
Weixler, Antonius, on authenticity, 6–7
"We Love the Place, O God" (1827), 136. *See also* Bullock, Rev. William
Whitbourne, Sir Richard, 115, 138
White, Christine, 154
White, Gareth, 78, 88, 149–50, 173, 202
Whybrow, Nicolas, 112–13
Wildworks. *See* Mitchell, Bill
Wiles, David, 8
Wood, Eric Emin, 90–3, 102

Yagi, Michelle, 170–1
Yuen, Cheryl L., 69–70

Zaiontz, Keren, on presumptive intimacy in immersive theatre, 158–9
Zhulina, Alisa, 93, 101–2
Žižek, Slavoj, 87–8
Zuckerman, Ethan, xi–xii; on the unreal, xii. *See also* QAnon